POCKET SIZE 2

THE MENACE OF
ALIA RELLAPOR, PART TWO

The Akiko Series, Issues 8~13

SIRIUS ENTERTAINMENT
UNADILLA, NEW YORK

*This book is dedicated
to my son, Matthew*

AKIKO POCKET SIZE 2 AUGUST, 2004.
FIRST PRINTING. PUBLISHED BY SIRIUS ENTERTAINMENT, INC.
LAWRENCE SALAMONE, PRESIDENT. ROBB HORAN, PUBLISHER.
KEITH DAVIDSEN, EDITOR. CORRESPONDENCE: P.O. BOX X, UNADILLA, NY 13849.

THE STORY SO FAR

Welcome to Akiko Pocket Size Two, the second of three trade paperbacks comprising Akiko's first epic-length adventure story, "The Menace of Alia Rellapor." Those of you who haven't yet read the first installment will be relieved to know that there are only a few plot points you'll need to know to get the most out of this volume. Indeed, the entire story was written with the goal of making it as easy as possible for new readers to become familiar with the story no matter where they happened to begin reading.

The concept behind the series is this: a young girl by the name of Akiko is taken off to a planet called Smoo, where she leads a crew of companions on a series of adventures. Her friends from Smoo include Spuckler (a rugged space-pirate), Gax (Spuckler's trusty robot), Mr. Beeba (a nervous academic), and Poog (an inscrutable floating alien). Once you get to know this gang, the rest of the story falls into place with a minimum of details.

In Volume One, Akiko was put in charge of a mission to rescue King Froptoppit's son, the Prince of Smoo, who has been kidnapped by his own mother, a mysterious woman by the name of Alia Rellapor. The seemingly straightforward mission is beset with problems, however, as Akiko and her friends are thwarted at every turn by pirates, sea monsters, and other threats they encounter on their way to Alia Rellapor's castle.

In the sequence immediately preceding the first page of this volume, Akiko's crew had just received a map from a kindly Queen by the name of Pwip. Bidding the Queen farewell, they take the map in hand and set their sights on reaching a structure known as the Great Wall of Trudd. If they can find a way of getting to the other side of this massive barrier, they will finally enter into the realm of Alia Rellapor.

And that's about all the preparation you'll need to join them here mid-quest. If you have any questions or comments, feel free to contact me directly by e-mail at the address below. I'd love to hear what you think, and will do my best to reply to you personally.

mark@markcrilley.com

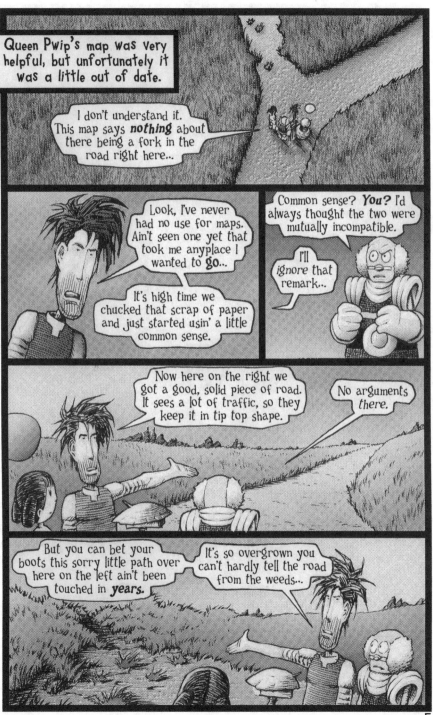

Queen Pwip's map was very helpful, but unfortunately it was a little out of date.

I don't understand it. This map says **nothing** about there being a fork in the road right here...

Look, I've never had no use for maps. Ain't seen one yet that took me anyplace I wanted to **go**...

It's high time we chucked that scrap of paper and just started usin' a little common sense.

Common sense? **You?** I'd always thought the two were mutually incompatible.

I'll *ignore* that remark...

Now here on the right we got a good, solid piece of road. It sees a lot of traffic, so they keep it in tip top shape.

No arguments there.

But you can bet your boots this sorry little path over here on the left ain't been touched in **years**.

It's so overgrown you can't hardly tell the road from the weeds...

5

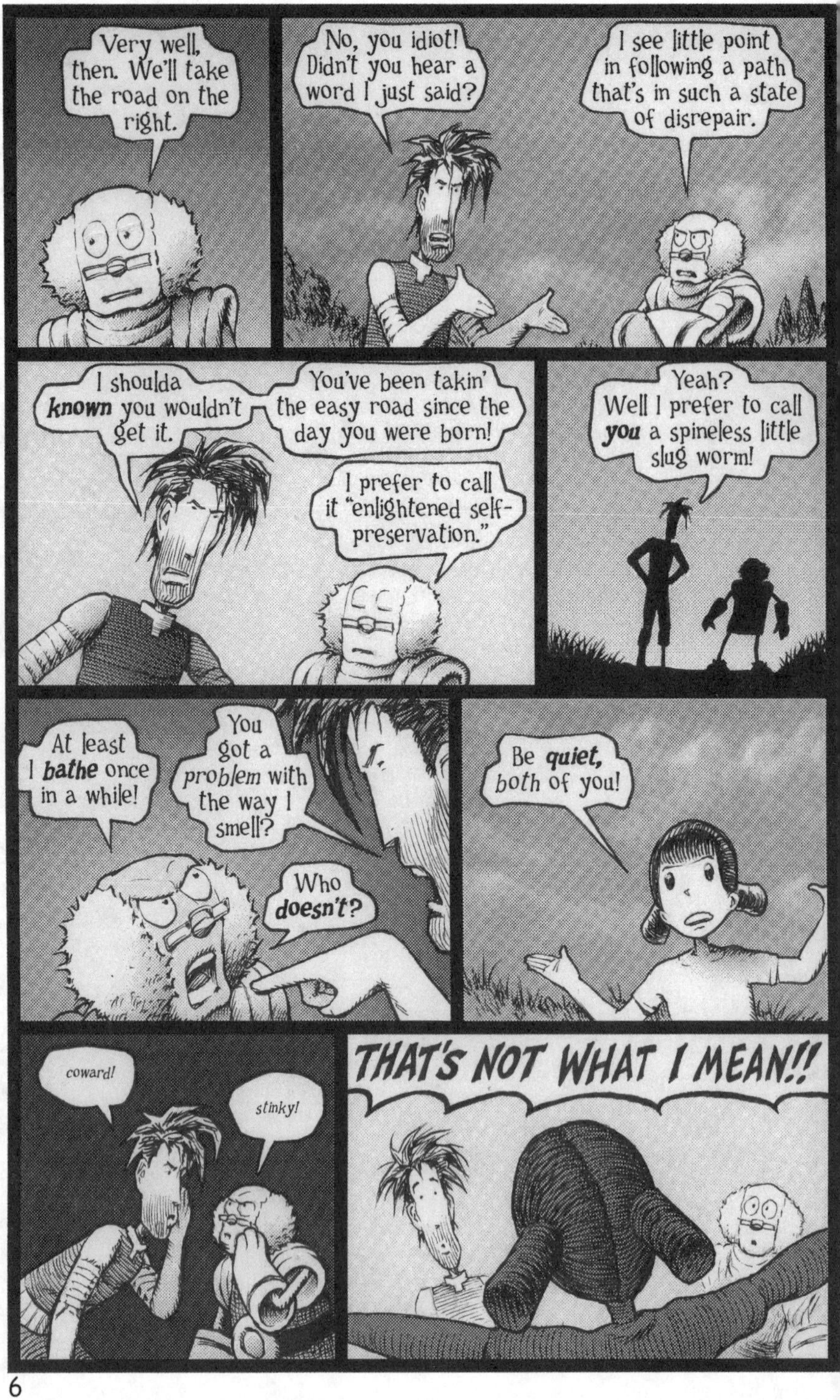
Very well, then. We'll take the road on the right.
No, you idiot! Didn't you hear a word I just said?
I see little point in following a path that's in such a state of disrepair.
I shoulda **known** you wouldn't get it.
You've been takin' the easy road since the day you were born!
I prefer to call it "enlightened self-preservation."
Yeah? Well I prefer to call **you** a spineless little slug worm!
At least I **bathe** once in a while!
You got a *problem* with the way I smell?
Who **doesn't?**
Be **quiet,** *both* of you!
coward!
stinky!
THAT'S NOT WHAT I MEAN!!

What's, uh...

...what's on your mind, 'Kiko?

Look, I've got *enough* to worry about without having to be the *referee* for you guys all the time!

Just *take it* easy or else I'll have to...

...I don't know, put you both on **time out** or something.

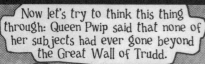

Now let's try to think this thing through: Queen Pwip said that none of her subjects had ever gone beyond the Great Wall of Trudd.

Indeed.

So it stands to reason that if there's a road leading to the Wall, it hasn't been used for a *very* long time.

That's what you were trying to tell us, right, Spuckler?

Actually, I just thought the road on the left looked more *interesting.*

But **your** reason sounds pretty good, too.

That *settles* it, then. We're taking the road on the *left.*

PBSHFP!

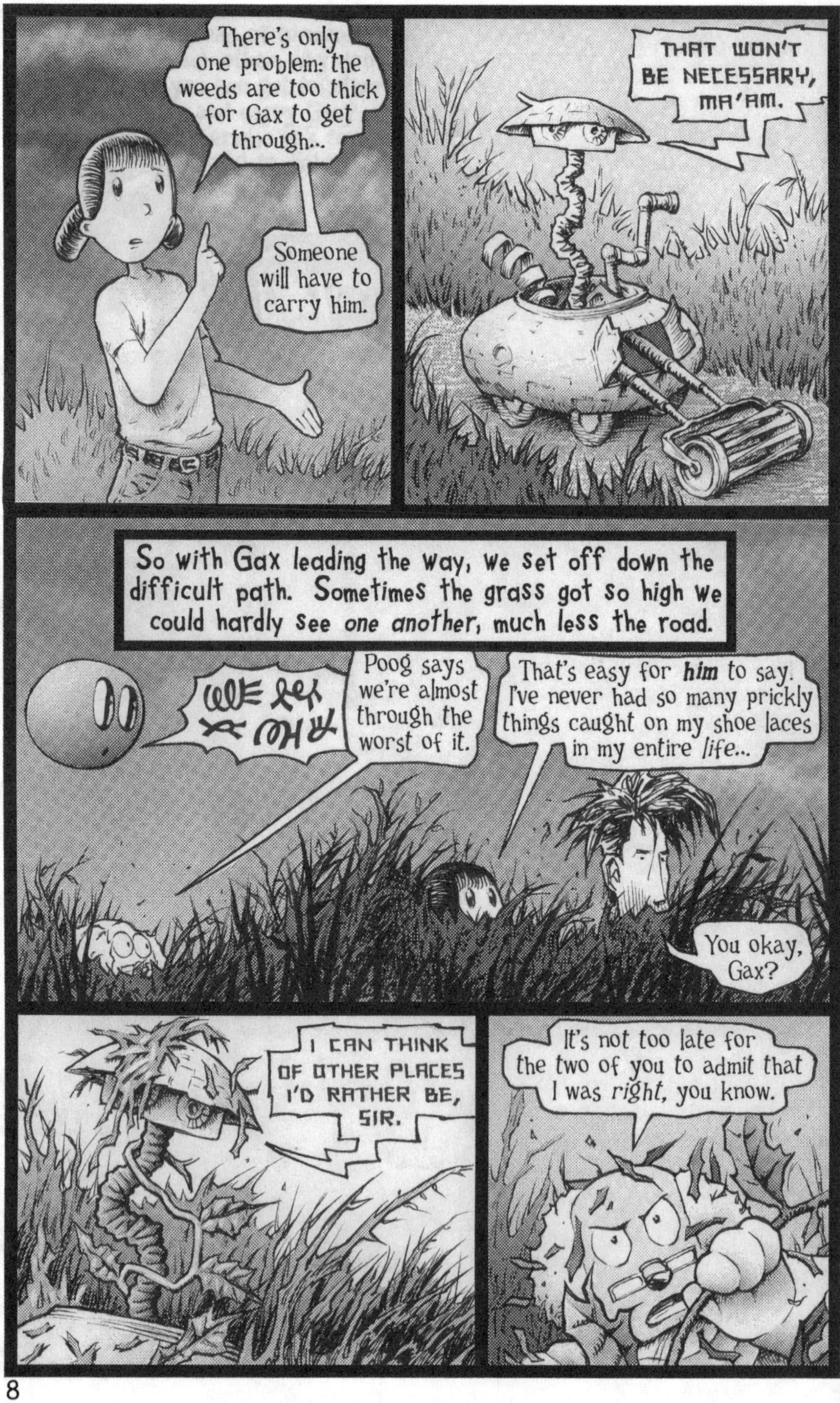
There's only one problem: the weeds are too thick for Gax to get through...
Someone will have to carry him.
THAT WON'T BE NECESSARY, MA'AM.
So with Gax leading the way, we set off down the difficult path. Sometimes the grass got so high we could hardly see *one another*, much less the road.
Poog says we're almost through the worst of it.
That's easy for **him** to say. I've never had so many prickly things caught on my shoe laces in my entire *life*...
You okay, Gax?
I CAN THINK OF OTHER PLACES I'D RATHER BE, SIR.
It's not too late for the two of you to admit that I was *right*, you know.

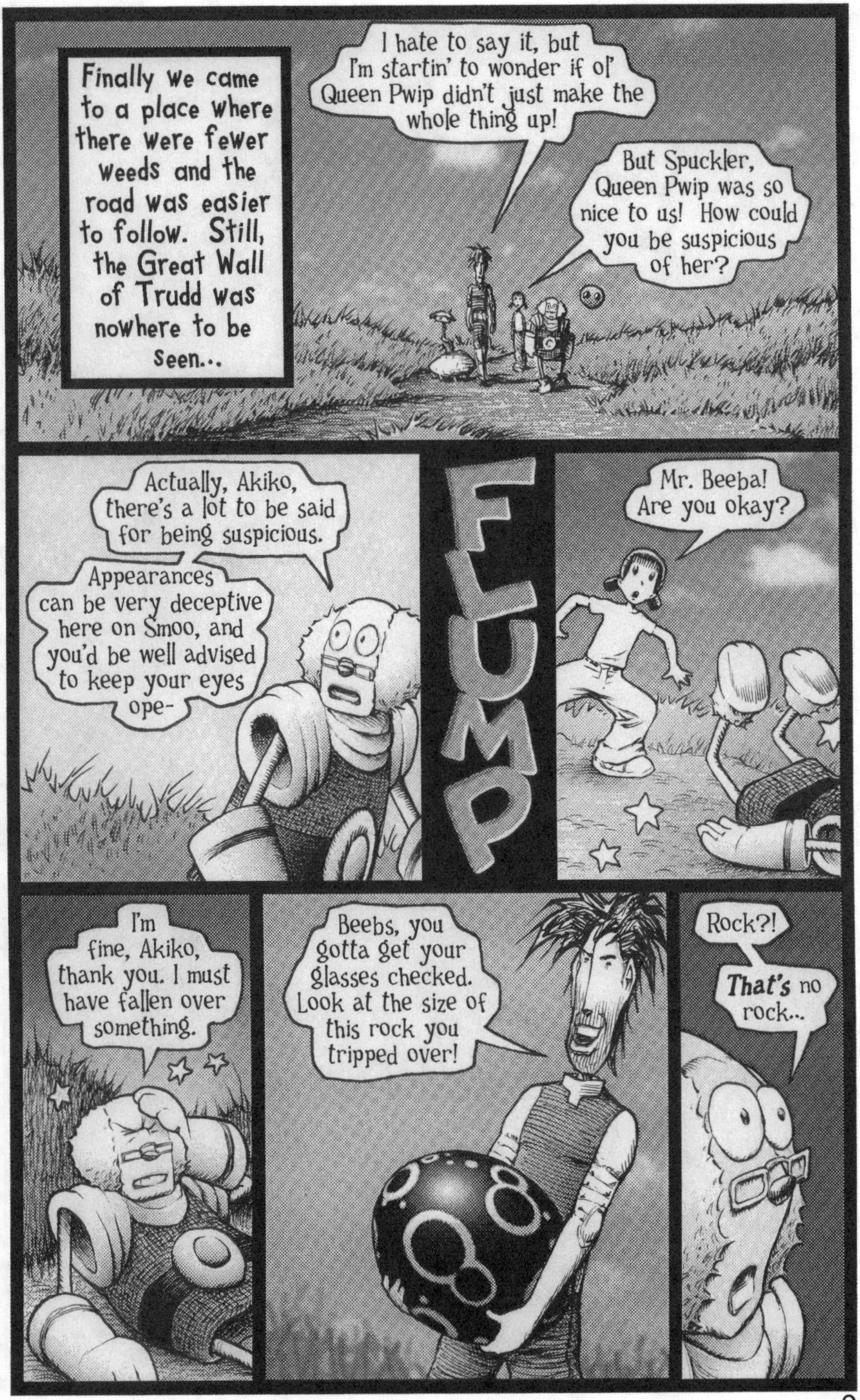
Finally we came to a place where there were fewer weeds and the road was easier to follow. Still, the Great Wall of Trudd was nowhere to be seen...
I hate to say it, but I'm startin' to wonder if ol' Queen Pwip didn't just make the whole thing up!
But Spuckler, Queen Pwip was so nice to us! How could you be suspicious of her?
Actually, Akiko, there's a lot to be said for being suspicious.
Appearances can be very deceptive here on Smoo, and you'd be well advised to keep your eyes ope-
FLUMP
Mr. Beeba! Are you okay?
I'm fine, Akiko, thank you. I must have fallen over something.
Beebs, you gotta get your glasses checked. Look at the size of this rock you tripped over!
Rock?!
That's no rock...

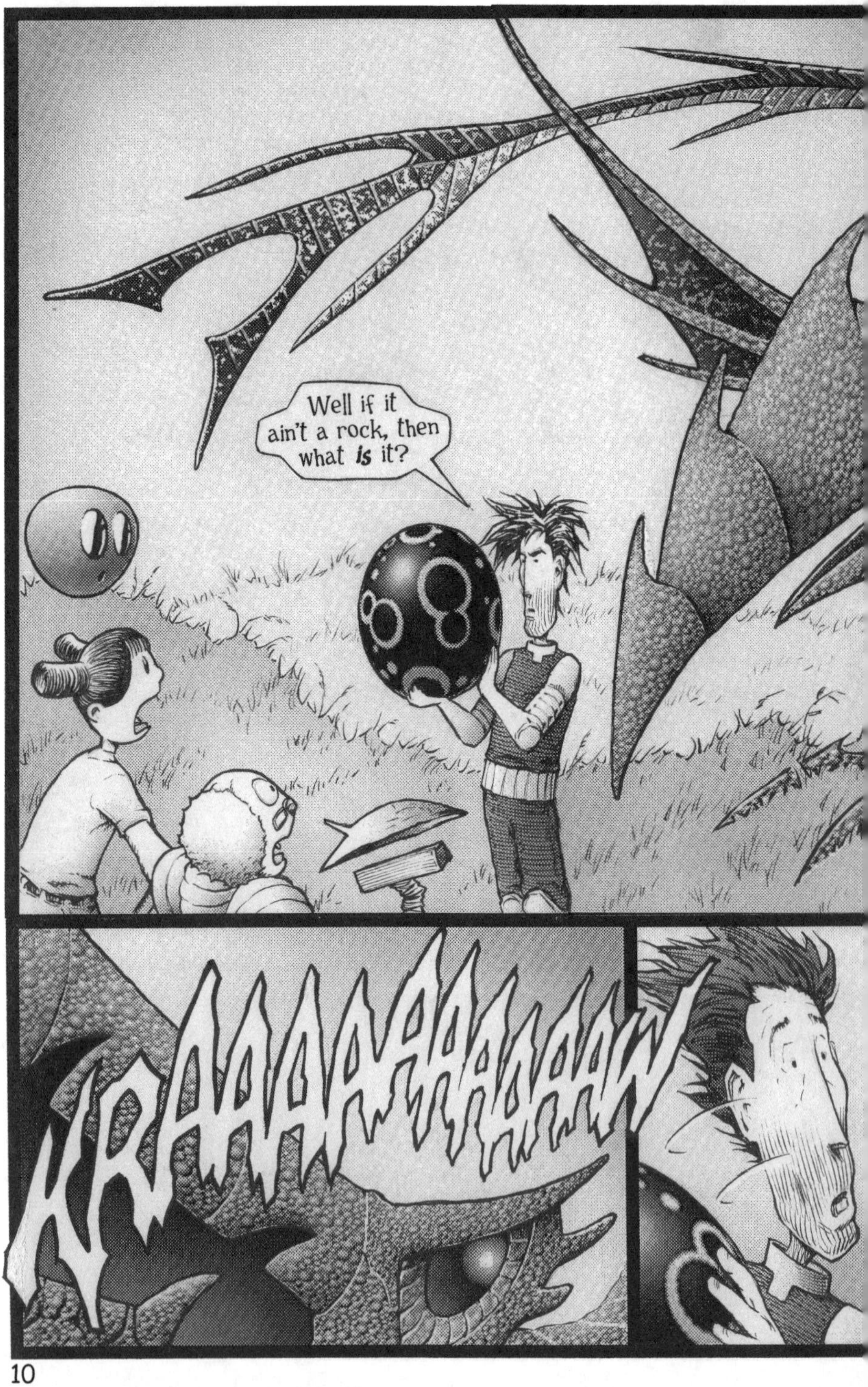
Well if it ain't a rock, then what *is* it?
KRAAAAAAAAAAW

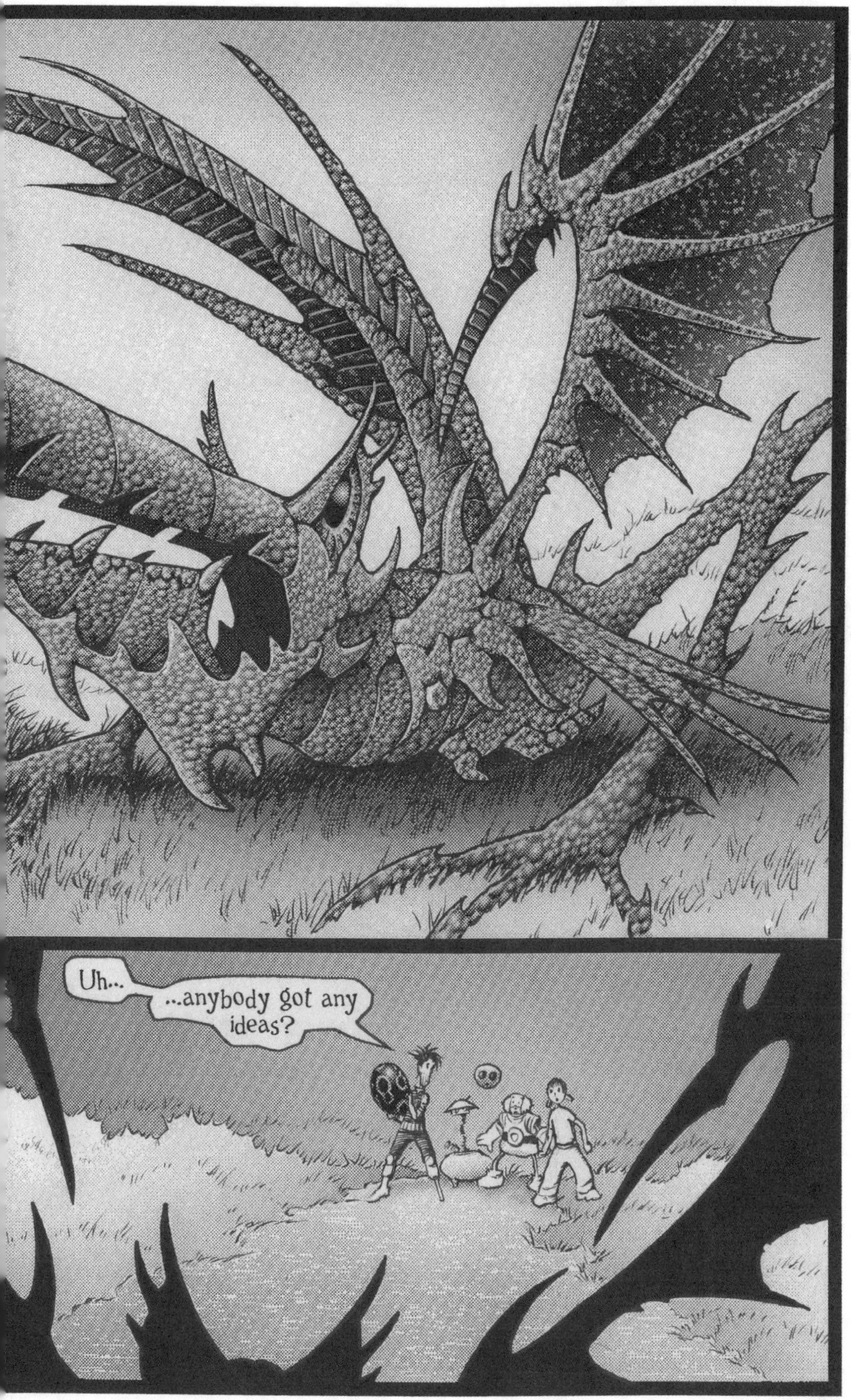
Uh...
...anybody got any ideas?

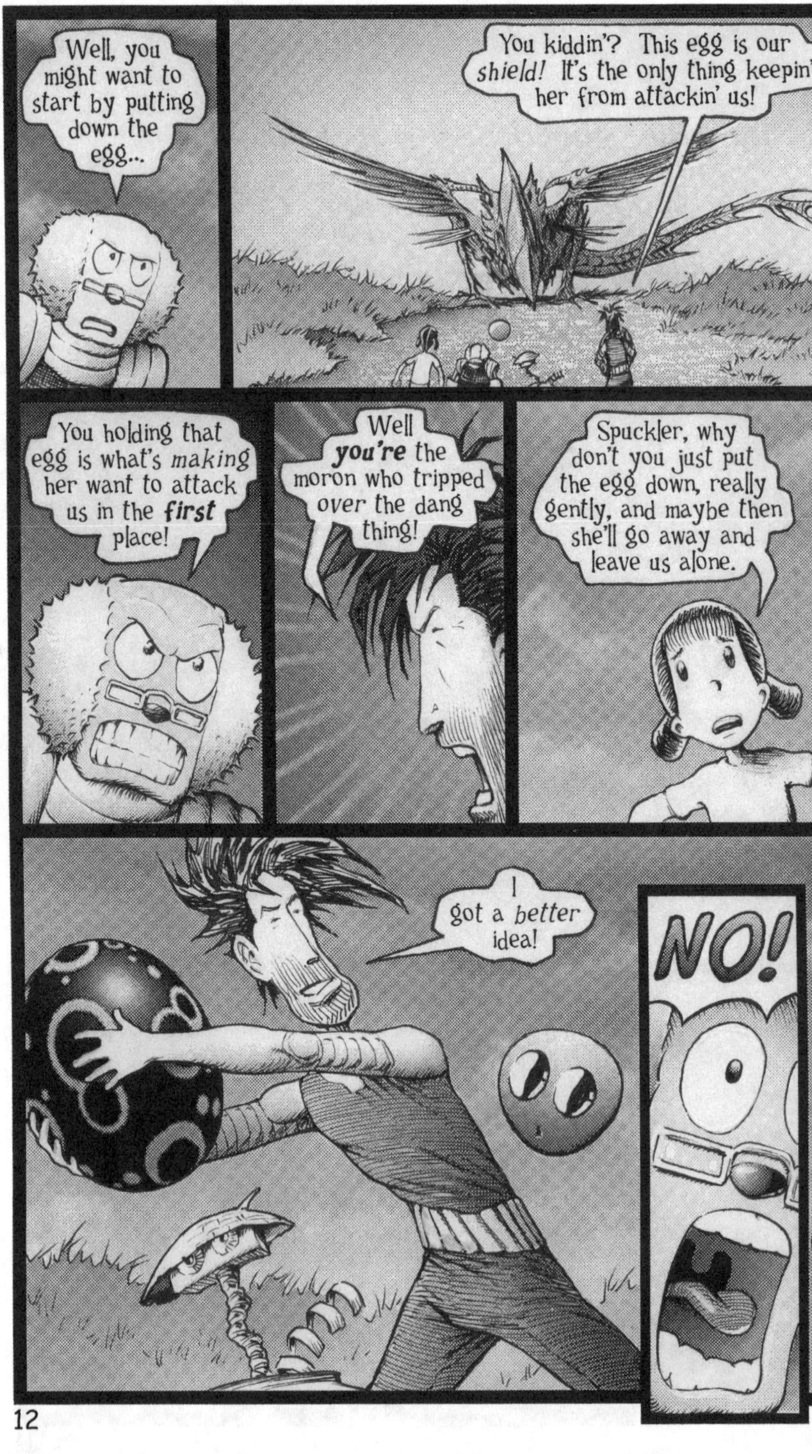

Well, you might want to start by putting down the egg...
You kiddin'? This egg is our *shield!* It's the only thing keepin' her from attackin' us!
You holding that egg is what's *making* her want to attack us in the **first** place!
Well ***you're*** the moron who tripped *over* the dang thing!
Spuckler, why don't you just put the egg down, really gently, and maybe then she'll go away and leave us alone.
I got a *better* idea!
NO!

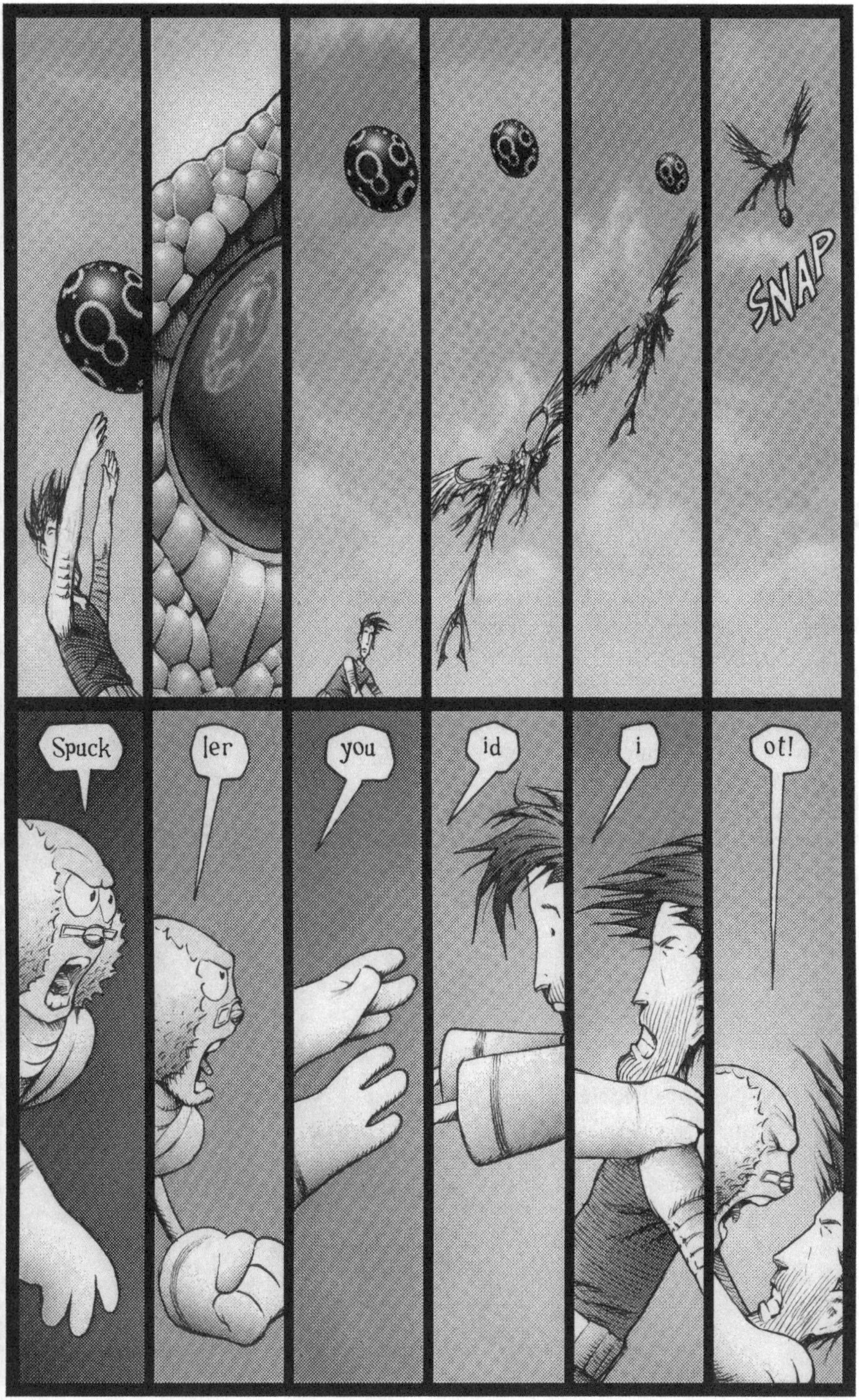
SNAP
Spuck
ler
you
id
i
ot!

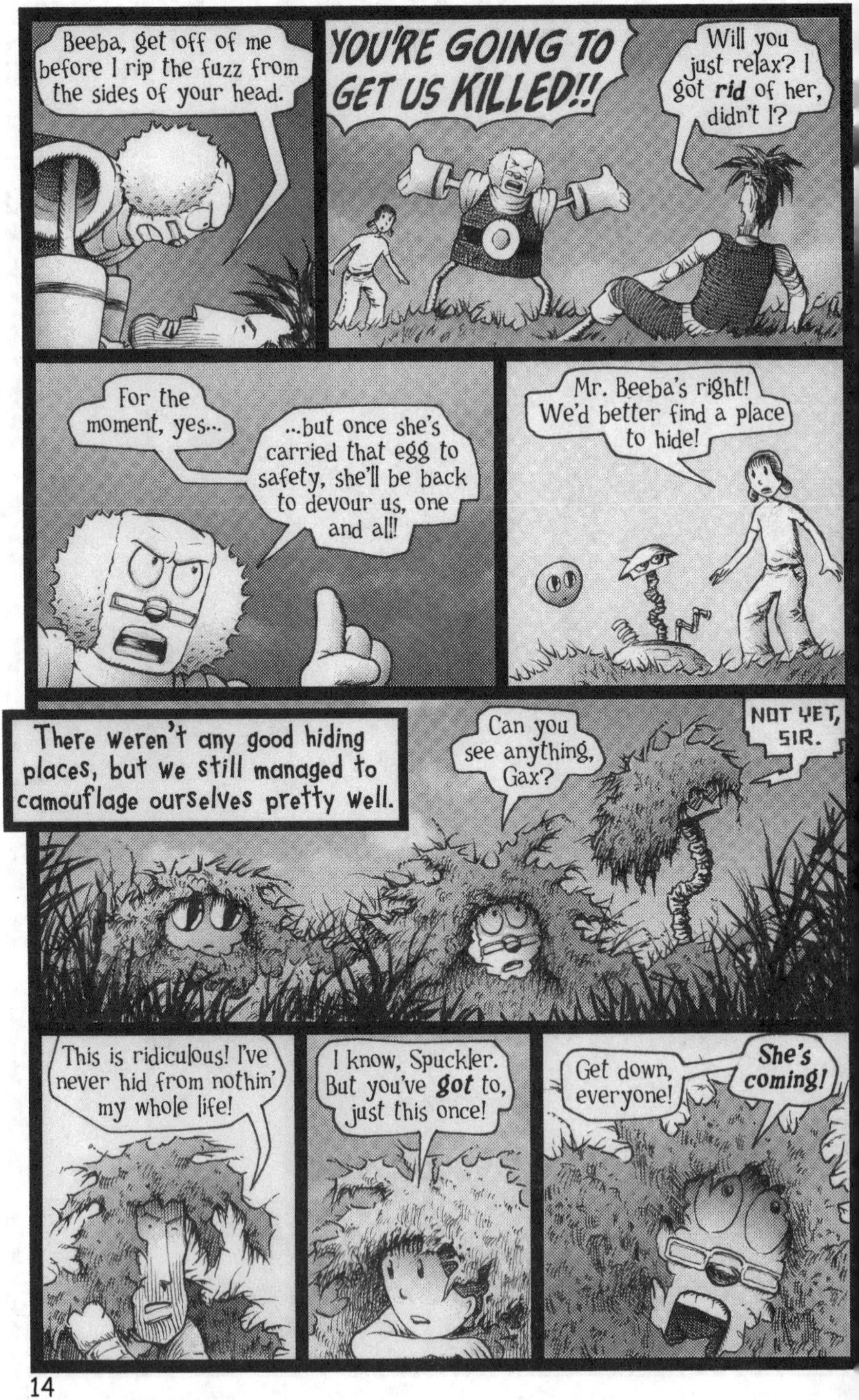
Beeba, get off of me before I rip the fuzz from the sides of your head.
YOU'RE GOING TO GET US KILLED!!
Will you just relax? I got rid of her, didn't I?
For the moment, yes...
...but once she's carried that egg to safety, she'll be back to devour us, one and all!
Mr. Beeba's right! We'd better find a place to hide!
There weren't any good hiding places, but we still managed to camouflage ourselves pretty well.
Can you see anything, Gax?
NOT YET, SIR.
This is ridiculous! I've never hid from nothin' my whole life!
I know, Spuckler. But you've got to, just this once!
Get down, everyone!
She's coming!

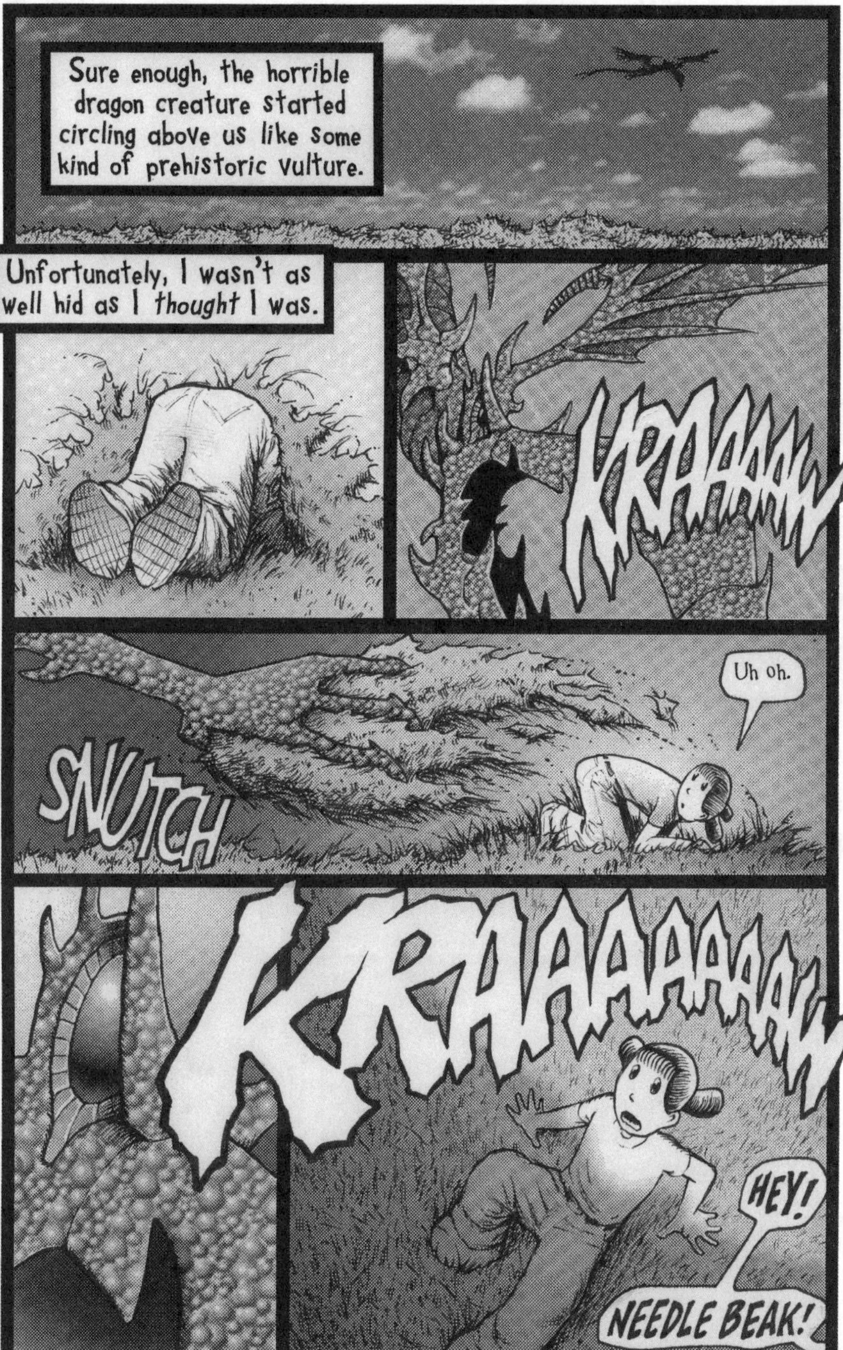
Sure enough, the horrible dragon creature started circling above us like some kind of prehistoric vulture.
Unfortunately, I wasn't as well hid as I *thought* I was.
KRAAAAW
SNUTCH
Uh oh.
KRAAAAAAAW
HEY!
NEEDLE BEAK!

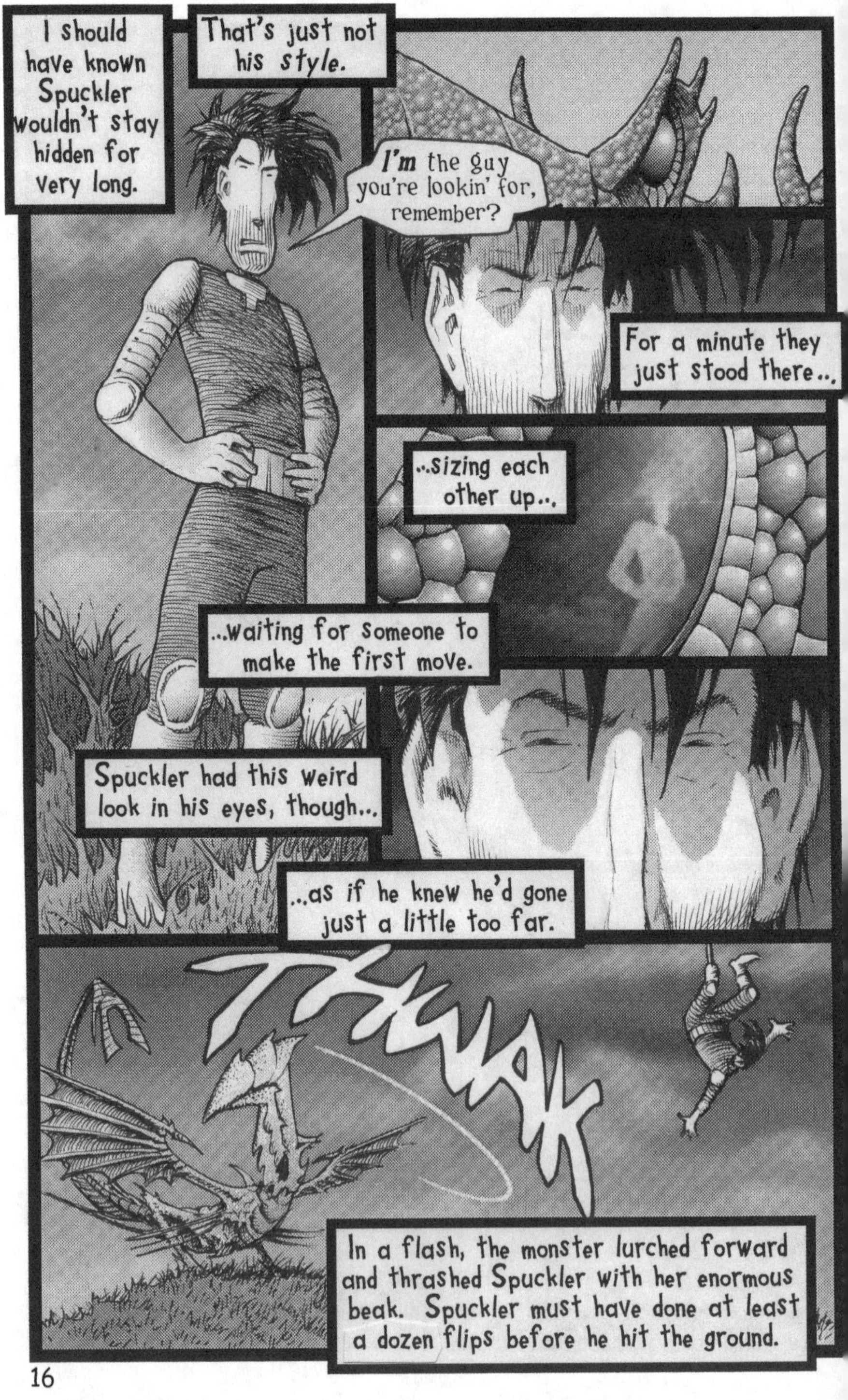
I should have known Spuckler wouldn't stay hidden for very long.
That's just not his *style.*
I'm the guy you're lookin' for, remember?
For a minute they just stood there...
...sizing each other up...
...waiting for someone to make the first move.
Spuckler had this weird look in his eyes, though...
...as if he knew he'd gone just a little too far.
THWAK
In a flash, the monster lurched forward and thrashed Spuckler with her enormous beak. Spuckler must have done at least a dozen flips before he hit the ground.

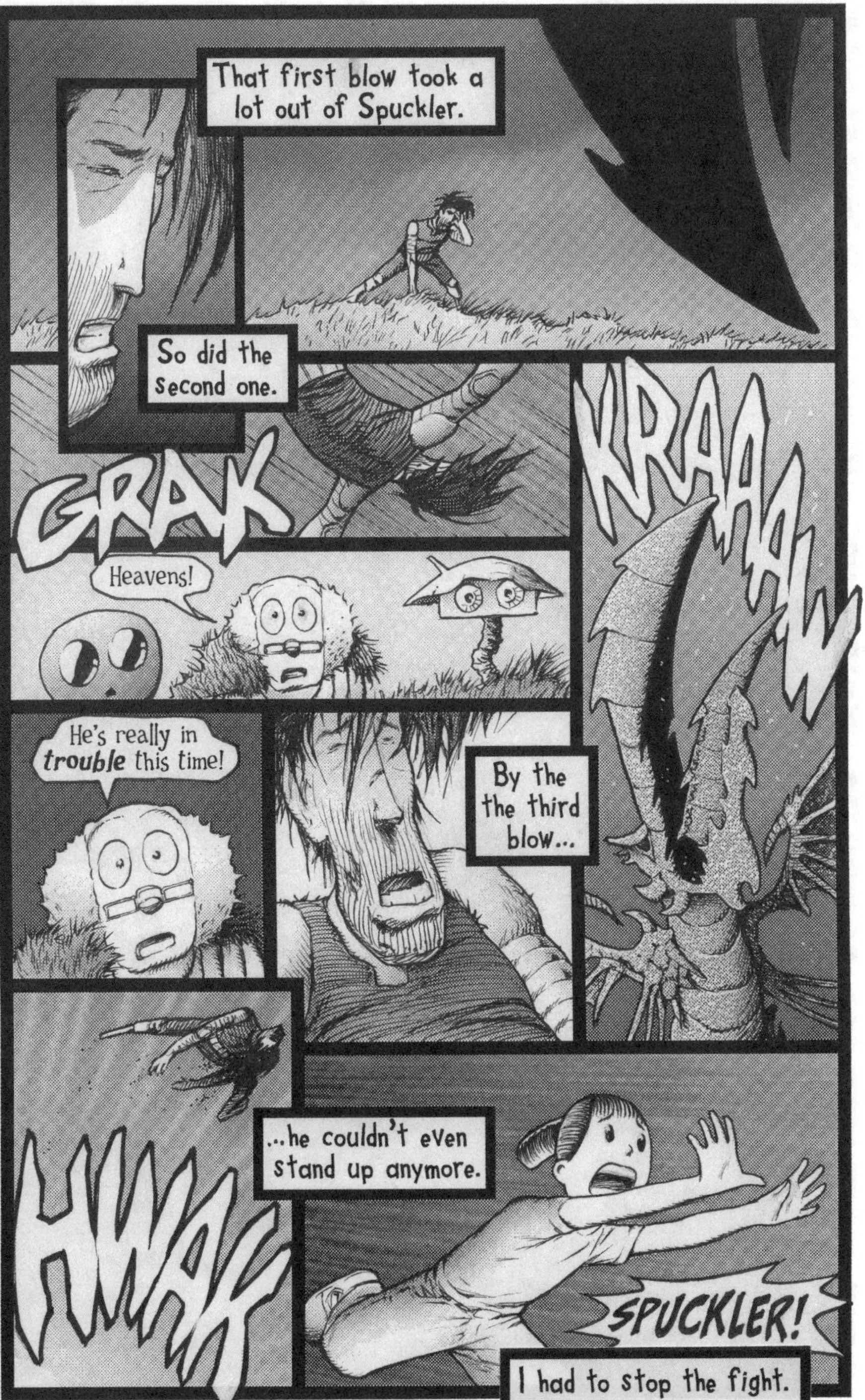
That first blow took a lot out of Spuckler.
So did the second one.
GRAK
KRAAAW
Heavens!
He's really in *trouble* this time!
By the the third blow...
HWAK
...he couldn't even stand up anymore.
SPUCKLER!
I had to stop the fight.

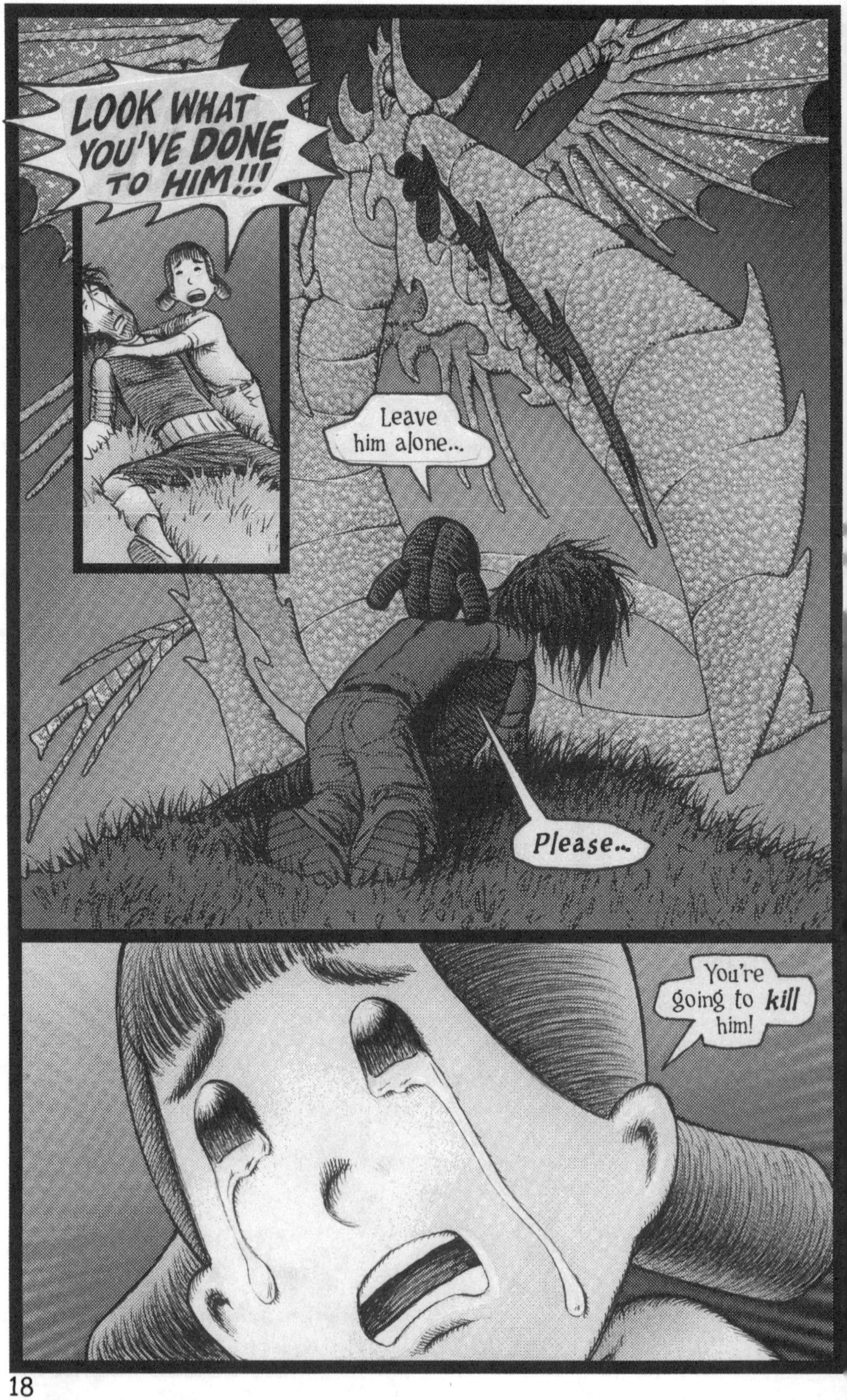

LOOK WHAT YOU'VE DONE TO HIM!!!
Leave him alone...
Please..
You're going to kill him!

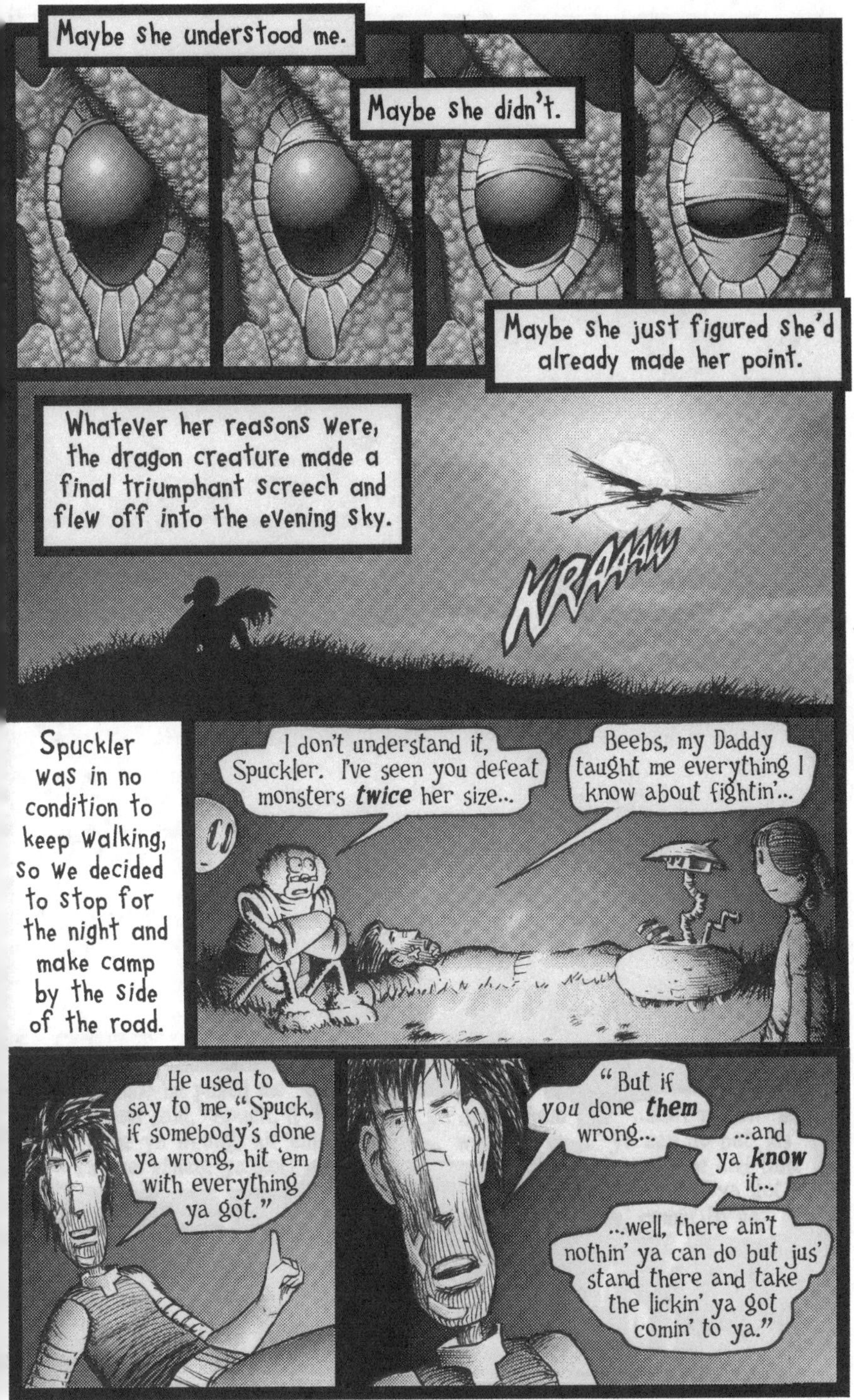

Maybe she understood me.
Maybe she didn't.
Maybe she just figured she'd already made her point.
Whatever her reasons were, the dragon creature made a final triumphant screech and flew off into the evening sky.
KRAAAW
Spuckler was in no condition to keep walking, so we decided to stop for the night and make camp by the side of the road.
I don't understand it, Spuckler. I've seen you defeat monsters **twice** her size...
Beebs, my Daddy taught me everything I know about fightin'...
He used to say to me, "Spuck, if somebody's done ya wrong, hit 'em with everything ya got."
"But if *you* done **them** wrong...
...and ya **know** it...
...well, there ain't nothin' ya can do but jus' stand there and take the lickin' ya got comin' to ya."

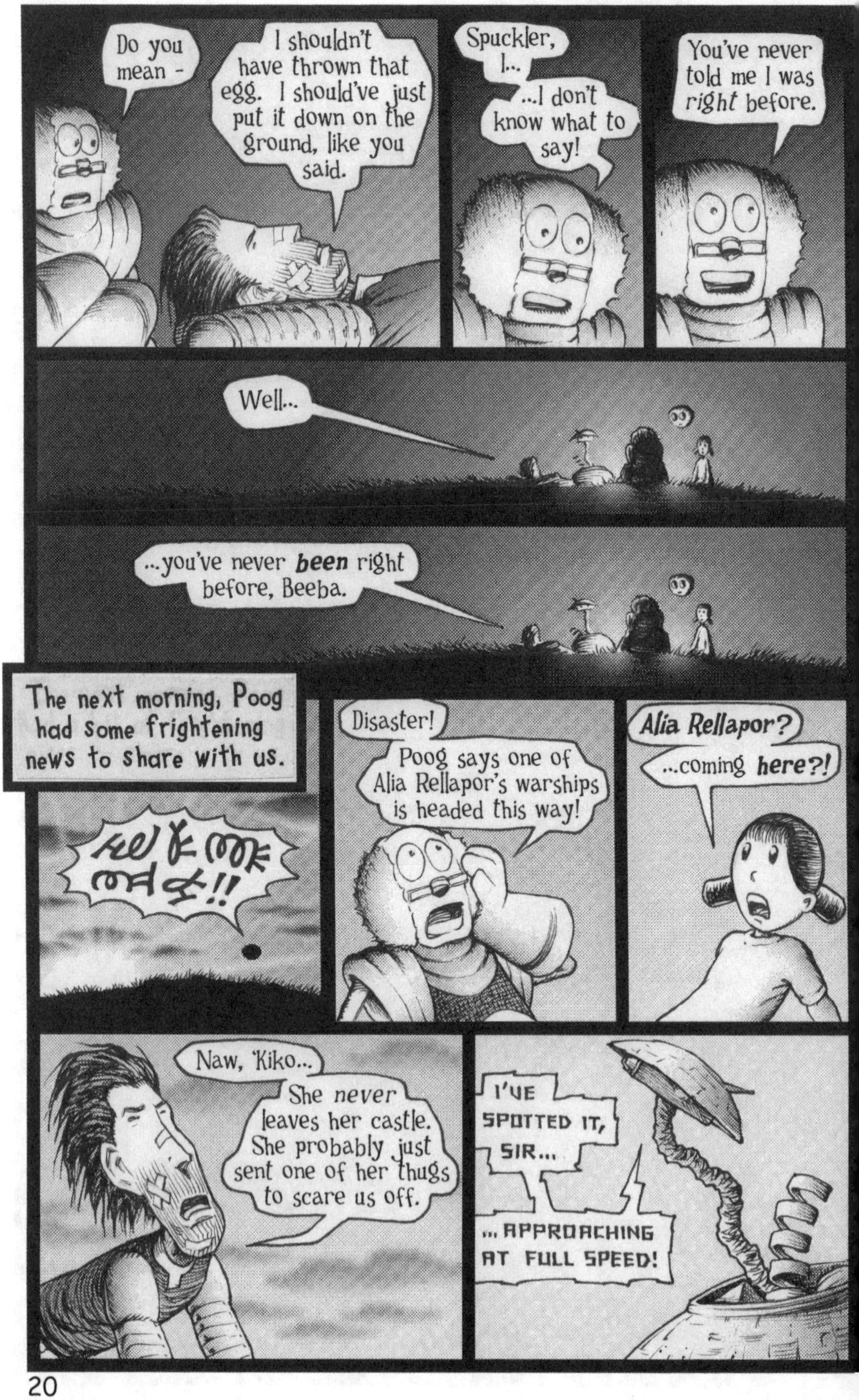
Do you mean -
I shouldn't have thrown that egg. I should've just put it down on the ground, like you said.
Spuckler, I...
...I don't know what to say!
You've never told me I was *right* before.
Well...
...you've never **been** right before, Beeba.
The next morning, Poog had some frightening news to share with us.
Disaster!
Poog says one of Alia Rellapor's warships is headed this way!
Alia Rellapor?
...coming ***here?!***
Naw, 'Kiko...
She *never* leaves her castle. She probably just sent one of her thugs to scare us off.
I'VE SPOTTED IT, SIR...
... APPROACHING AT FULL SPEED!

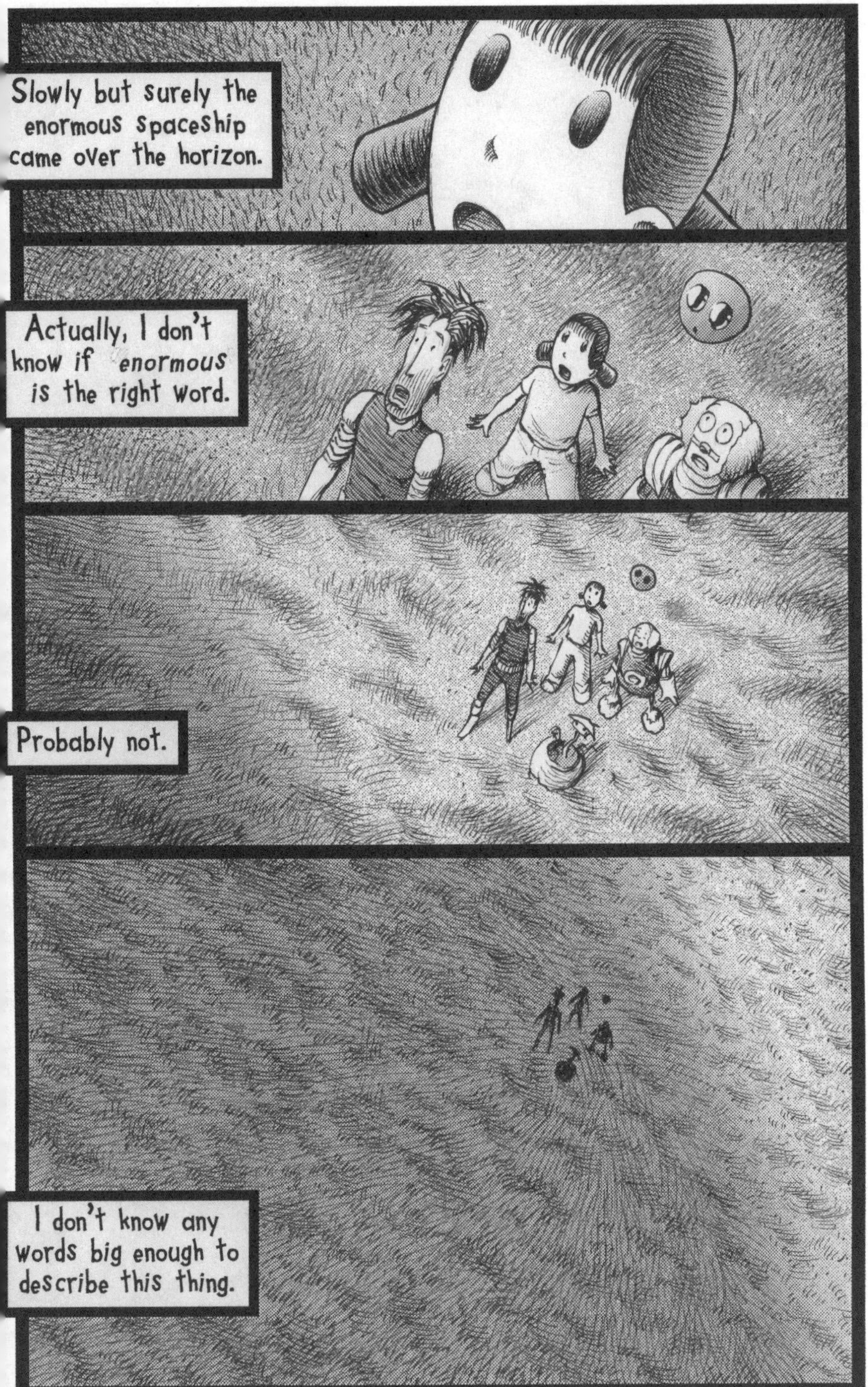
Slowly but surely the enormous spaceship came over the horizon.
Actually, I don't know if *enormous* is the right word.
Probably not.
I don't know any words big enough to describe this thing.

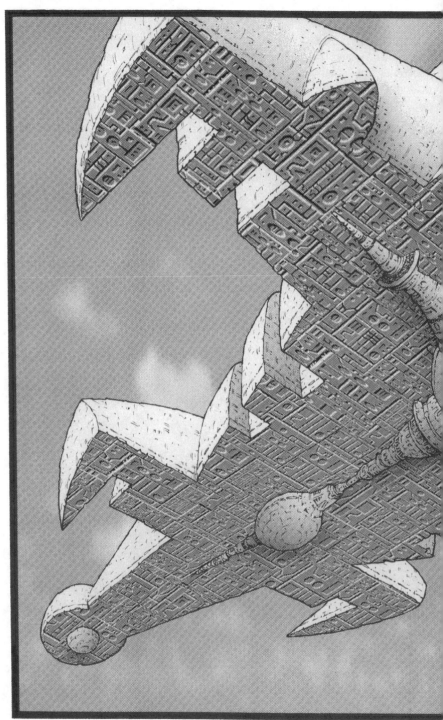

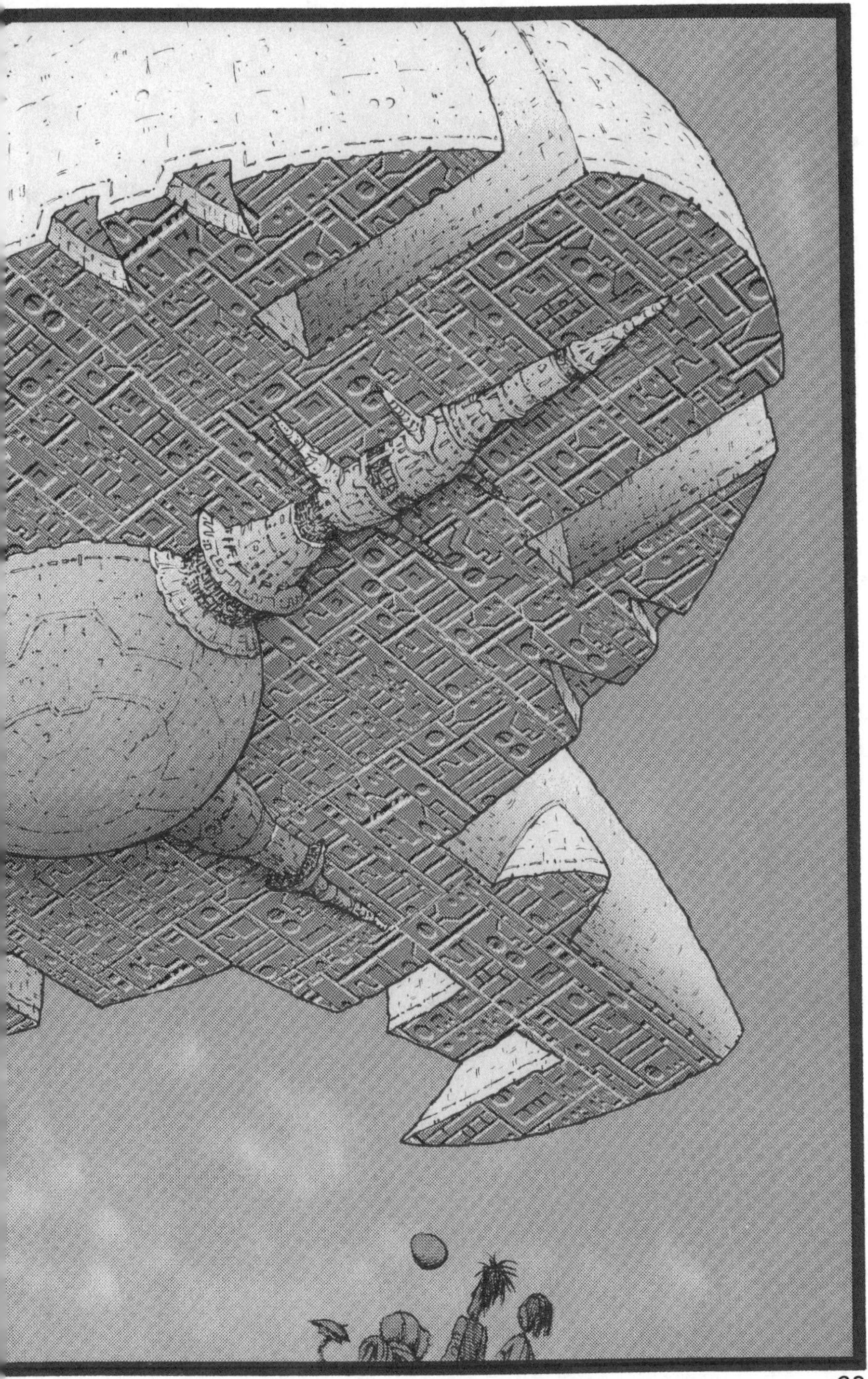

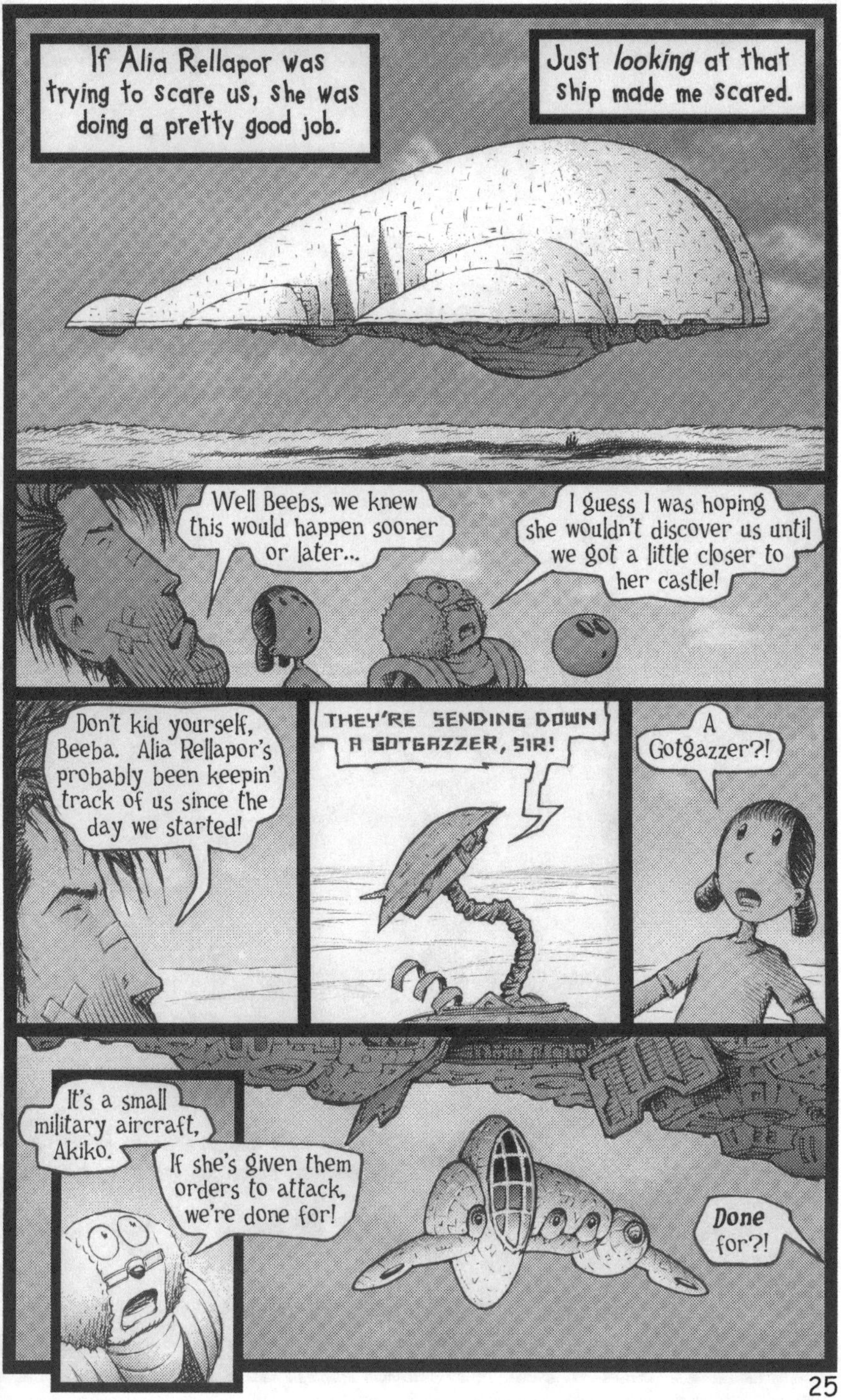

If Alia Rellapor was trying to scare us, she was doing a pretty good job.
Just *looking* at that ship made me scared.
Well Beebs, we knew this would happen sooner or later...
I guess I was hoping she wouldn't discover us until we got a little closer to her castle!
Don't kid yourself, Beeba. Alia Rellapor's probably been keepin' track of us since the day we started!
THEY'RE SENDING DOWN A GOTGAZZER, SIR!
A Gotgazzer?!
It's a small military aircraft, Akiko.
If she's given them orders to attack, we're done for!
Done for?!

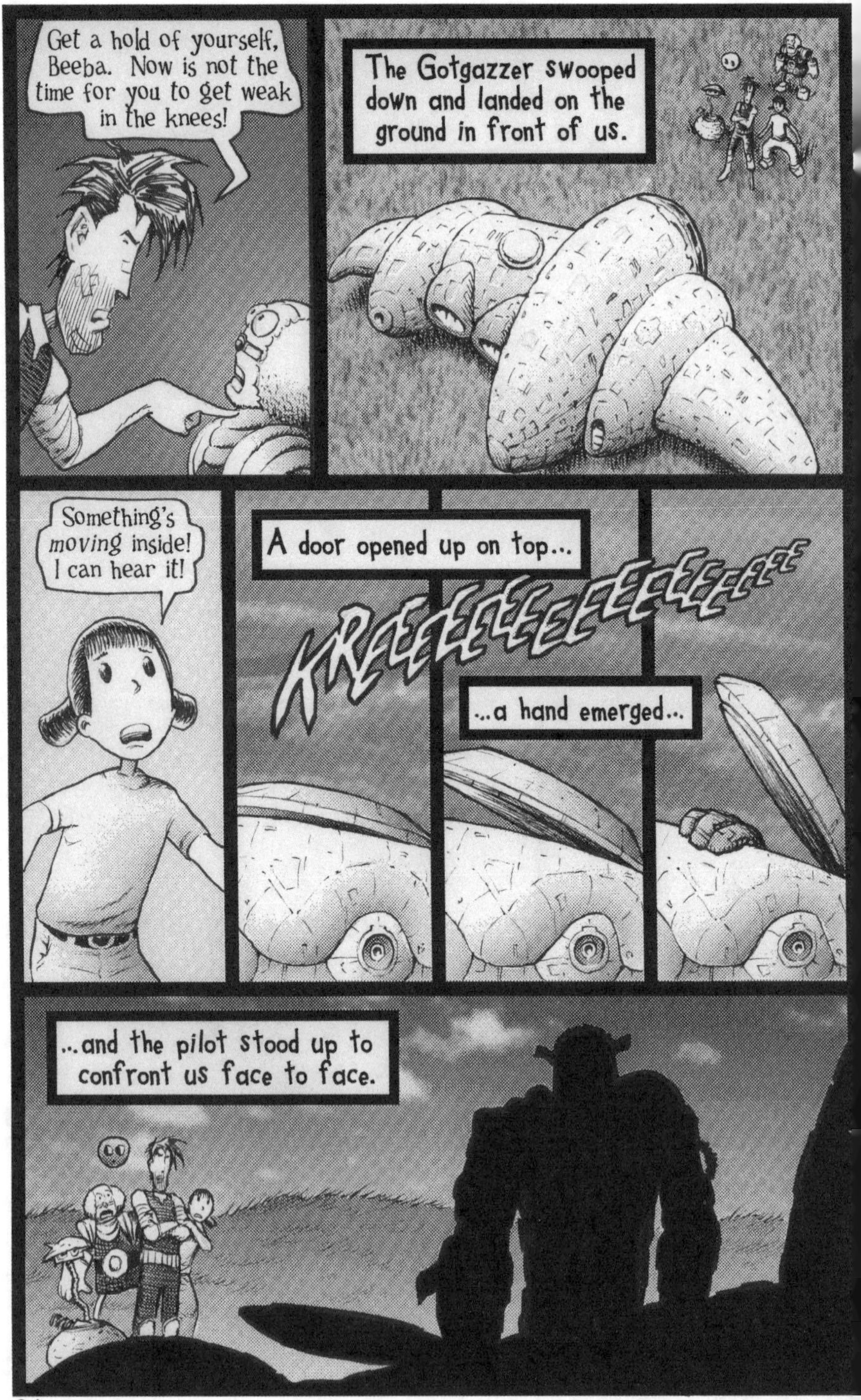

Get a hold of yourself, Beeba. Now is not the time for you to get weak in the knees!
The Gotgazzer swooped down and landed on the ground in front of us.
Something's *moving* inside! I can hear it!
A door opened up on top...
KREEEEEEEEEEEEEEEEE
...a hand emerged...
...and the pilot stood up to confront us face to face.

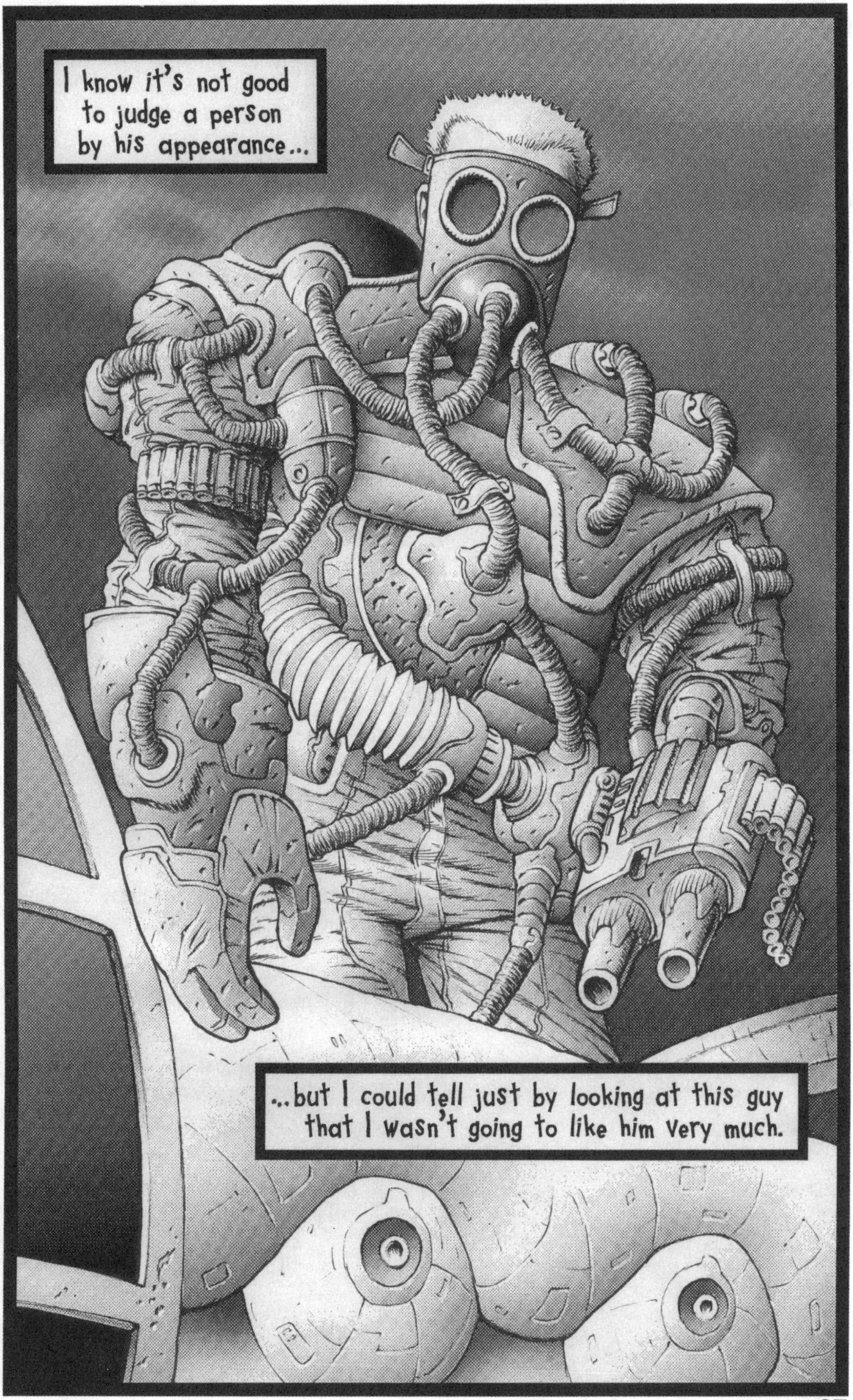
I know it's not good to judge a person by his appearance...
...but I could tell just by looking at this guy that I wasn't going to like him very much.

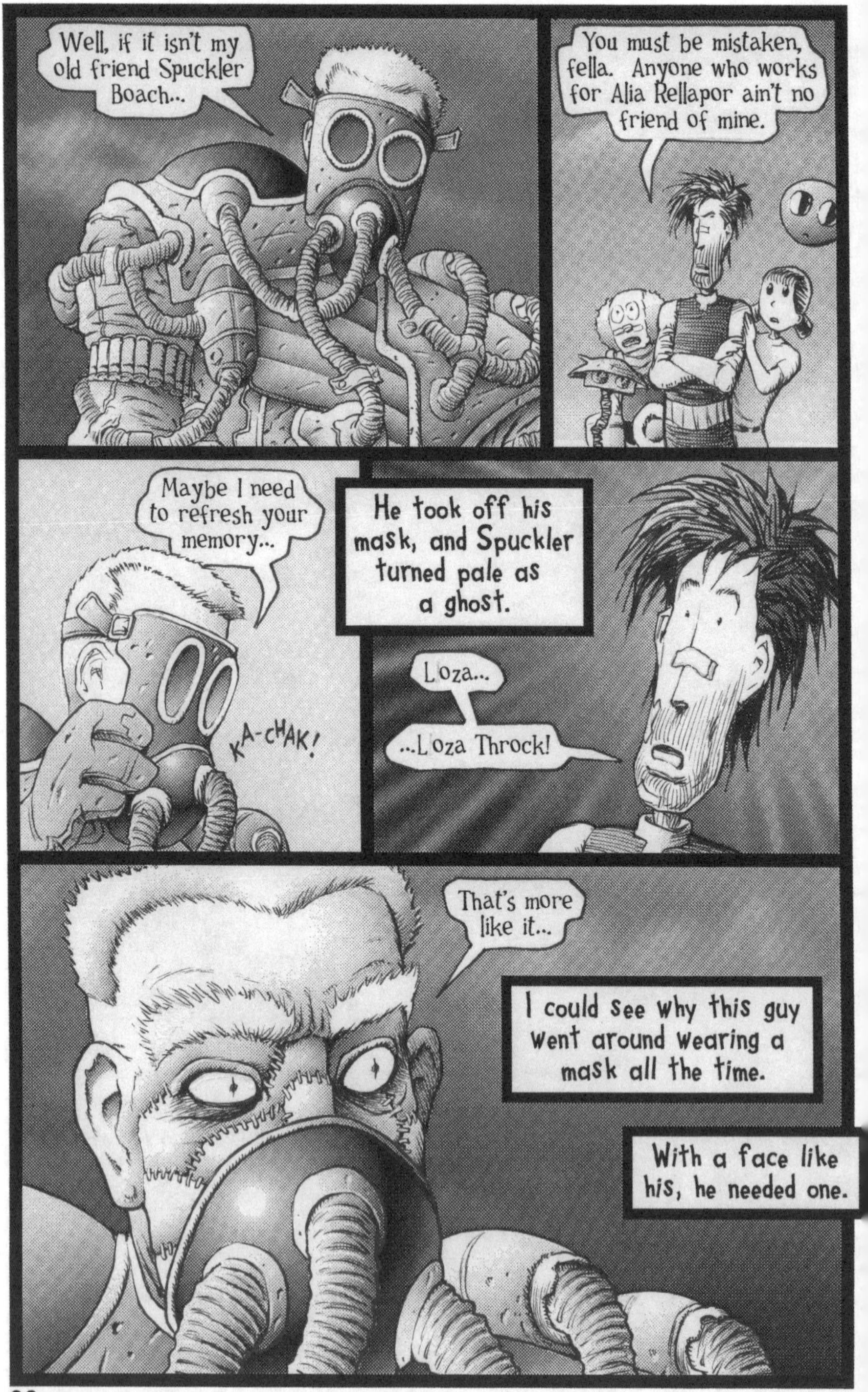
Well, if it isn't my old friend Spuckler Boach...
You must be mistaken, fella. Anyone who works for Alia Rellapor ain't no friend of mine.
Maybe I need to refresh your memory...
KA-CHAK!
He took off his mask, and Spuckler turned pale as a ghost.
Loza...
...Loza Throck!
That's more like it...
I could see why this guy went around wearing a mask all the time.
With a face like his, he needed one.

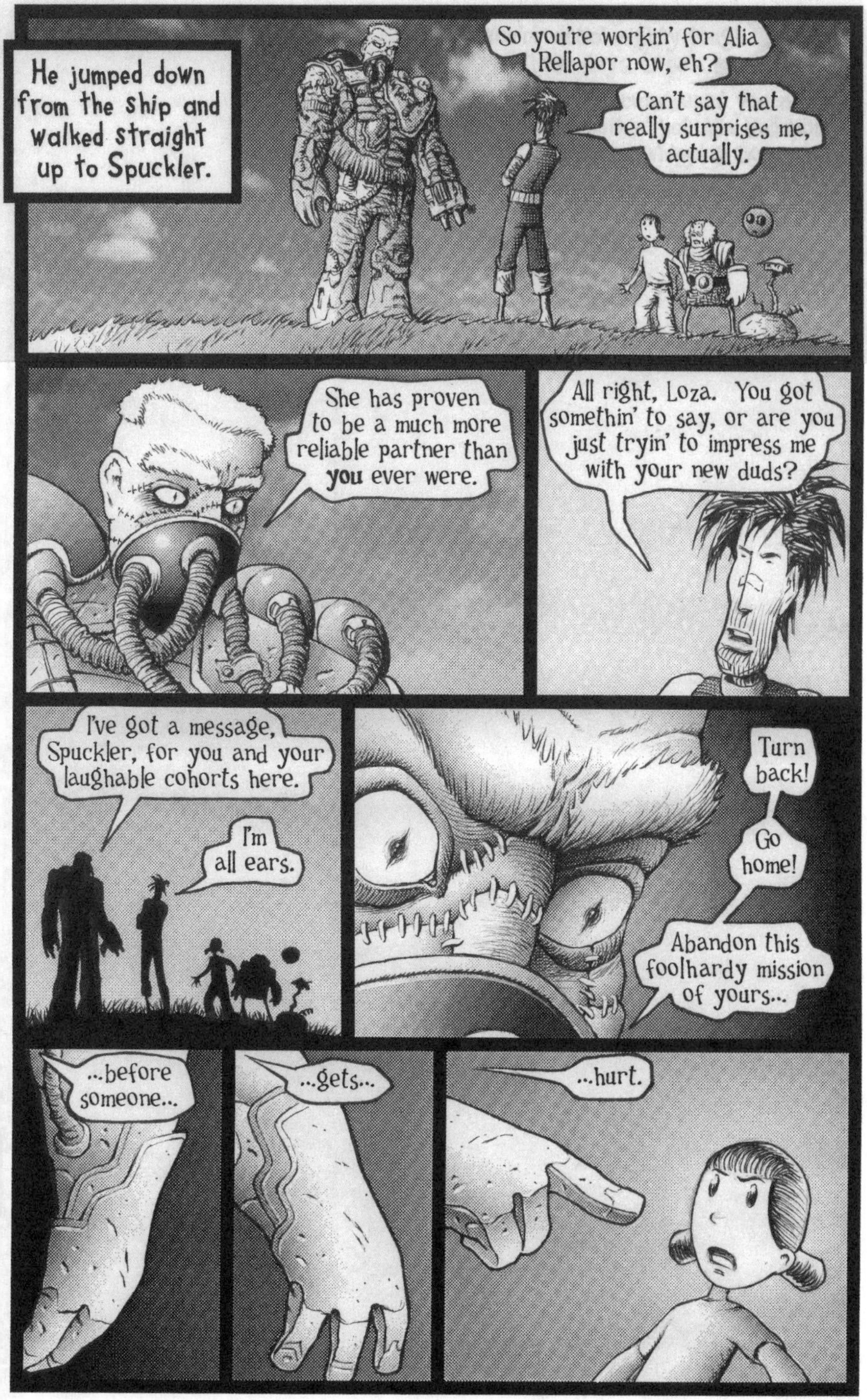
He jumped down from the ship and walked straight up to Spuckler.
So you're workin' for Alia Rellapor now, eh?
Can't say that really surprises me, actually.
She has proven to be a much more reliable partner than **you** ever were.
All right, Loza. You got somethin' to say, or are you just tryin' to impress me with your new duds?
I've got a message, Spuckler, for you and your laughable cohorts here.
I'm all ears.
Turn back!
Go home!
Abandon this foolhardy mission of yours...
...before someone...
...gets...
...hurt.

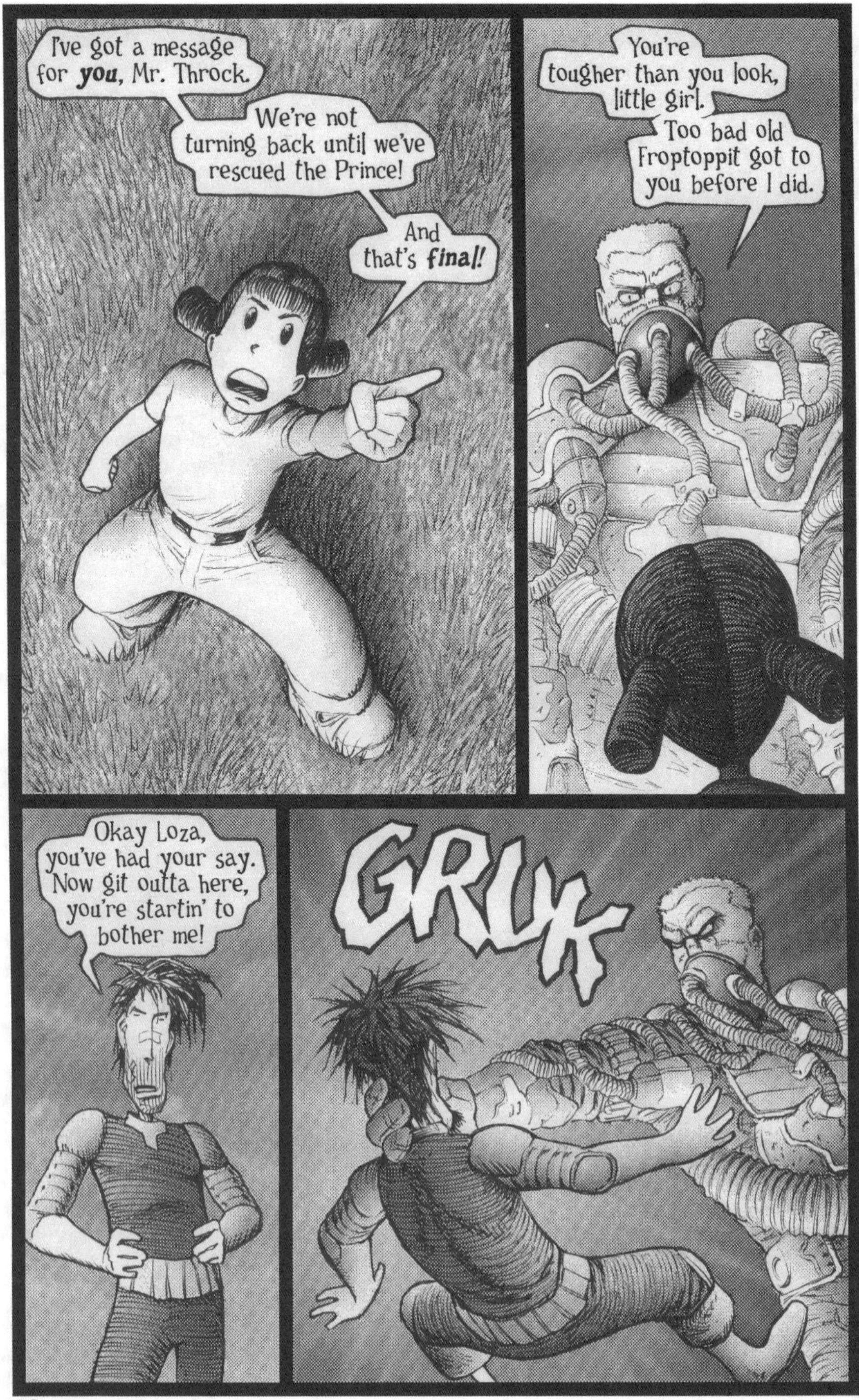
I've got a message for **you**, Mr. Throck.
We're not turning back until we've rescued the Prince!
And that's **final**!
You're tougher than you look, little girl.
Too bad old Froptoppit got to you before I did.
Okay Loza, you've had your say. Now git outta here, you're startin' to bother me!
GRUK

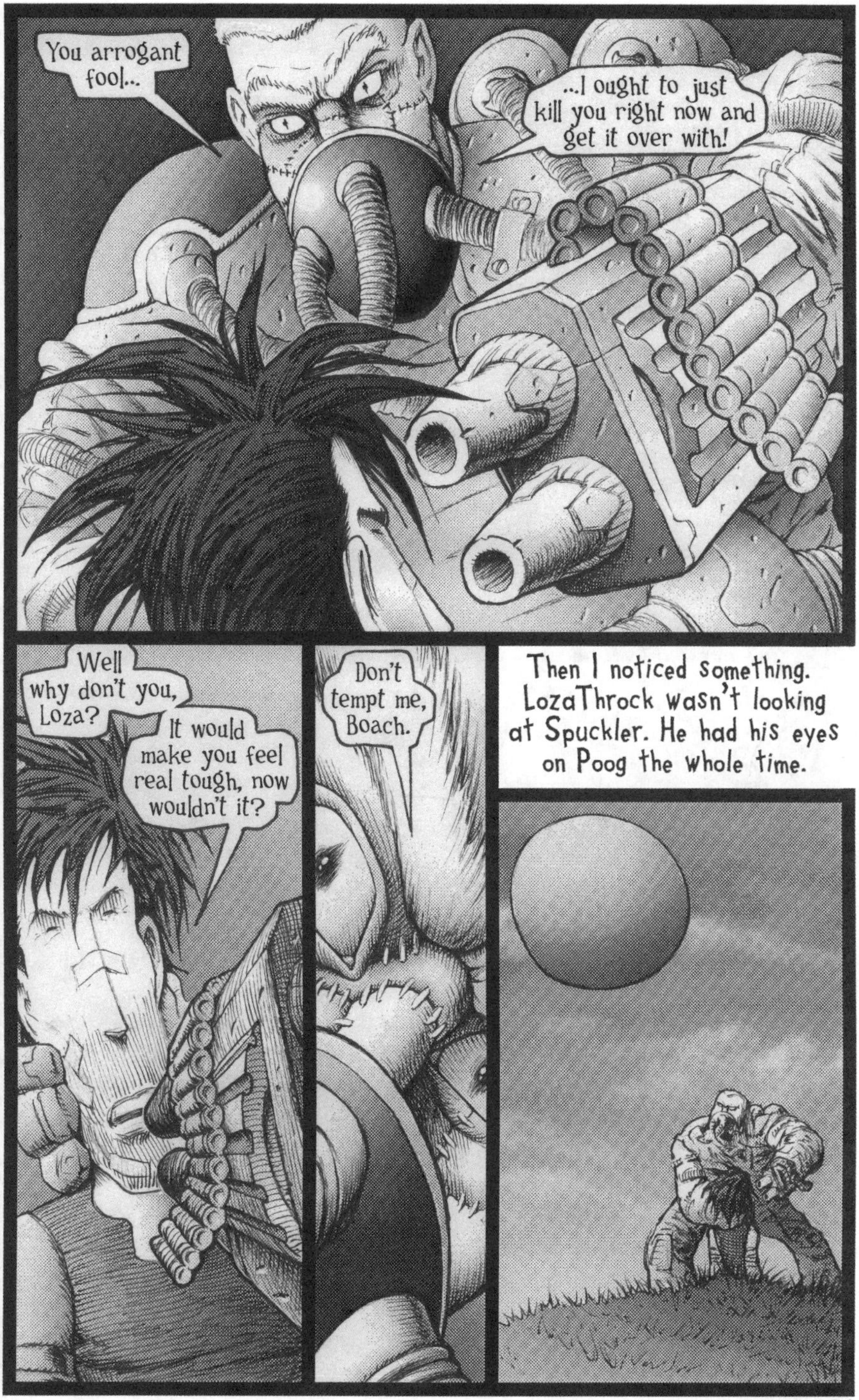

You arrogant fool...
...I ought to just kill you right now and get it over with!
Well why don't you, Loza?
It would make you feel real tough, now wouldn't it?
Don't tempt me, Boach.
Then I noticed something. LozaThrock wasn't looking at Spuckler. He had his eyes on Poog the whole time.

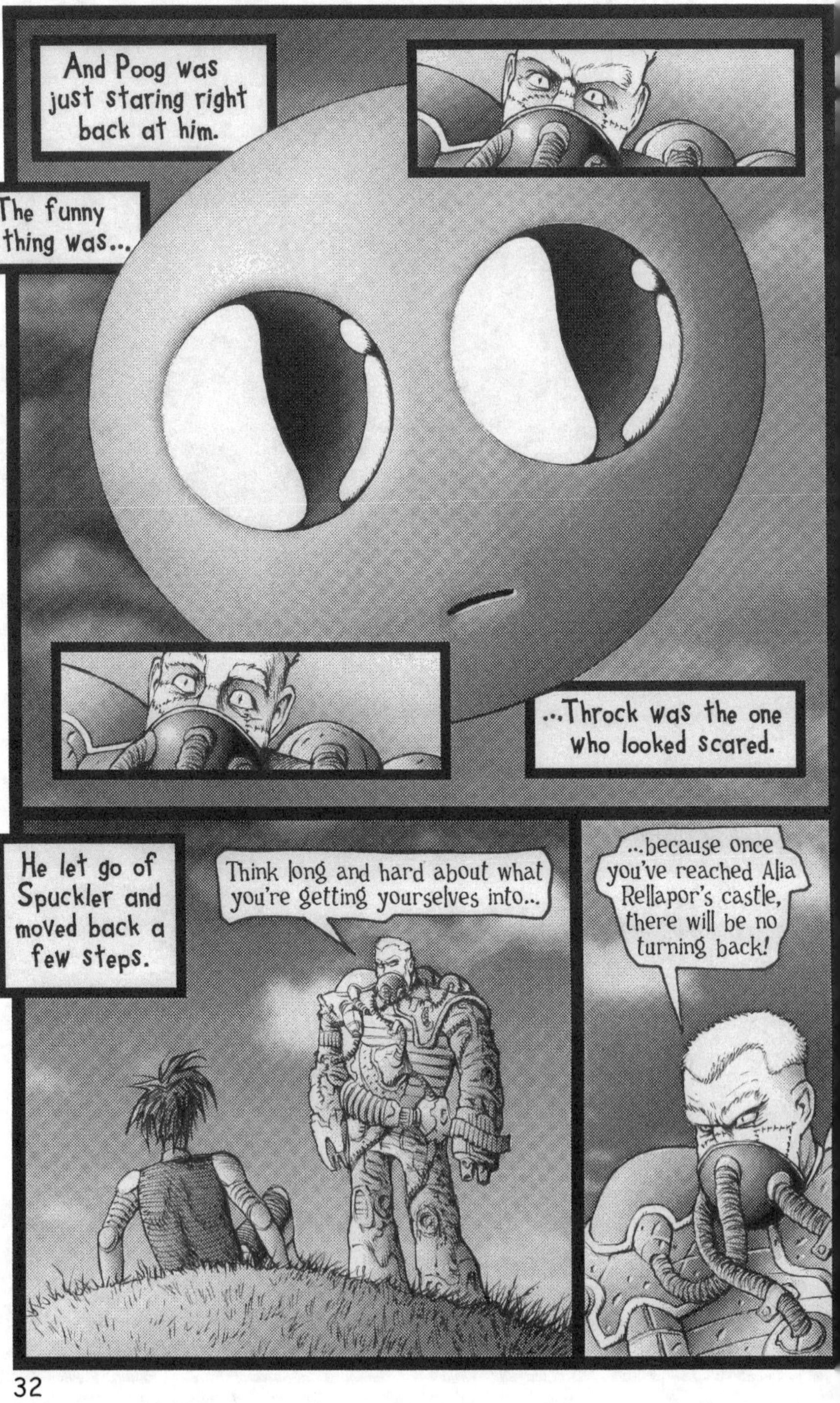
And Poog was just staring right back at him.
The funny thing was...
...Throck was the one who looked scared.
He let go of Spuckler and moved back a few steps.
Think long and hard about what you're getting yourselves into...
...because once you've reached Alia Rellapor's castle, there will be no turning back!

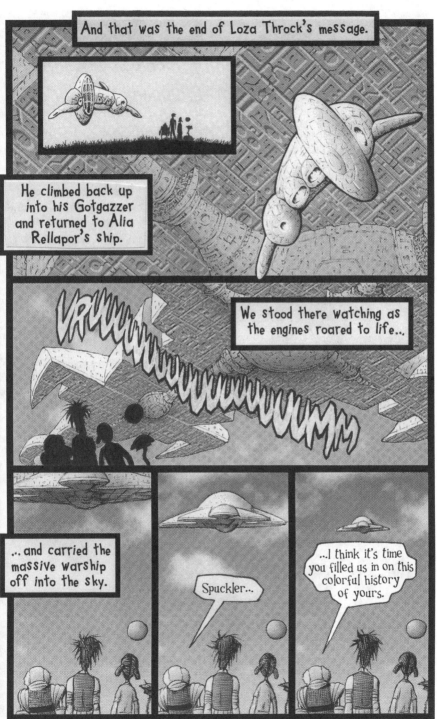

And that was the end of Loza Throck's message.

He climbed back up into his Gotgazzer and returned to Alia Rellapor's ship.

We stood there watching as the engines roared to life...

VRUUUUUUUUUUUMMMM

...and carried the massive warship off into the sky.

Spuckler...

...I think it's time you filled us in on this colorful history of yours.

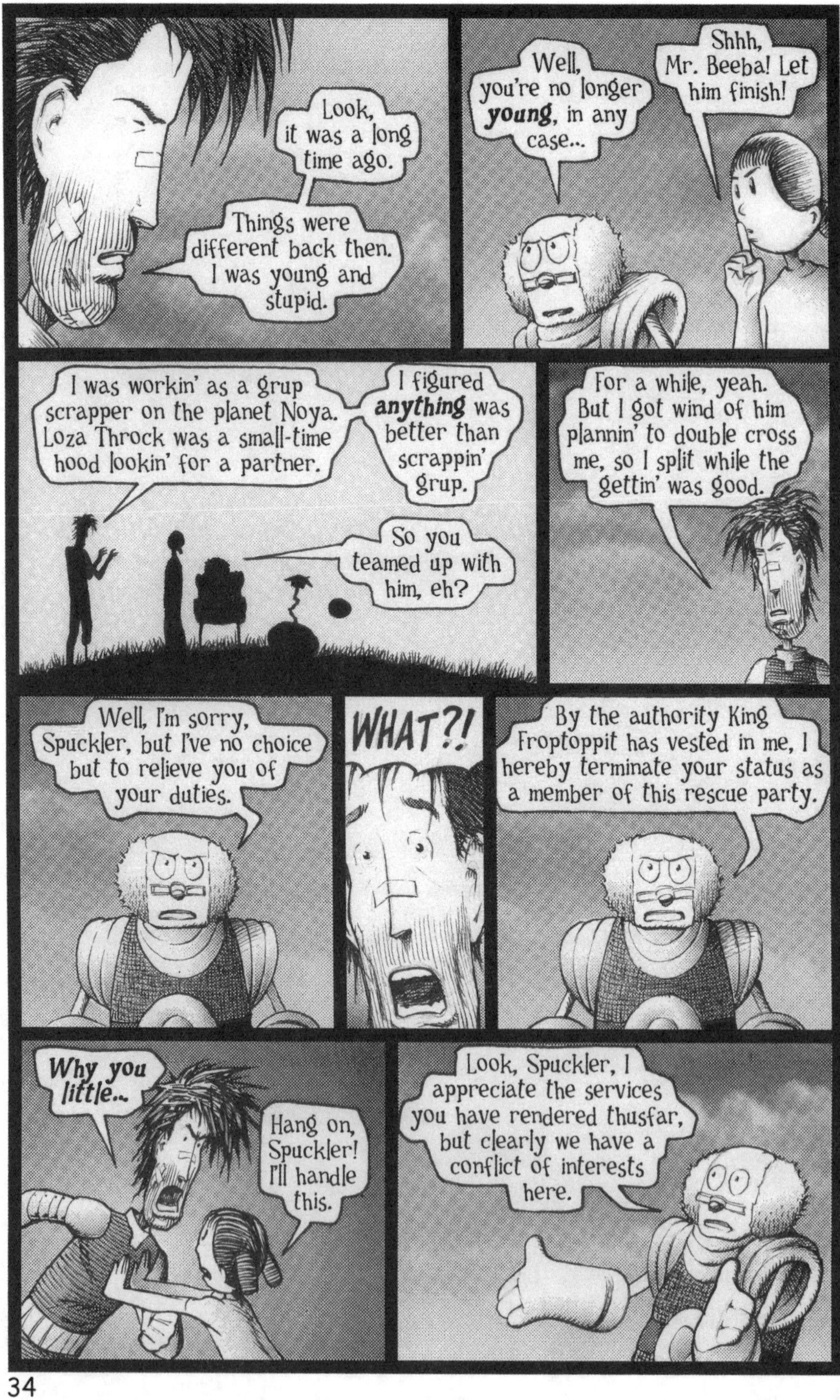
Look, it was a long time ago.
Things were different back then. I was young and stupid.
Well, you're no longer **young**, in any case...
Shhh, Mr. Beeba! Let him finish!
I was workin' as a grup scrapper on the planet Noya. Loza Throck was a small-time hood lookin' for a partner.
I figured **anything** was better than scrappin' grup.
So you teamed up with him, eh?
For a while, yeah. But I got wind of him plannin' to double cross me, so I split while the gettin' was good.
Well, I'm sorry, Spuckler, but I've no choice but to relieve you of your duties.
WHAT?!
By the authority King Froptoppit has vested in me, I hereby terminate your status as a member of this rescue party.
Why you little...
Hang on, Spuckler! I'll handle this.
Look, Spuckler, I appreciate the services you have rendered thusfar, but clearly we have a conflict of interests here.

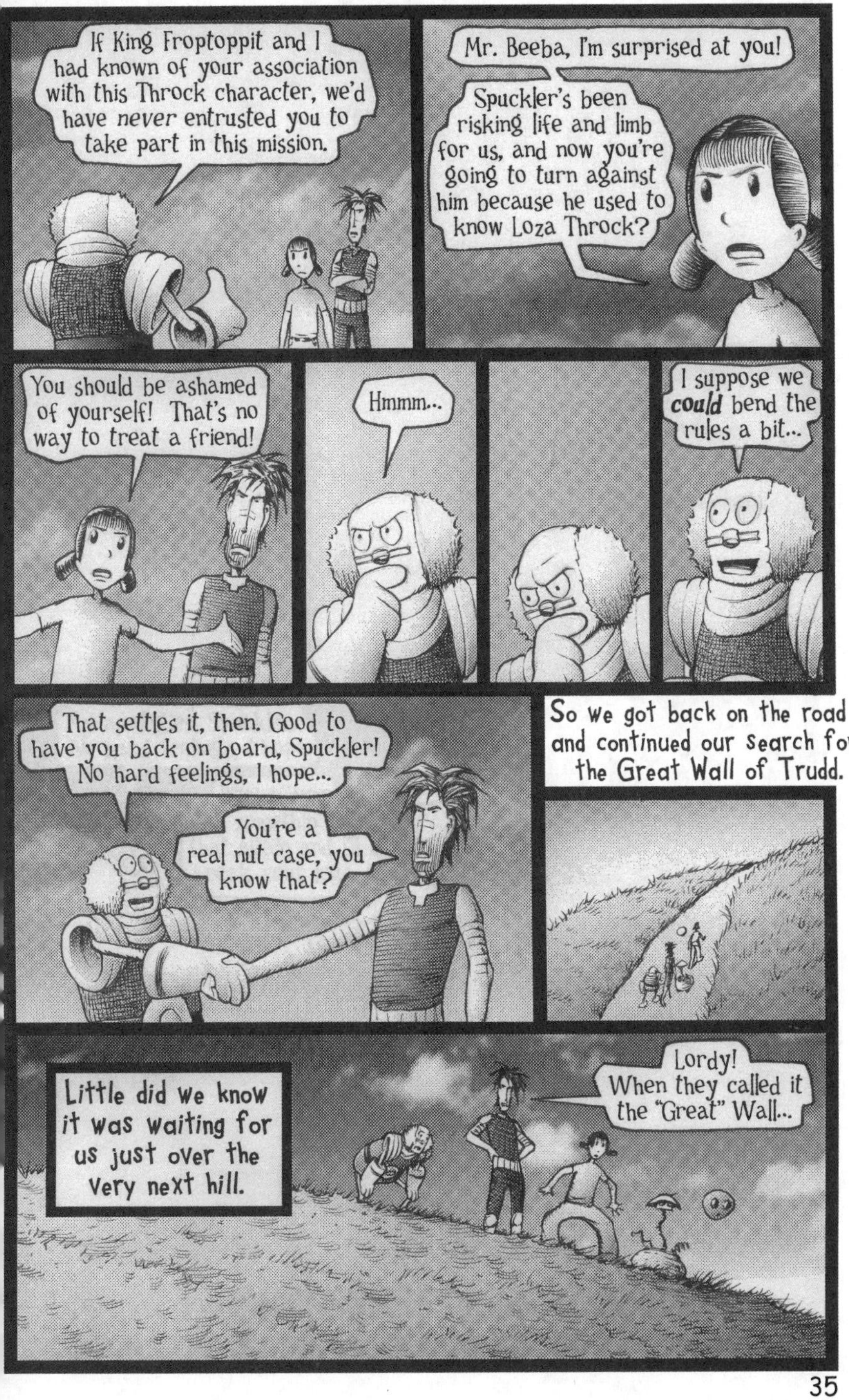

If King Froptoppit and I had known of your association with this Throck character, we'd have *never* entrusted you to take part in this mission.
Mr. Beeba, I'm surprised at you!
Spuckler's been risking life and limb for us, and now you're going to turn against him because he used to know Loza Throck?
You should be ashamed of yourself! That's no way to treat a friend!
Hmmm...
I suppose we **could** bend the rules a bit...
That settles it, then. Good to have you back on board, Spuckler! No hard feelings, I hope...
You're a real nut case, you know that?
So we got back on the road and continued our search for the Great Wall of Trudd.
Little did we know it was waiting for us just over the very next hill.
Lordy! When they called it the "Great" Wall...

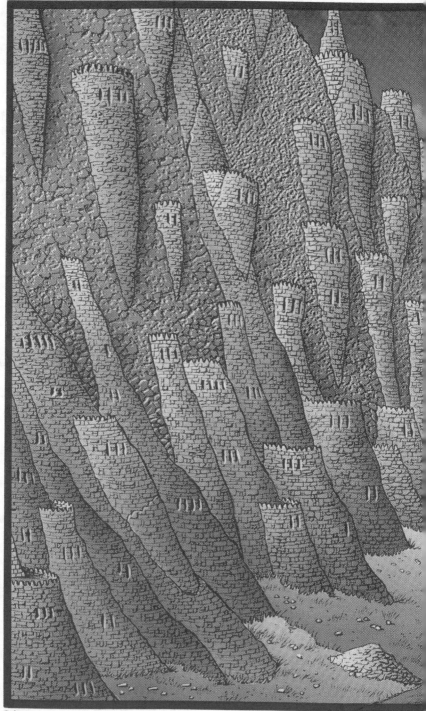

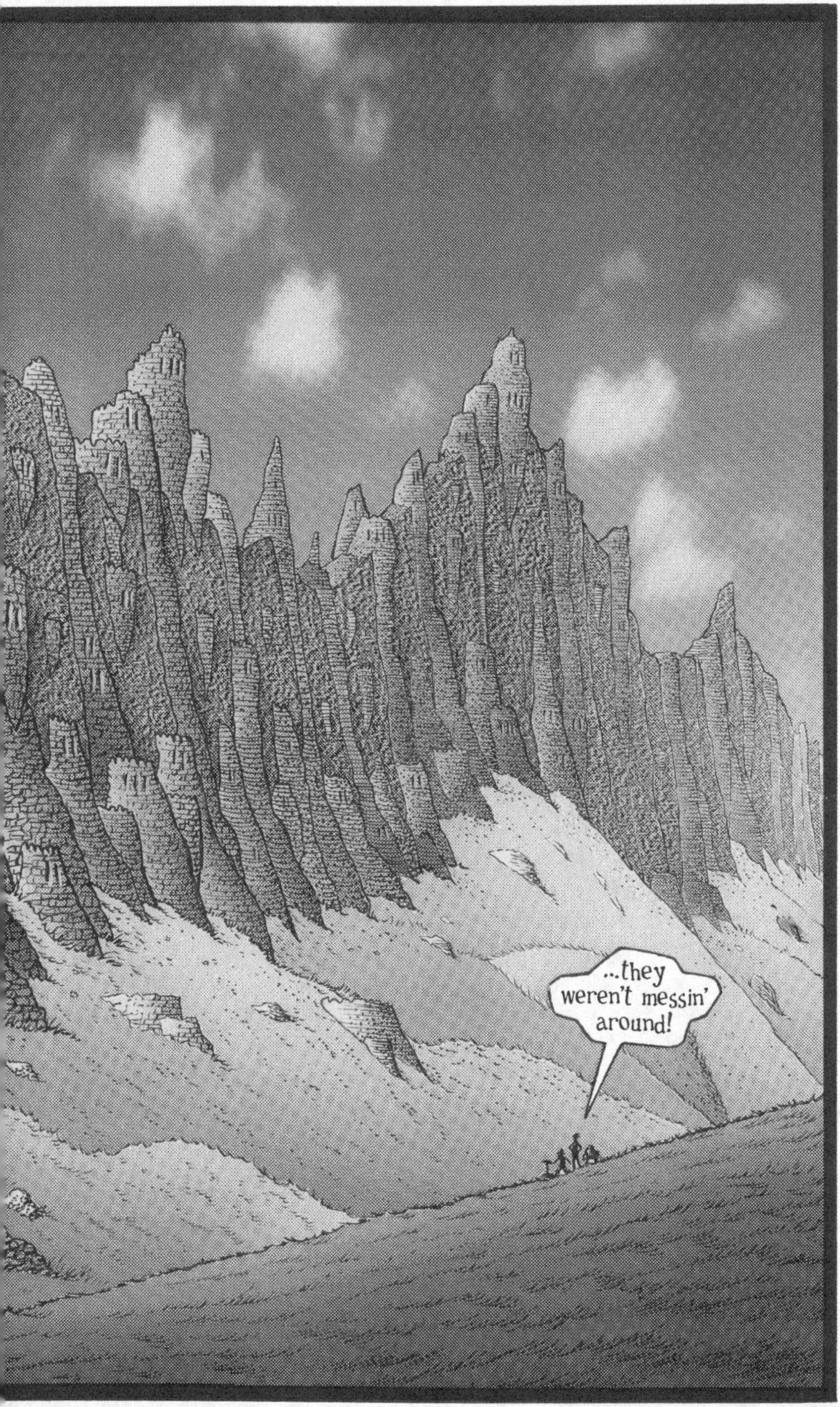
...they weren't messin' around!

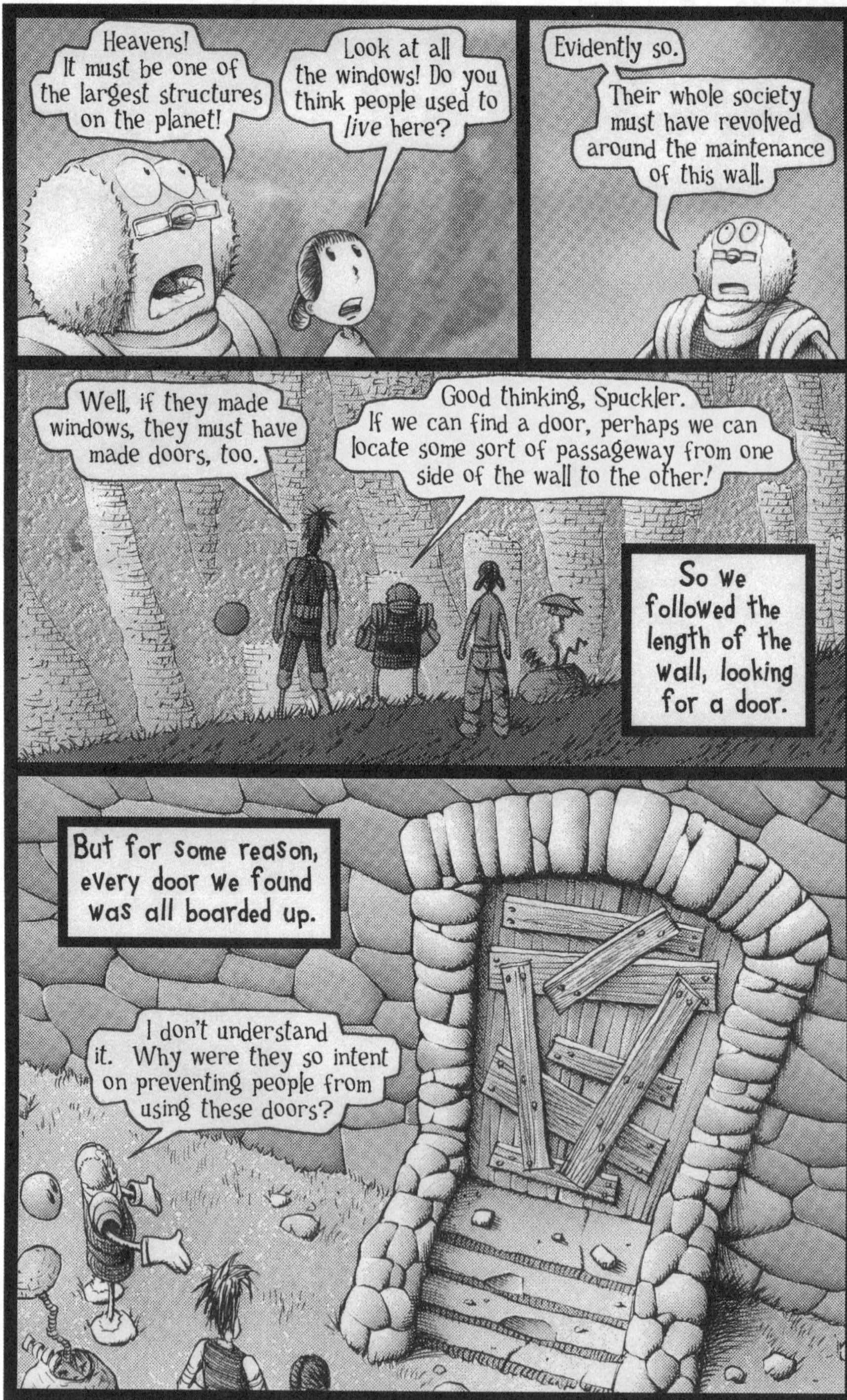
Heavens! It must be one of the largest structures on the planet!
Look at all the windows! Do you think people used to *live* here?
Evidently so.
Their whole society must have revolved around the maintenance of this wall.
Well, if they made windows, they must have made doors, too.
Good thinking, Spuckler. If we can find a door, perhaps we can locate some sort of passageway from one side of the wall to the other!
So we followed the length of the wall, looking for a door.
But for some reason, every door we found was all boarded up.
I don't understand it. Why were they so intent on preventing people from using these doors?

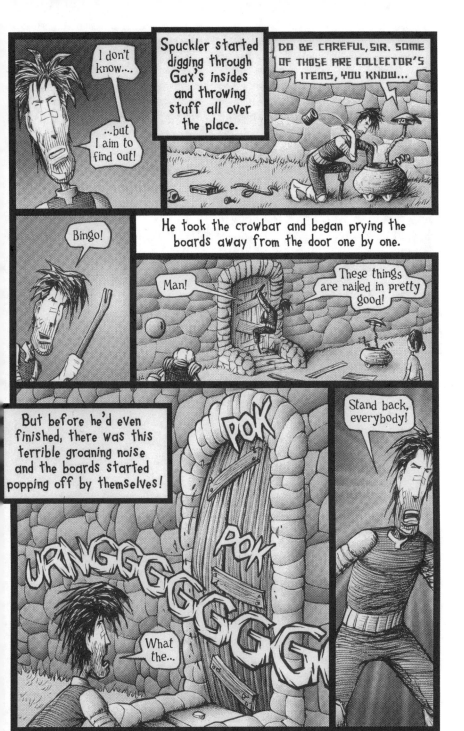

I don't know....

...but to I aim to find out!

Spuckler started digging through Gax's insides and throwing stuff all over the place.

DO BE CAREFUL, SIR. SOME OF THOSE ARE COLLECTOR'S ITEMS, YOU KNOW...

Bingo!

He took the crowbar and began prying the boards away from the door one by one.

Man!

These things are nailed in pretty good!

But before he'd even finished, there was this terrible groaning noise and the boards started popping off by themselves!

POK

POK

URNNGGGGGGGGGGGGGGGGGGGGGGG

What the...

Stand back, everybody!

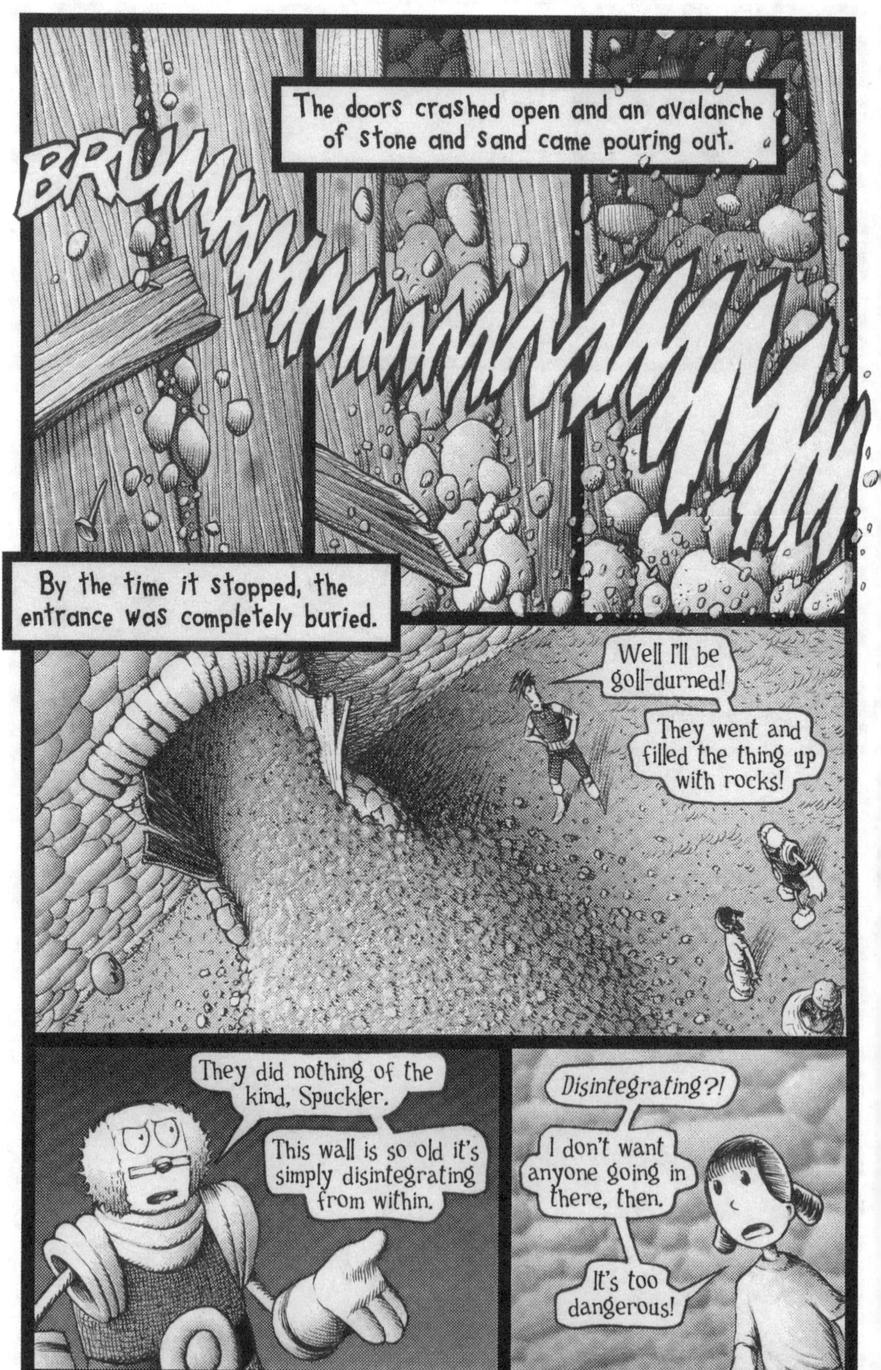
BRUMMMMMMMMMMMMM
The doors crashed open and an avalanche of stone and sand came pouring out.
By the time it stopped, the entrance was completely buried.
Well I'll be goll-durned!
They went and filled the thing up with rocks!
They did nothing of the kind, Spuckler.
This wall is so old it's simply disintegrating from within.
Disintegrating?!
I don't want anyone going in there, then.
It's too dangerous!

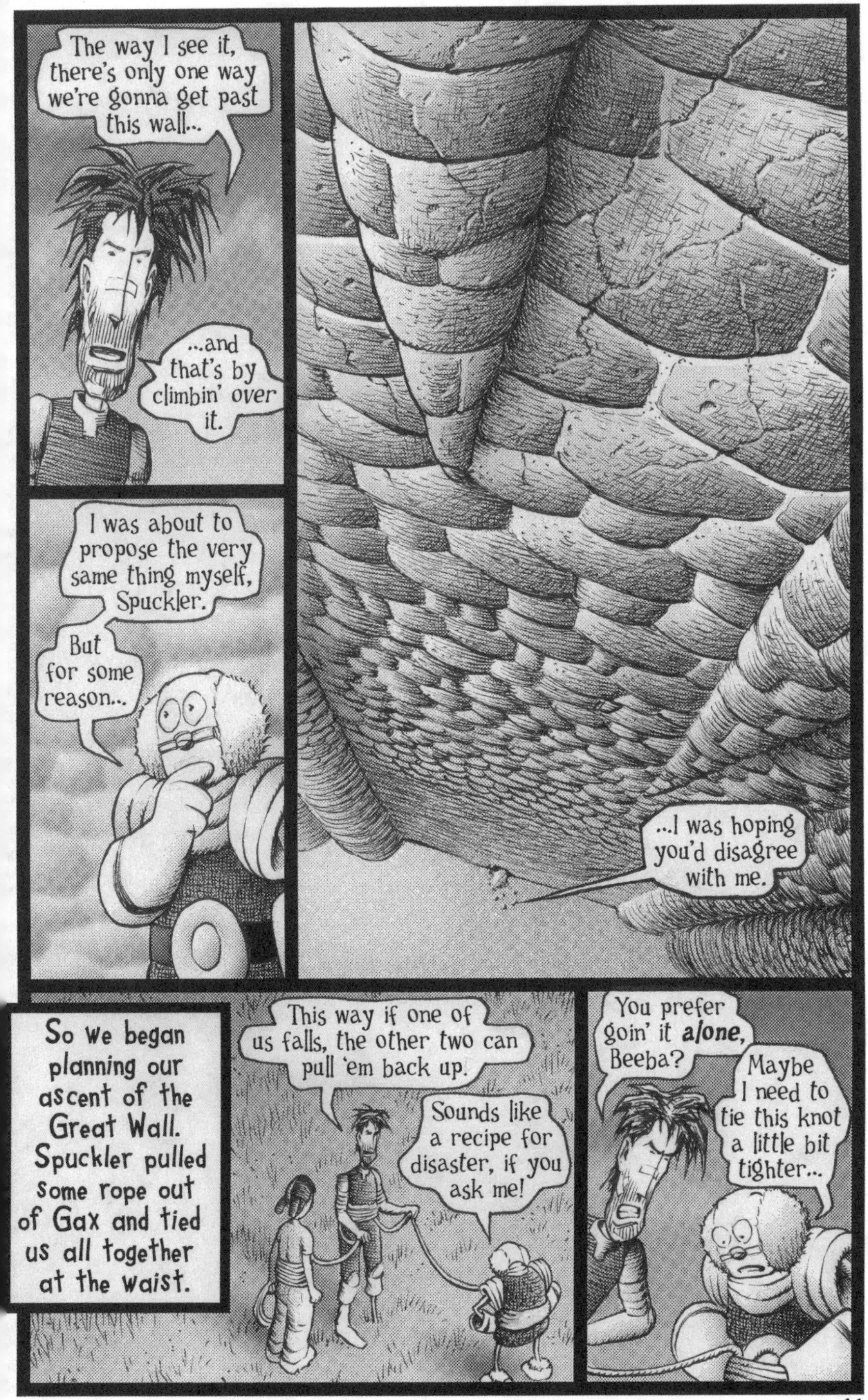
The way I see it, there's only one way we're gonna get past this wall...
...and that's by climbin' over it.
I was about to propose the very same thing myself, Spuckler.
But for some reason...
...I was hoping you'd disagree with me.
So we began planning our ascent of the Great Wall. Spuckler pulled some rope out of Gax and tied us all together at the waist.
This way if one of us falls, the other two can pull 'em back up.
Sounds like a recipe for disaster, if you ask me!
You prefer goin' it *alone*, Beeba?
Maybe I need to tie this knot a little bit tighter...

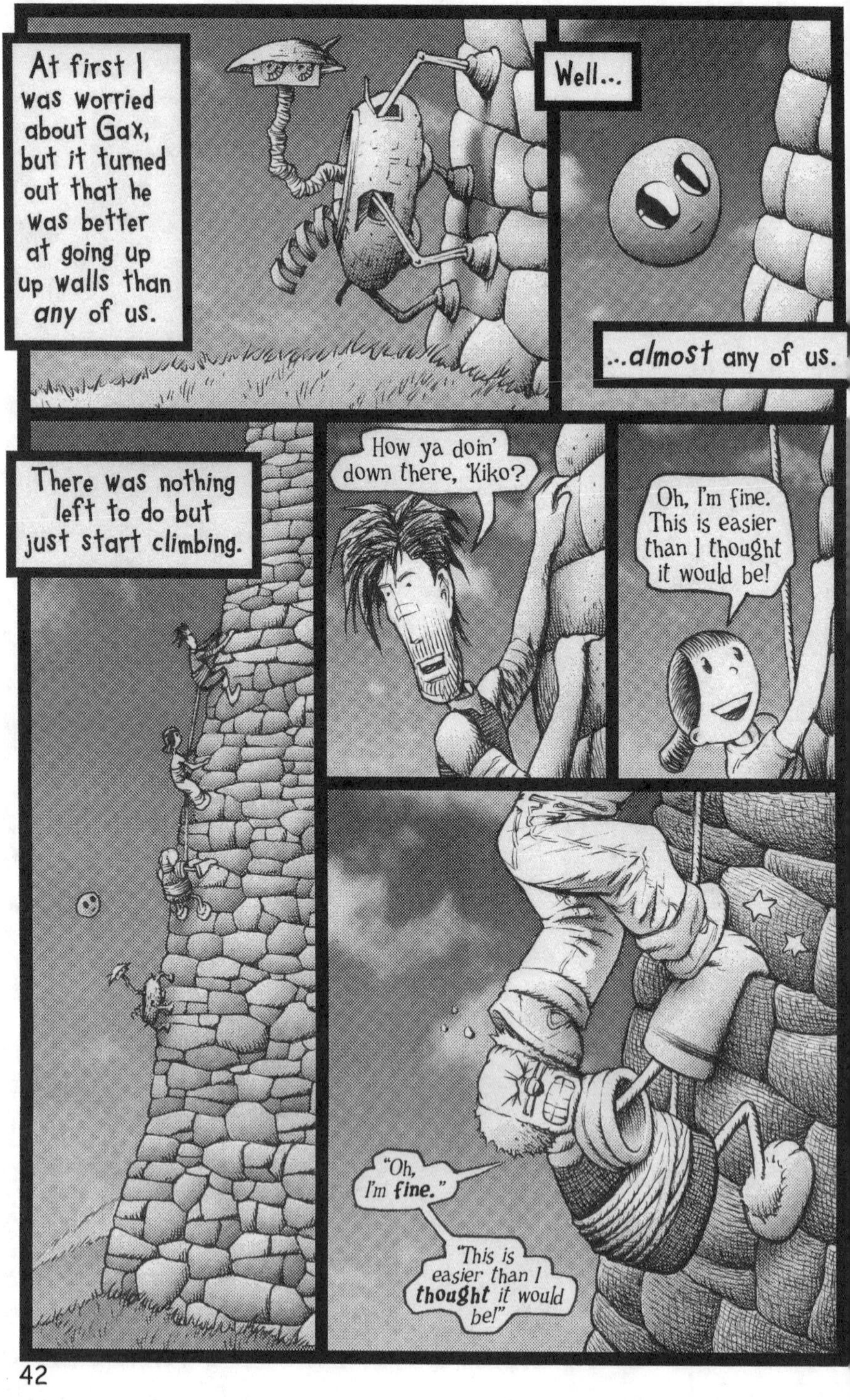

At first I was worried about Gax, but it turned out that he was better at going up up walls than *any* of us.
Well...
...*almost* any of us.
There was nothing left to do but just start climbing.
How ya doin' down there, 'Kiko?
Oh, I'm fine. This is easier than I thought it would be!
"Oh, I'm **fine.**"
"This is easier than I **thought** it would be!"

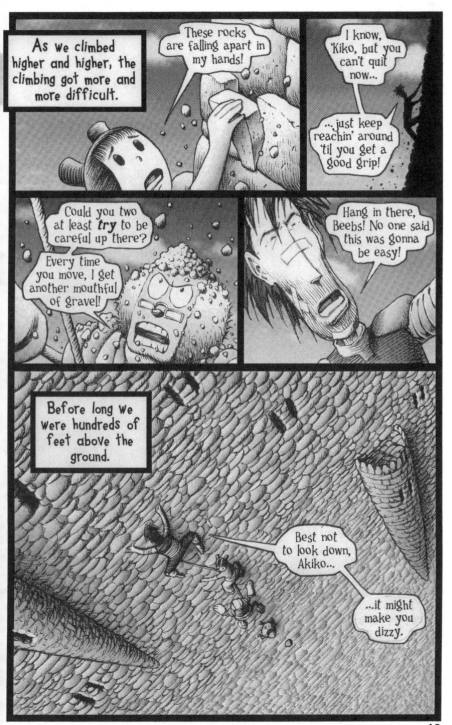

As we climbed higher and higher, the climbing got more and more difficult.

These rocks are falling apart in my hands!

I know, 'Kiko, but you can't quit now...

...just keep reachin' around 'til you get a good grip!

Could you two at least *try* to be careful up there?

Every time you move, I get another mouthful of gravel!

Hang in there, Beebs! No one said this was gonna be easy!

Before long we were hundreds of feet above the ground.

Best not to look down, Akiko...

...it might make you dizzy.

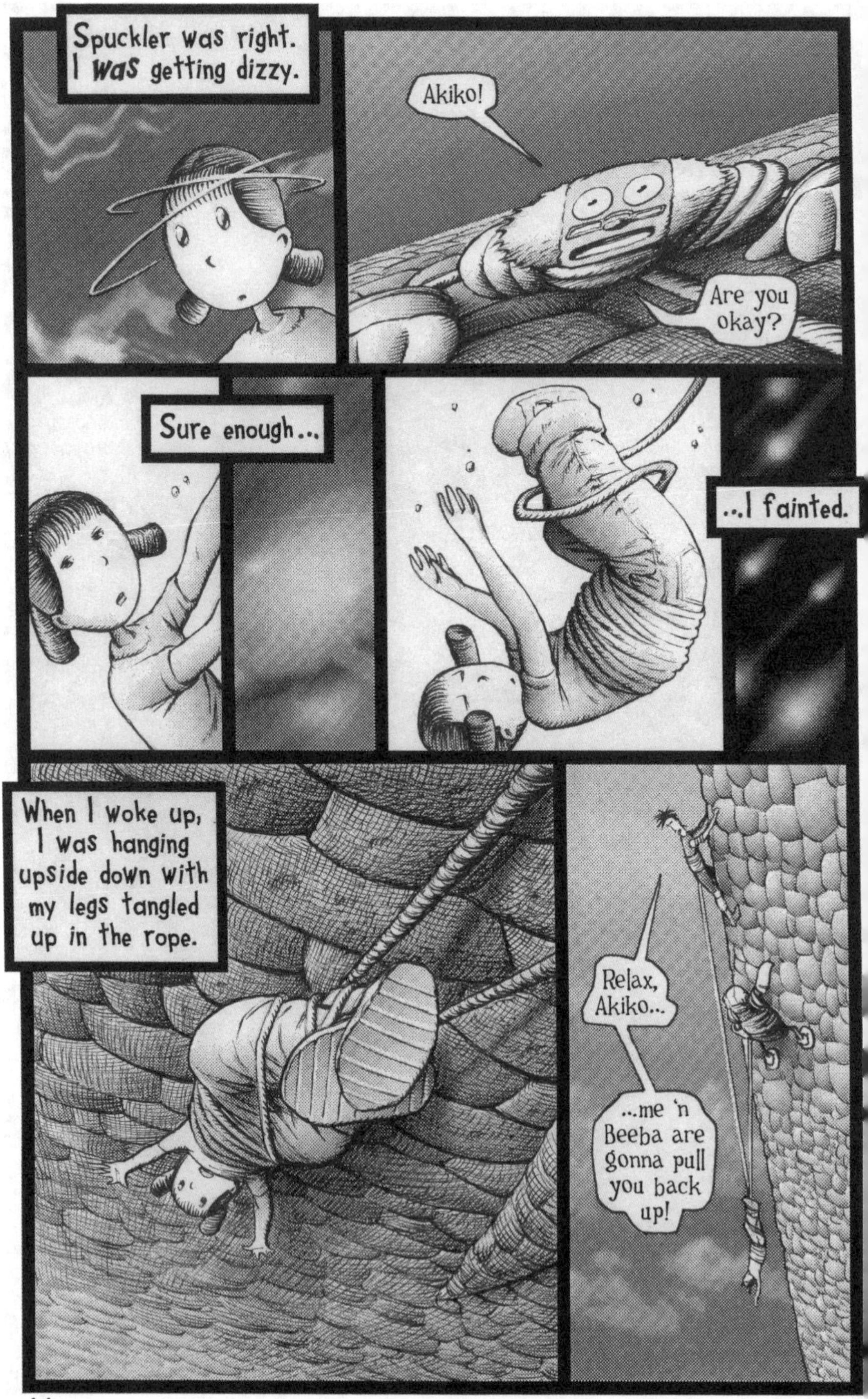
Spuckler was right. I *was* getting dizzy.
Akiko!
Are you okay?
Sure enough...
...I fainted.
When I woke up, I was hanging upside down with my legs tangled up in the rope.
Relax, Akiko...
...me 'n Beeba are gonna pull you back up!

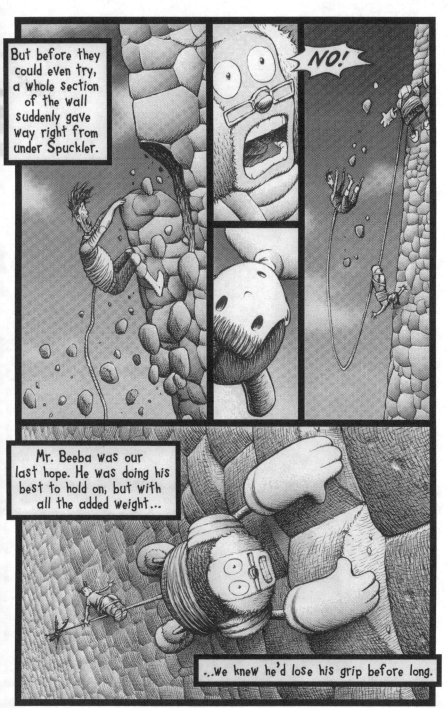

But before they could even try, a whole section of the wall suddenly gave way right from under Spuckler.

NO!

Mr. Beeba was our last hope. He was doing his best to hold on, but with all the added weight...

...we knew he'd lose his grip before long.

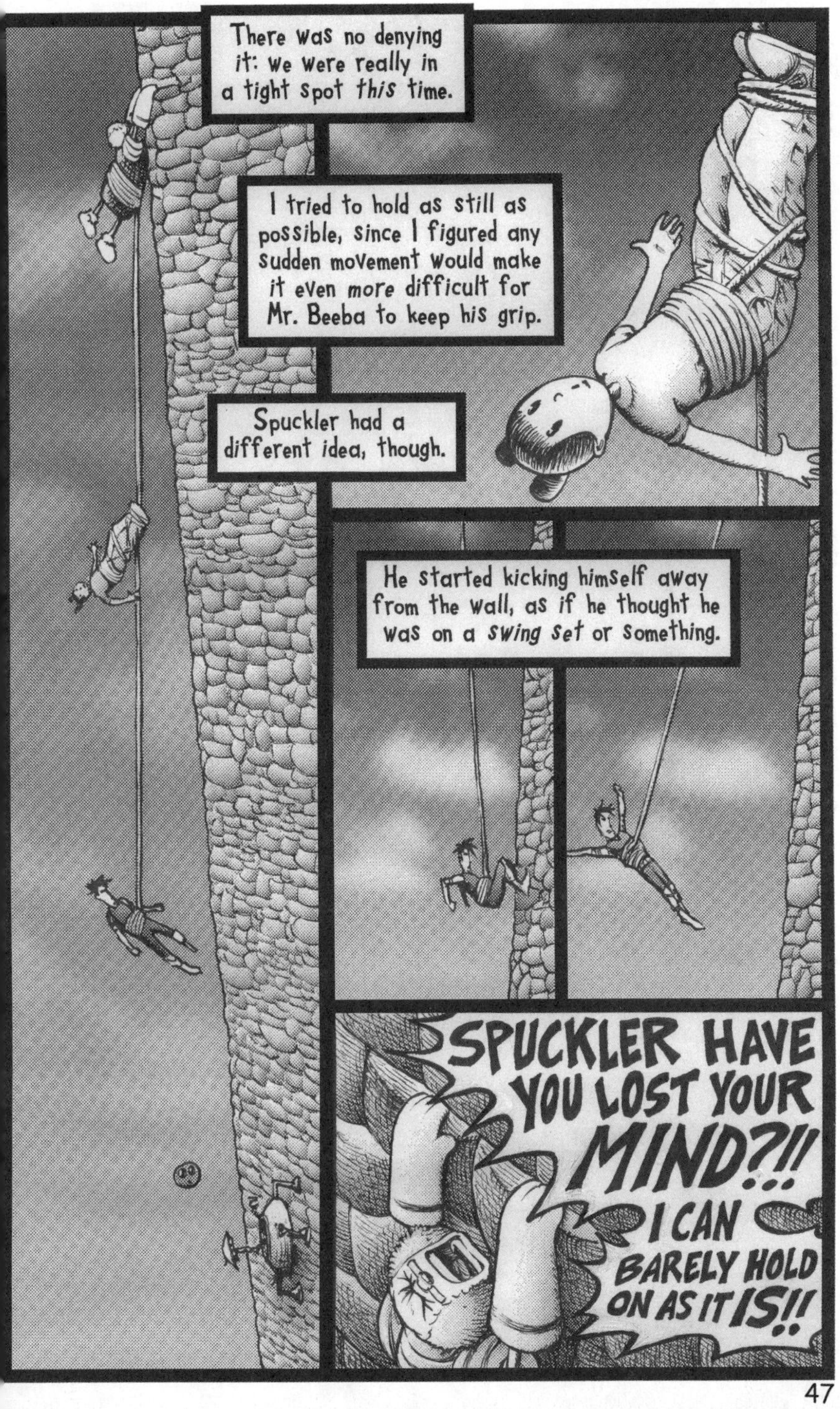
There was no denying it: we were really in a tight spot *this* time.
I tried to hold as still as possible, since I figured any sudden movement would make it even *more* difficult for Mr. Beeba to keep his grip.
Spuckler had a different *idea*, though.
He started kicking himself away from the wall, as if he thought he was on a *swing set* or something.
SPUCKLER HAVE YOU LOST YOUR MIND?!!
I CAN BARELY HOLD ON AS IT IS!!

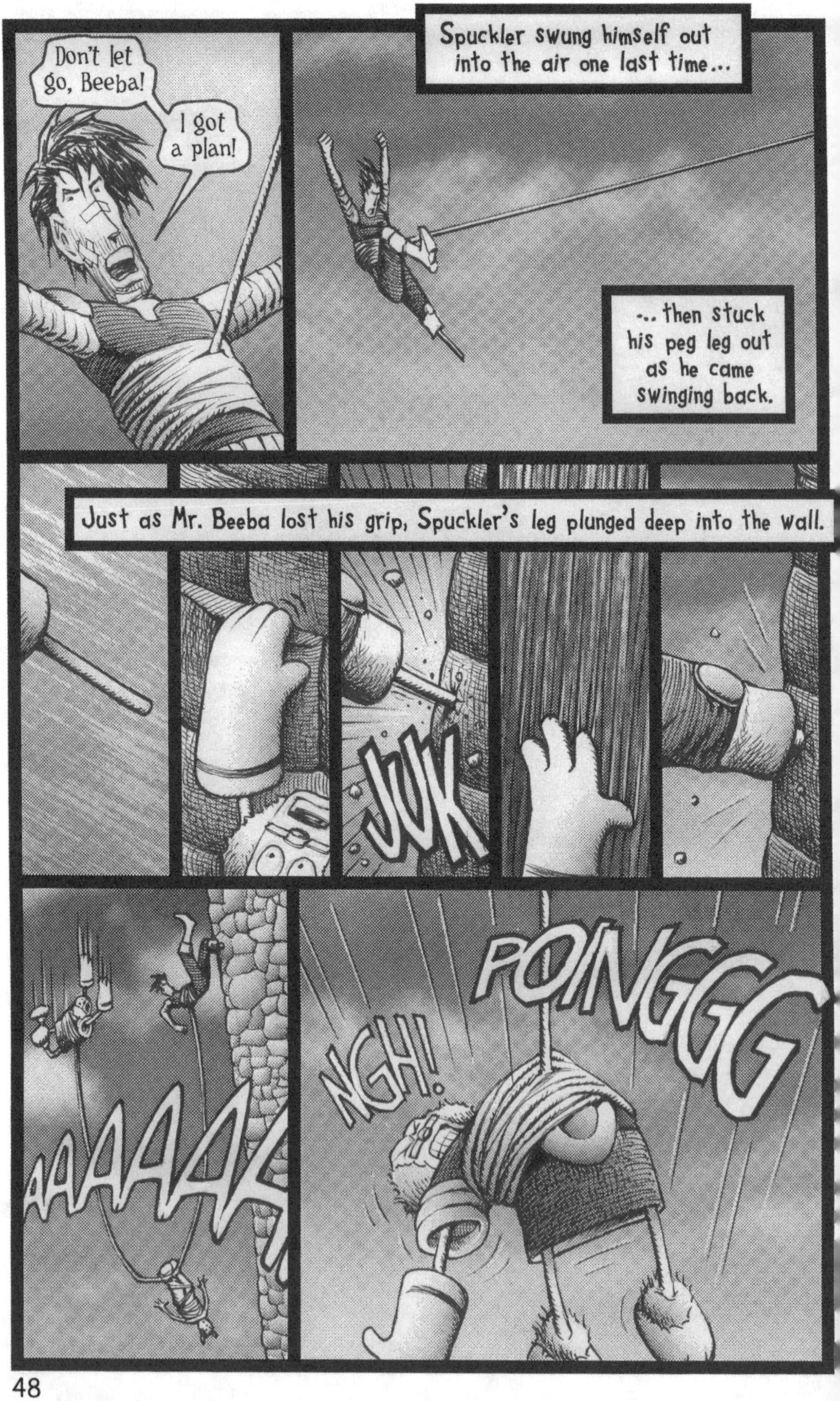
Don't let go, Beeba!
I got a plan!
Spuckler swung himself out into the air one last time...
-.. then stuck his peg leg out as he came swinging back.
Just as Mr. Beeba lost his grip, Spuckler's leg plunged deep into the wall.
JUK
AAAAAA
NGH!
POINGGG

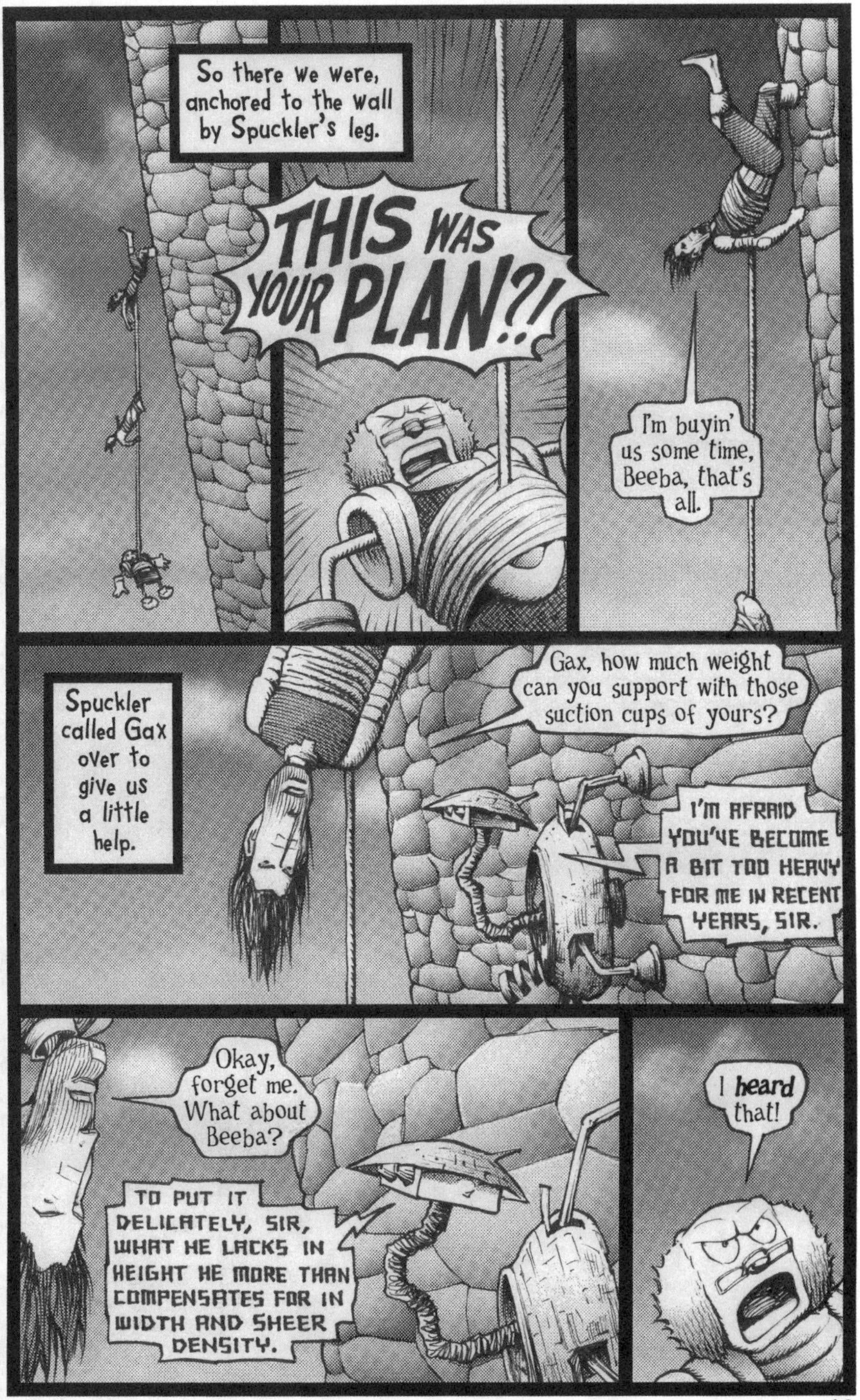
So there we were, anchored to the wall by Spuckler's leg.
THIS WAS YOUR PLAN?!
I'm buyin' us some time, Beeba, that's all.
Spuckler called Gax over to give us a little help.
Gax, how much weight can you support with those suction cups of yours?
I'M AFRAID YOU'VE BECOME A BIT TOO HEAVY FOR ME IN RECENT YEARS, SIR.
Okay, forget me. What about Beeba?
TO PUT IT DELICATELY, SIR, WHAT HE LACKS IN HEIGHT HE MORE THAN COMPENSATES FOR IN WIDTH AND SHEER DENSITY.
I heard that!

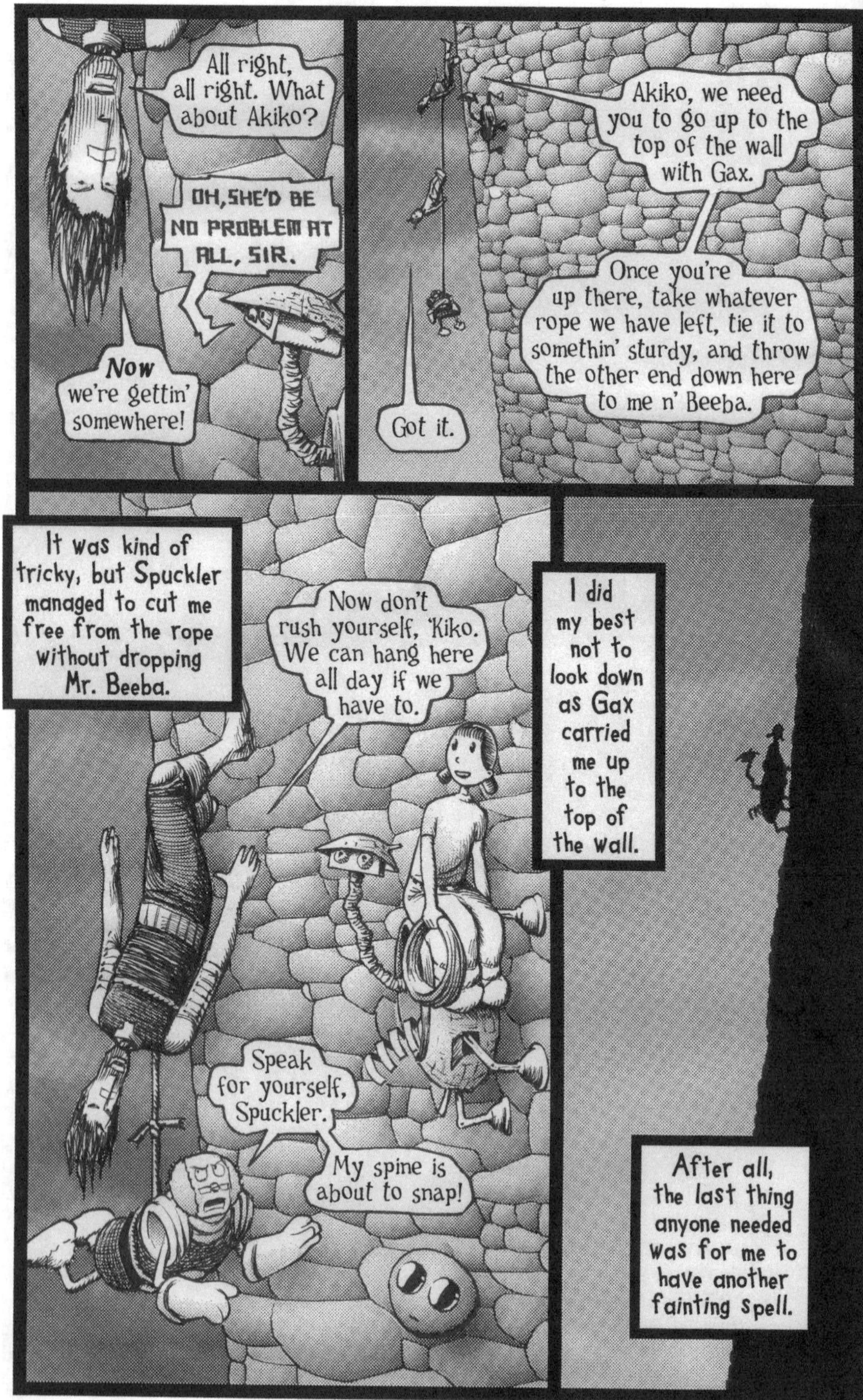

All right, all right. What about Akiko?
OH, SHE'D BE NO PROBLEM AT ALL, SIR.
Now we're gettin' somewhere!
Akiko, we need you to go up to the top of the wall with Gax.
Once you're up there, take whatever rope we have left, tie it to somethin' sturdy, and throw the other end down here to me n' Beeba.
Got it.
It was kind of tricky, but Spuckler managed to cut me free from the rope without dropping Mr. Beeba.
Now don't rush yourself, 'Kiko. We can hang here all day if we have to.
Speak for yourself, Spuckler.
My spine is about to snap!
I did my best not to look down as Gax carried me up to the top of the wall.
After all, the last thing anyone needed was for me to have another fainting spell.

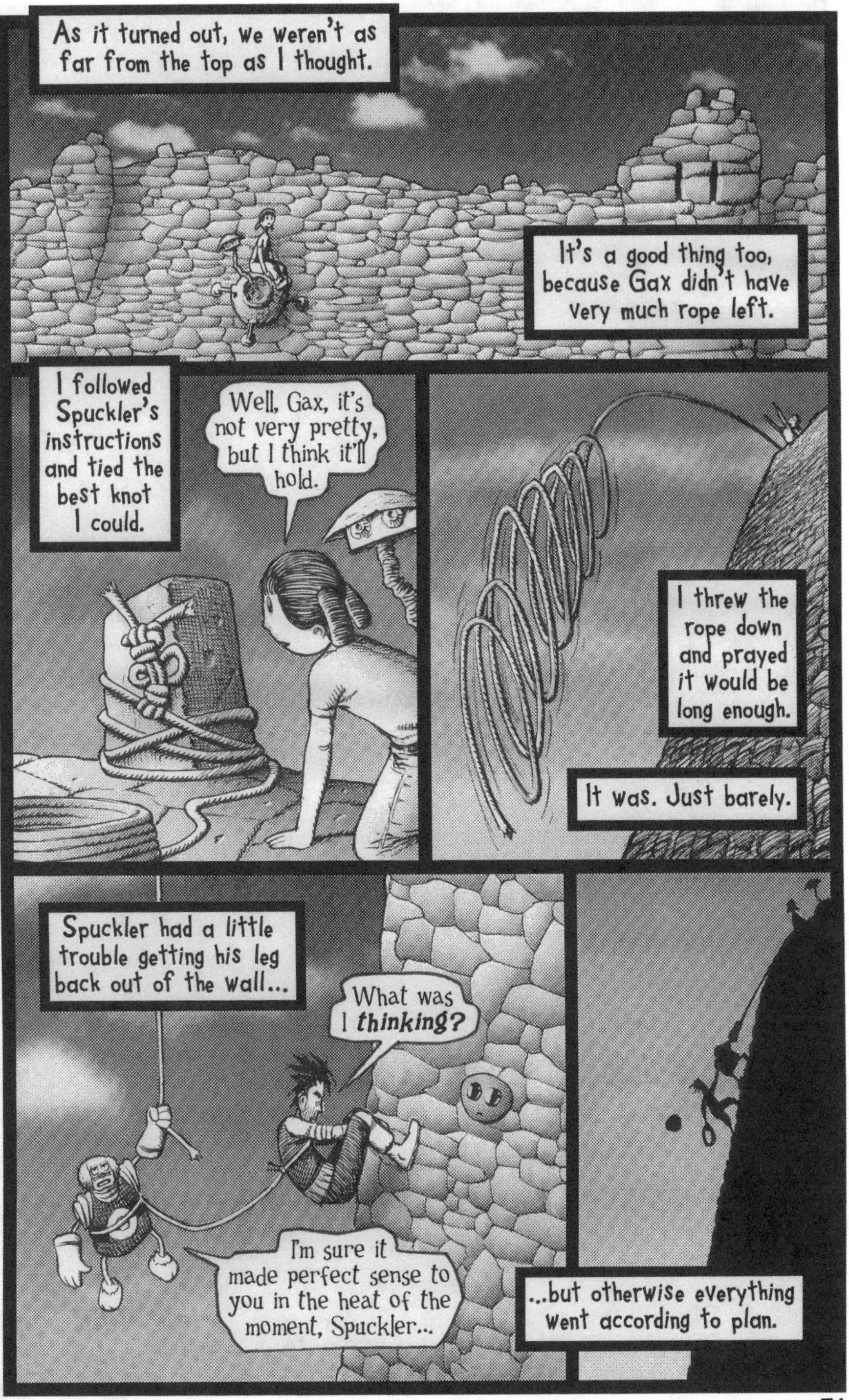

As it turned out, we weren't as far from the top as I thought.
It's a good thing too, because Gax didn't have very much rope left.
I followed Spuckler's instructions and tied the best knot I could.
Well, Gax, it's not very pretty, but I think it'll hold.
I threw the rope down and prayed it would be long enough.
It was. Just barely.
Spuckler had a little trouble getting his leg back out of the wall...
What was I *thinking?*
I'm sure it made perfect sense to you in the heat of the moment, Spuckler...
...but otherwise everything went according to plan.

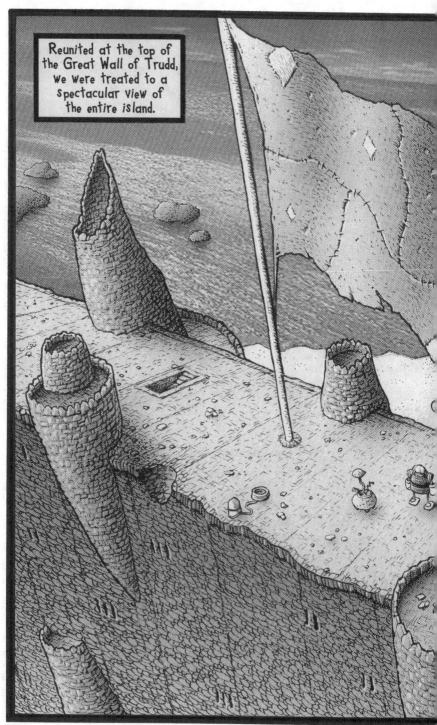

Reunited at the top of the Great Wall of Trudd, we were treated to a spectacular view of the entire island.

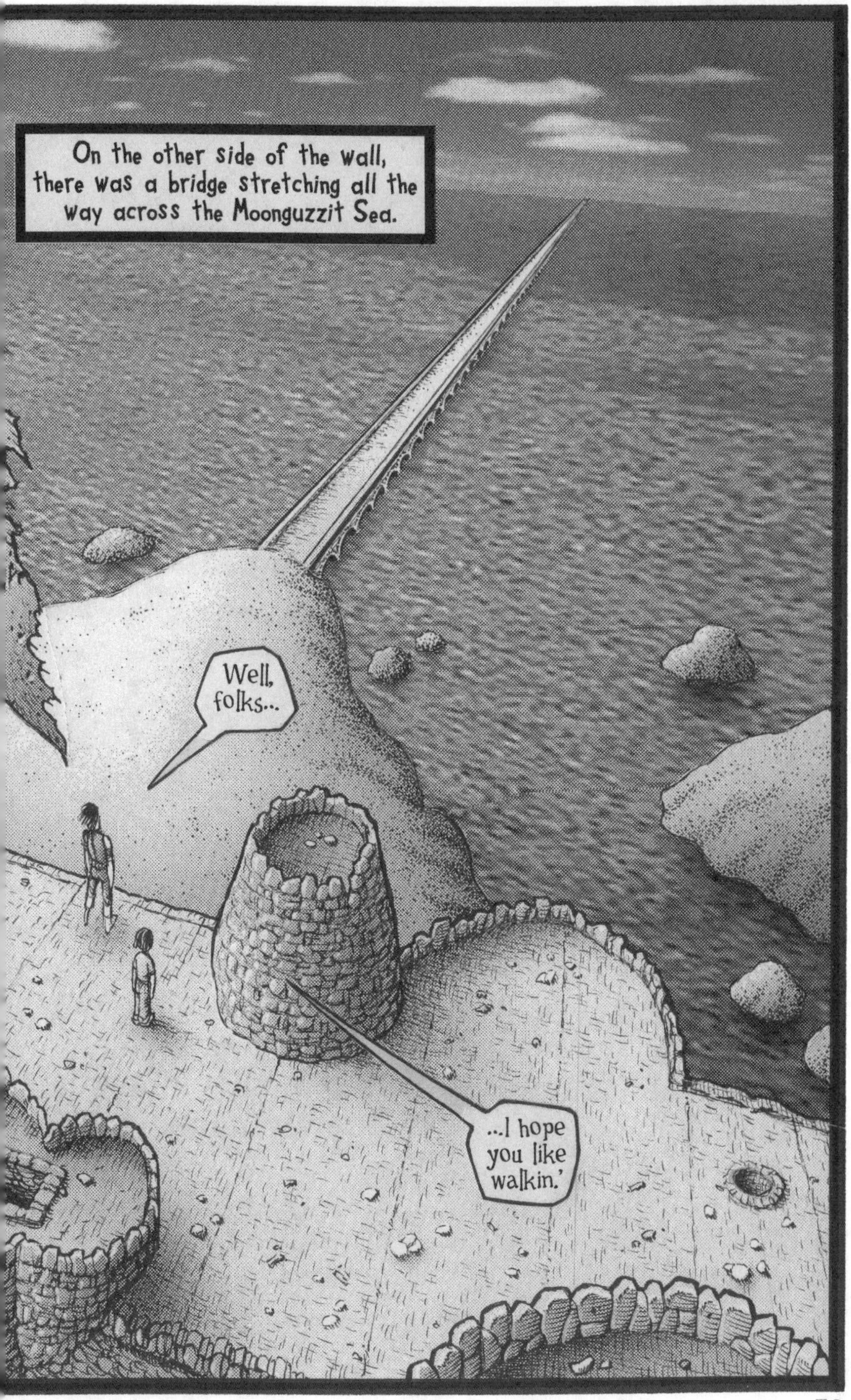
On the other side of the wall, there was a bridge stretching all the way across the Moonguzzit Sea.
Well, folks...
...I hope you like walkin.'

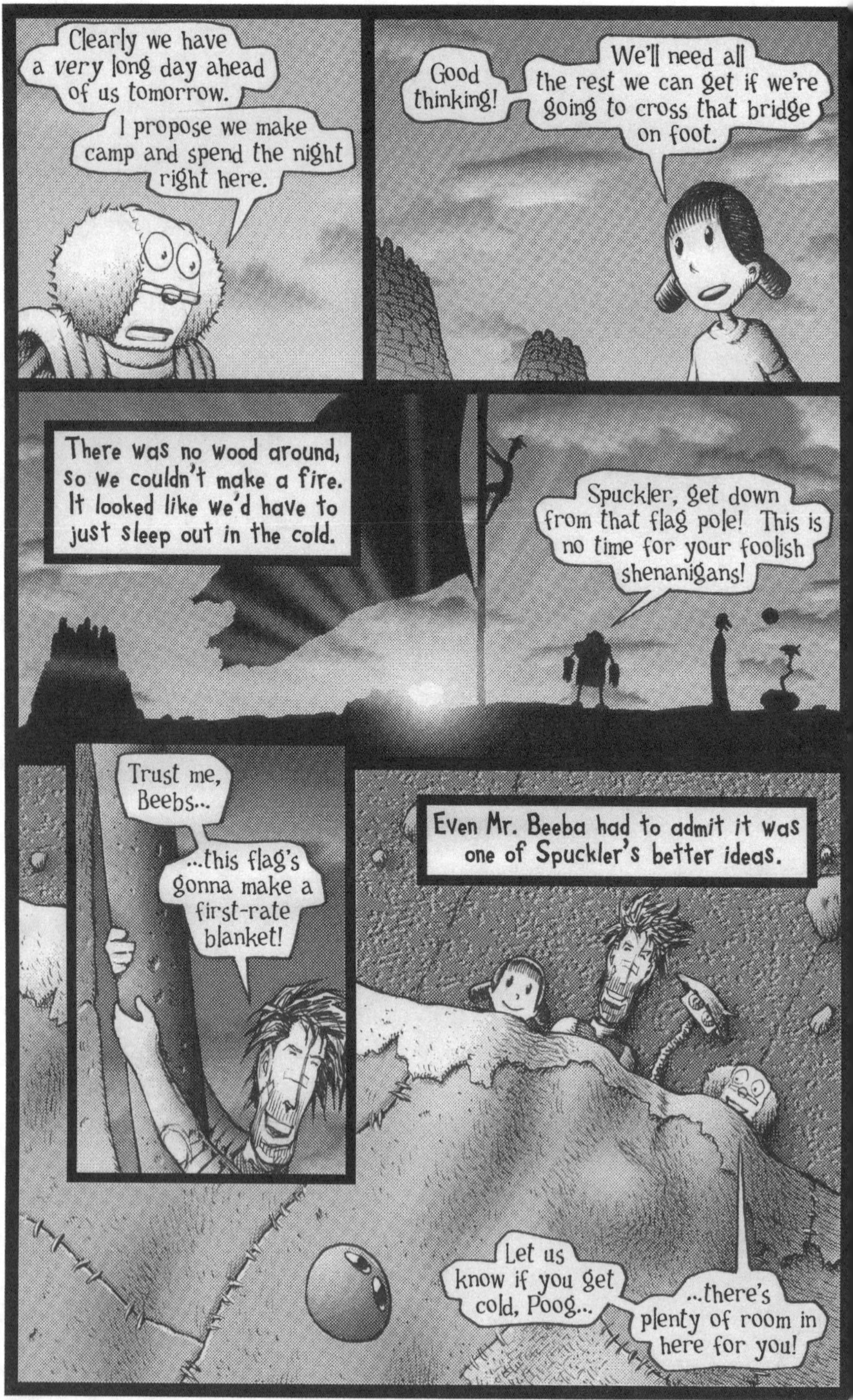
Clearly we have a very long day ahead of us tomorrow.
I propose we make camp and spend the night right here.
Good thinking!
We'll need all the rest we can get if we're going to cross that bridge on foot.
There was no wood around, so we couldn't make a fire. It looked like we'd have to just sleep out in the cold.
Spuckler, get down from that flag pole! This is no time for your foolish shenanigans!
Trust me, Beebs...
...this flag's gonna make a first-rate blanket!
Even Mr. Beeba had to admit it was one of Spuckler's better ideas.
Let us know if you get cold, Poog...
...there's plenty of room in here for you!

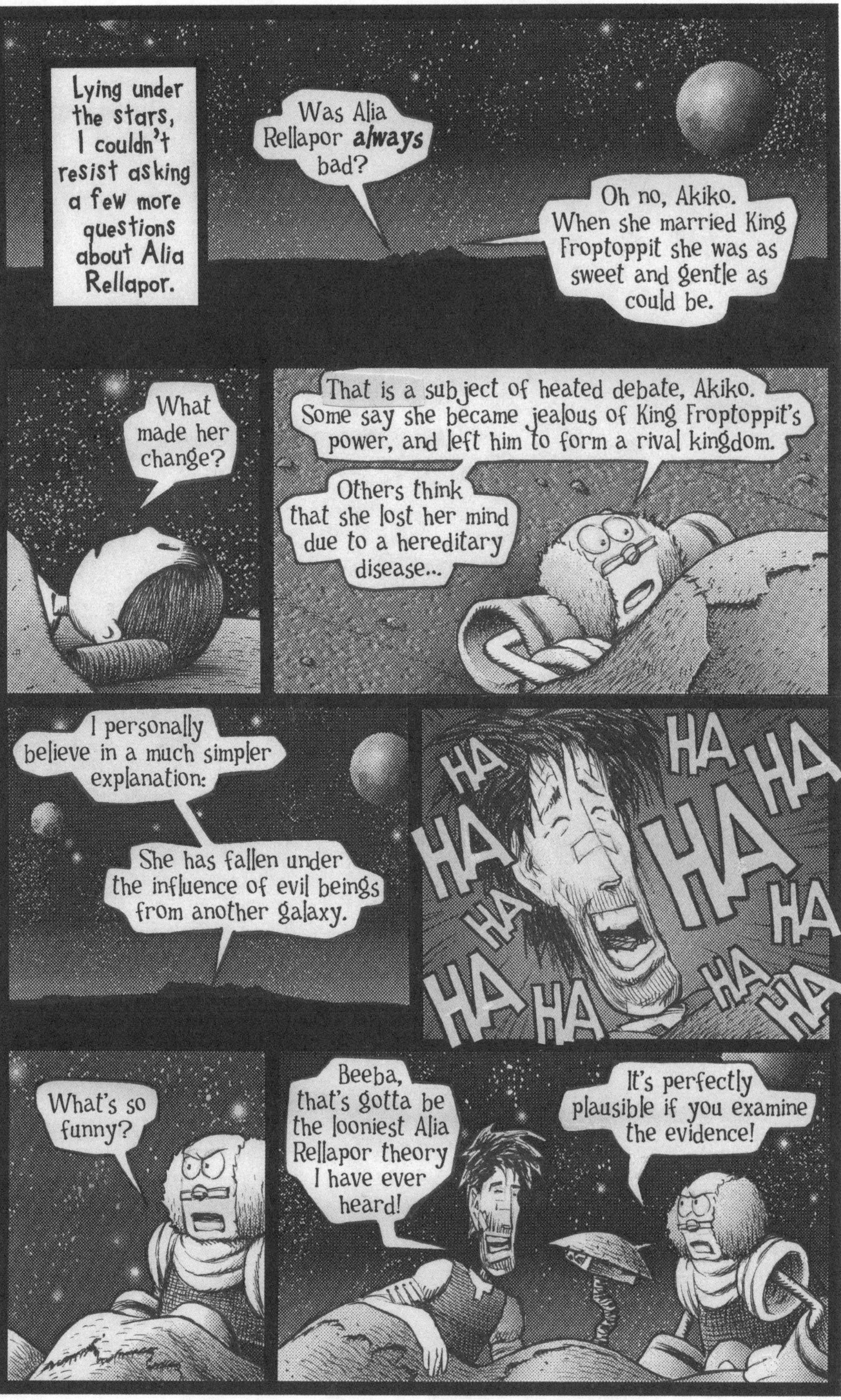
Lying under the stars, I couldn't resist asking a few more questions about Alia Rellapor.
Was Alia Rellapor **always** bad?
Oh no, Akiko. When she married King Froptoppit she was as sweet and gentle as could be.
What made her change?
That is a subject of heated debate, Akiko. Some say she became jealous of King Froptoppit's power, and left him to form a rival kingdom.
Others think that she lost her mind due to a hereditary disease...
I personally believe in a much simpler explanation:
She has fallen under the influence of evil beings from another galaxy.
HA HA HA HA HA HA HA HA HA HA HA HA HA
What's so funny?
Beeba, that's gotta be the looniest Alia Rellapor theory I have ever heard!
It's perfectly plausible if you examine the evidence!

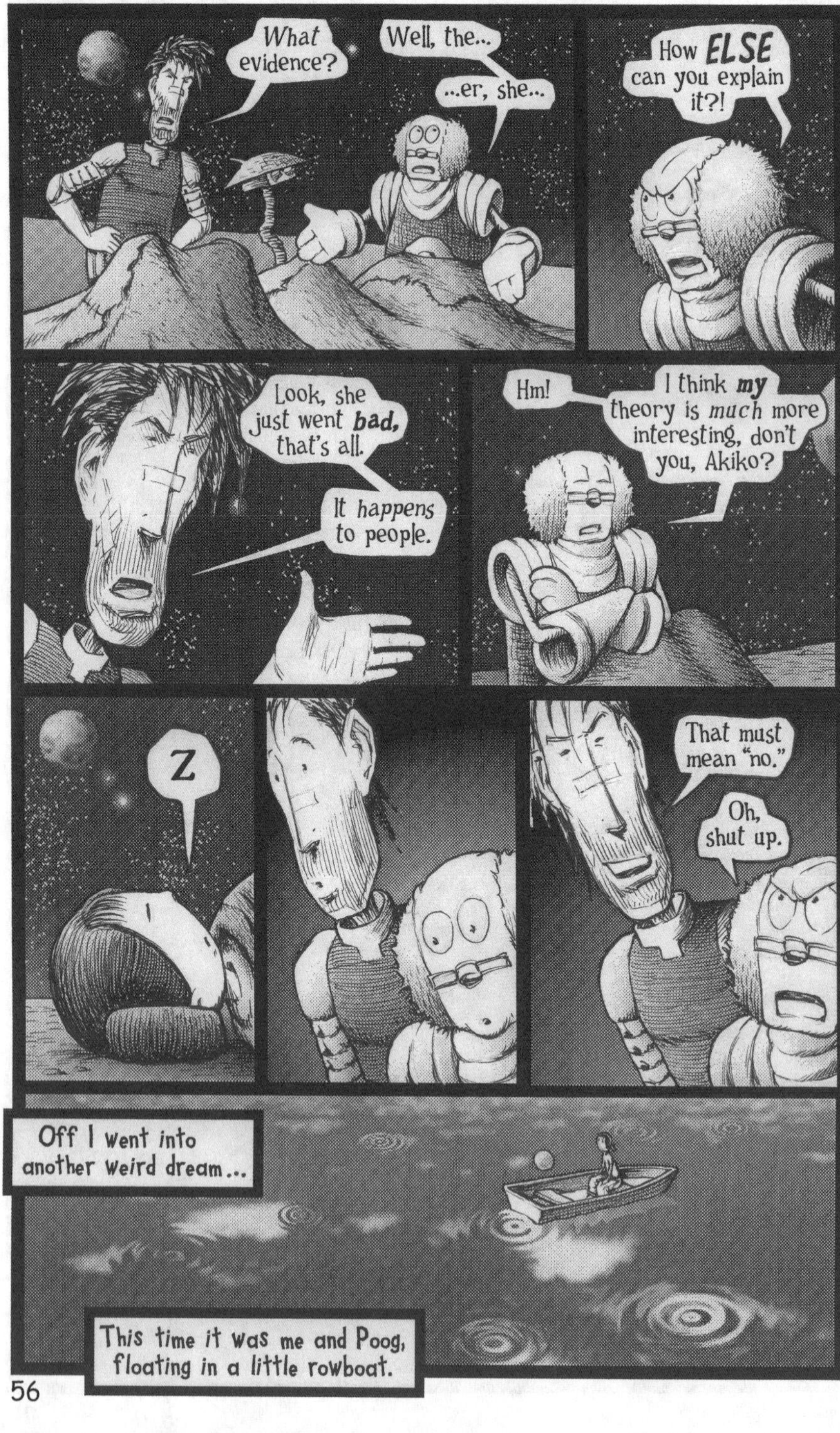
What evidence?
Well, the...
...er, she...
How ELSE can you explain it?!
Look, she just went bad, that's all.
It happens to people.
Hm!
I think my theory is much more interesting, don't you, Akiko?
Z
That must mean "no."
Oh, shut up.
Off I went into another weird dream...
This time it was me and Poog, floating in a little rowboat.

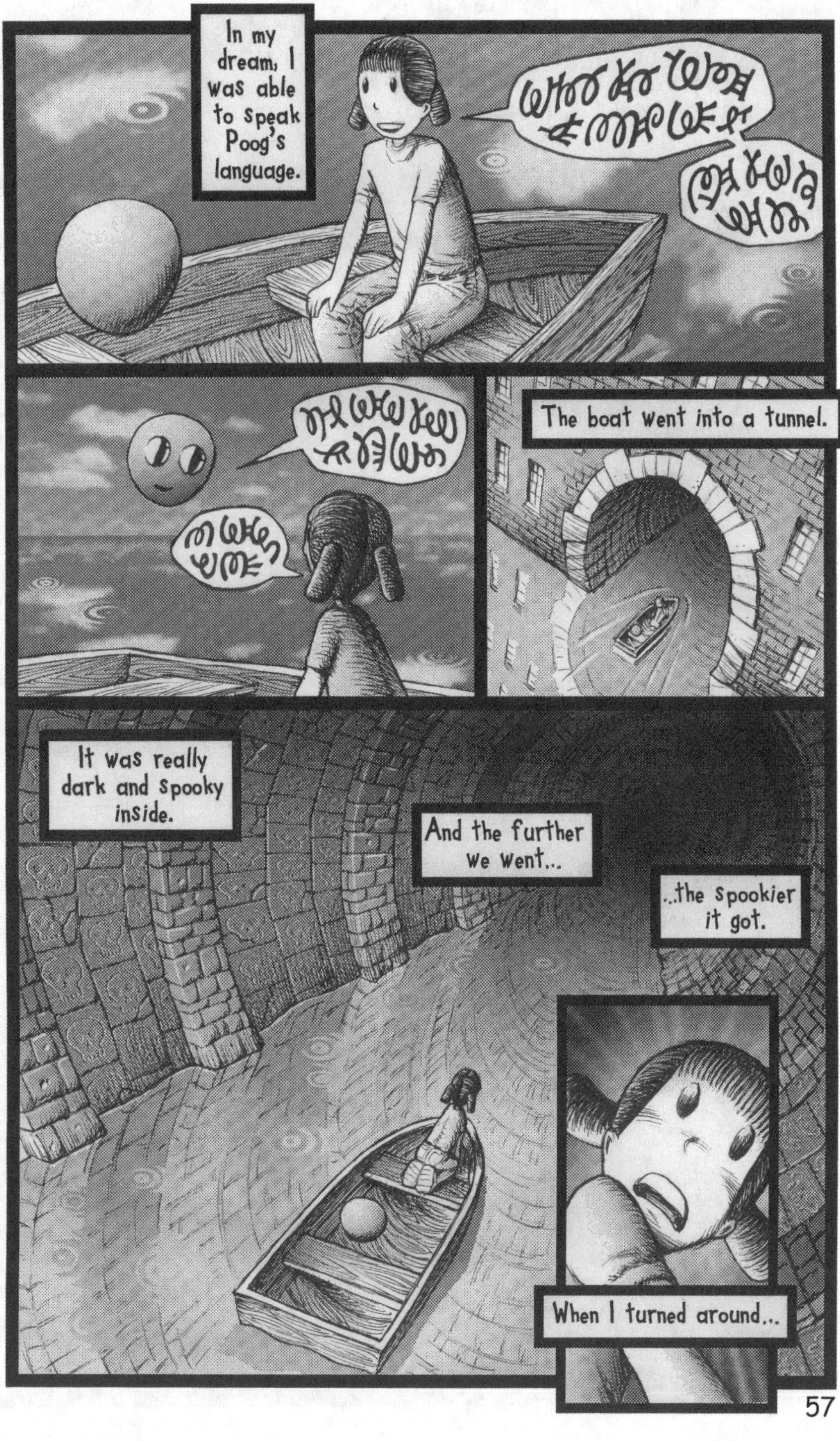
In my dream, I was able to speak Poog's language.
The boat went into a tunnel.
It was really dark and spooky inside.
And the further we went...
...the spookier it got.
When I turned around...

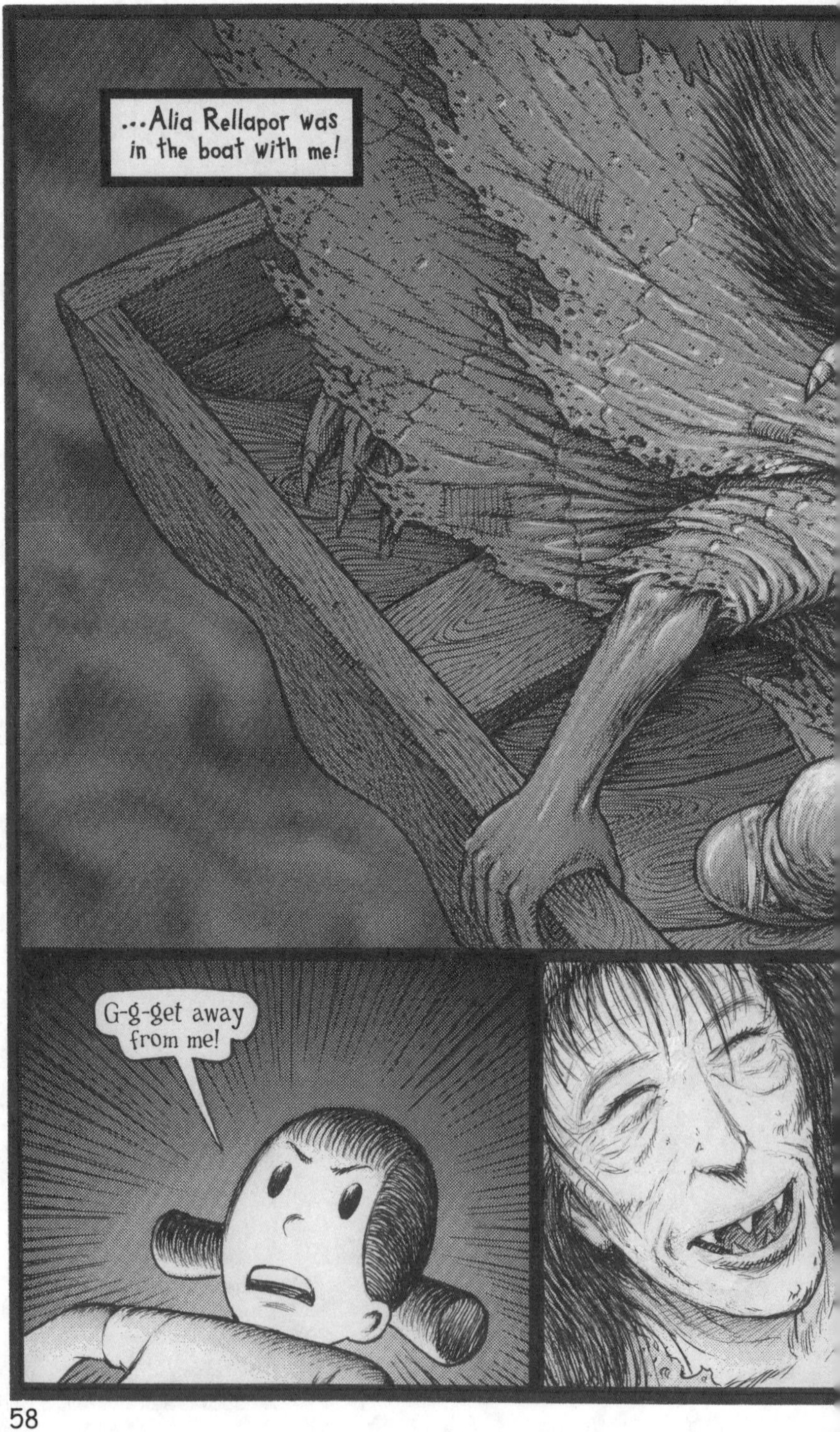
...Alia Rellapor was in the boat with me!
G-g-get away from me!

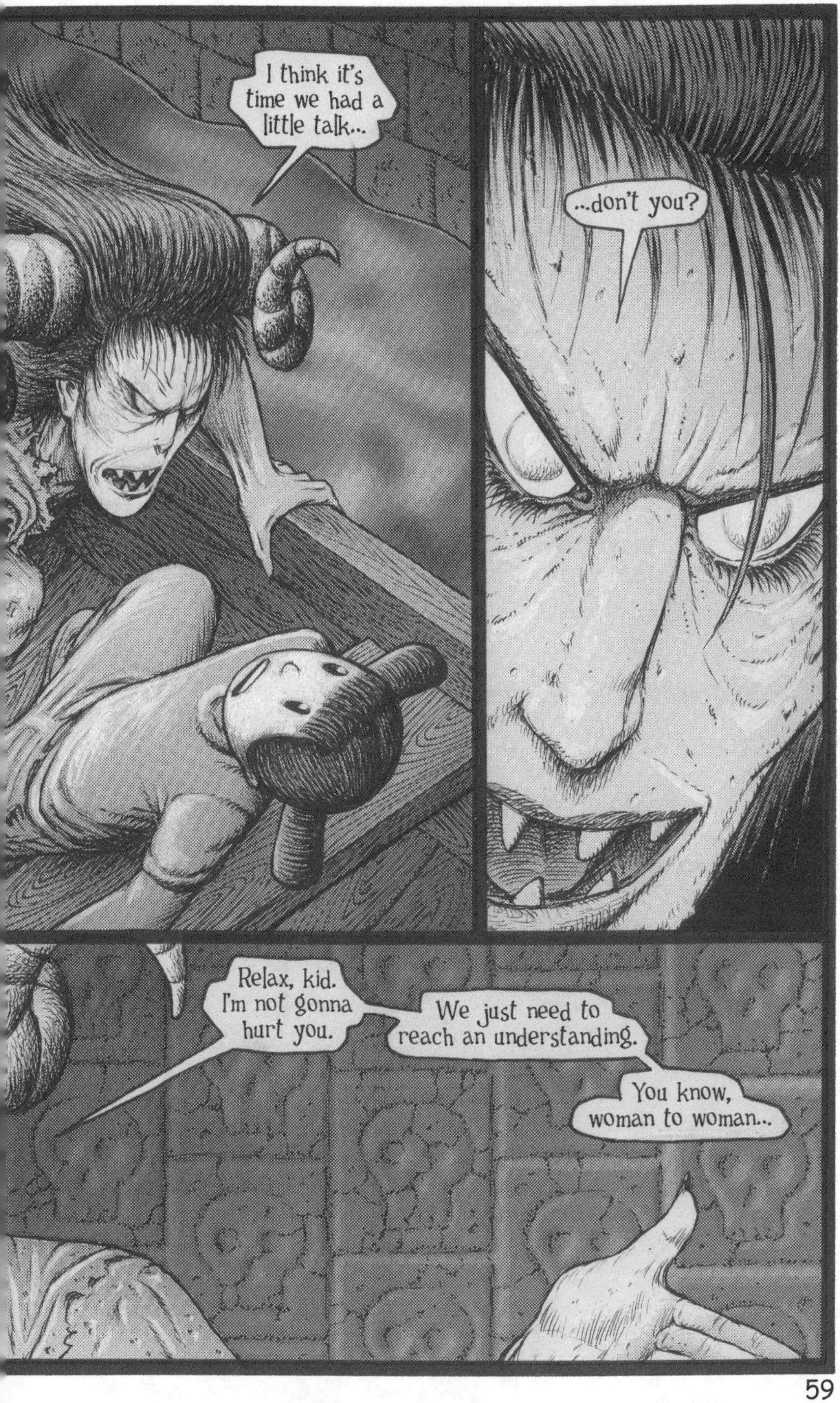
I think it's time we had a little talk...
...don't you?
Relax, kid. I'm not gonna hurt you.
We just need to reach an understanding.
You know, woman to woman...

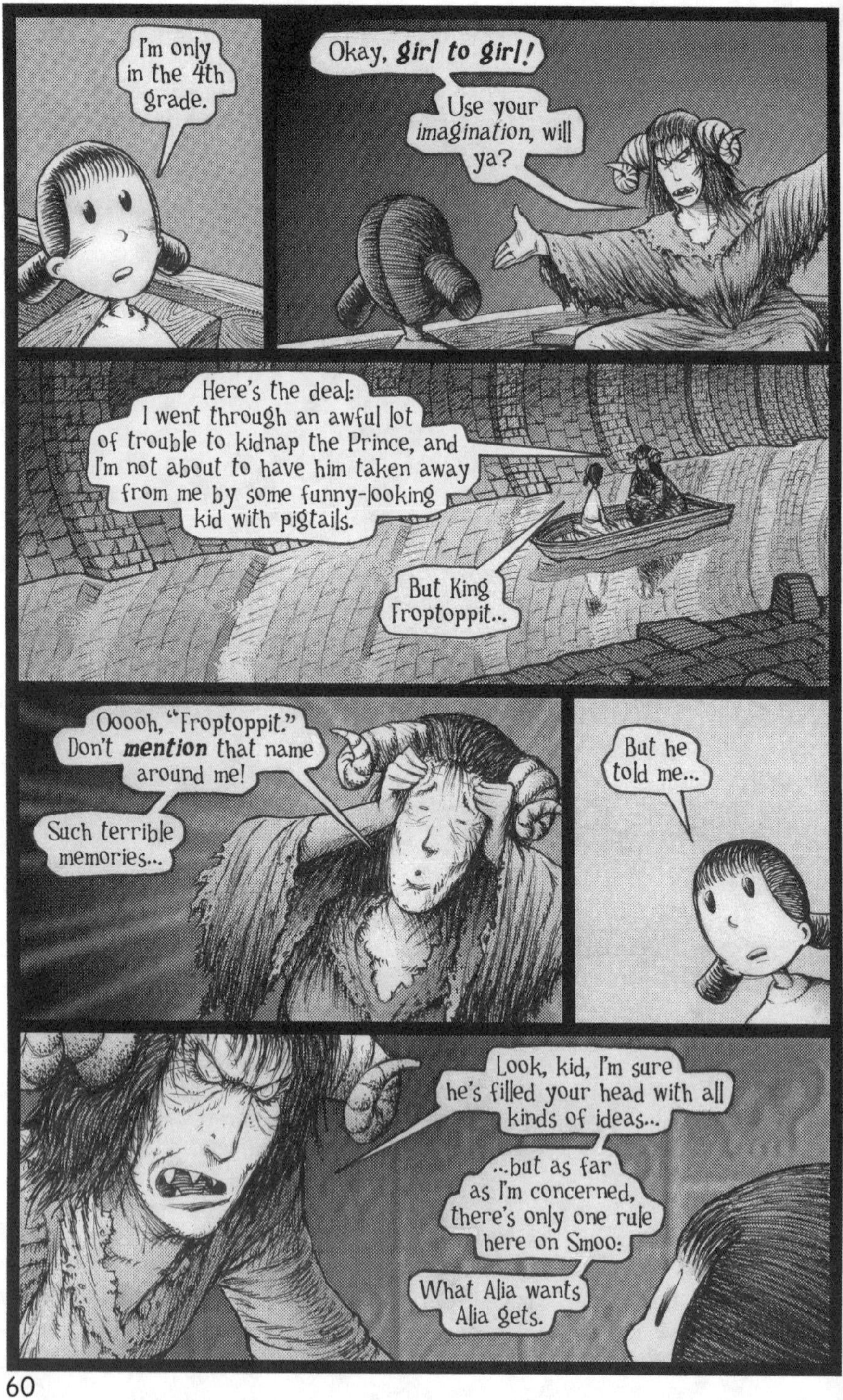
I'm only in the 4th grade.
Okay, ***girl to girl!***
Use your *imagination*, will ya?
Here's the deal: I went through an awful lot of trouble to kidnap the Prince, and I'm not about to have him taken away from me by some funny-looking kid with pigtails.
But King Froptoppit...
Ooooh, "Froptoppit." Don't ***mention*** that name around me!
Such terrible memories...
But he told me...
Look, kid, I'm sure he's filled your head with all kinds of ideas...
...but as far as I'm concerned, there's only one rule here on Smoo:
What Alia wants Alia gets.

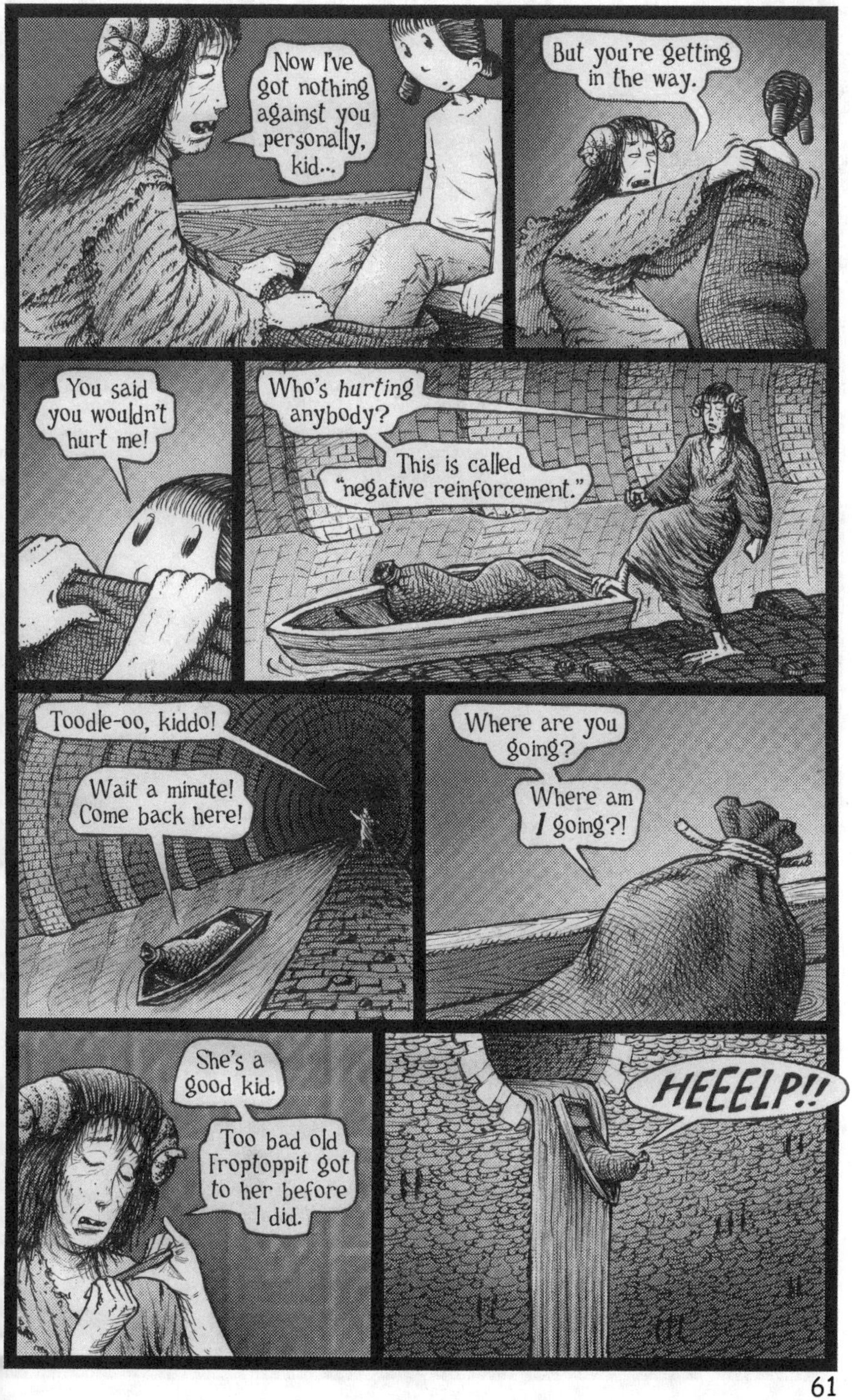
Now I've got nothing against you personally, kid...
But you're getting in the way.
You said you wouldn't hurt me!
Who's *hurting* anybody?
This is called "negative reinforcement."
Toodle-oo, kiddo!
Wait a minute! Come back here!
Where are you going?
Where am *I* going?!
She's a good kid.
Too bad old Froptoppit got to her before I did.
HEEELP!!

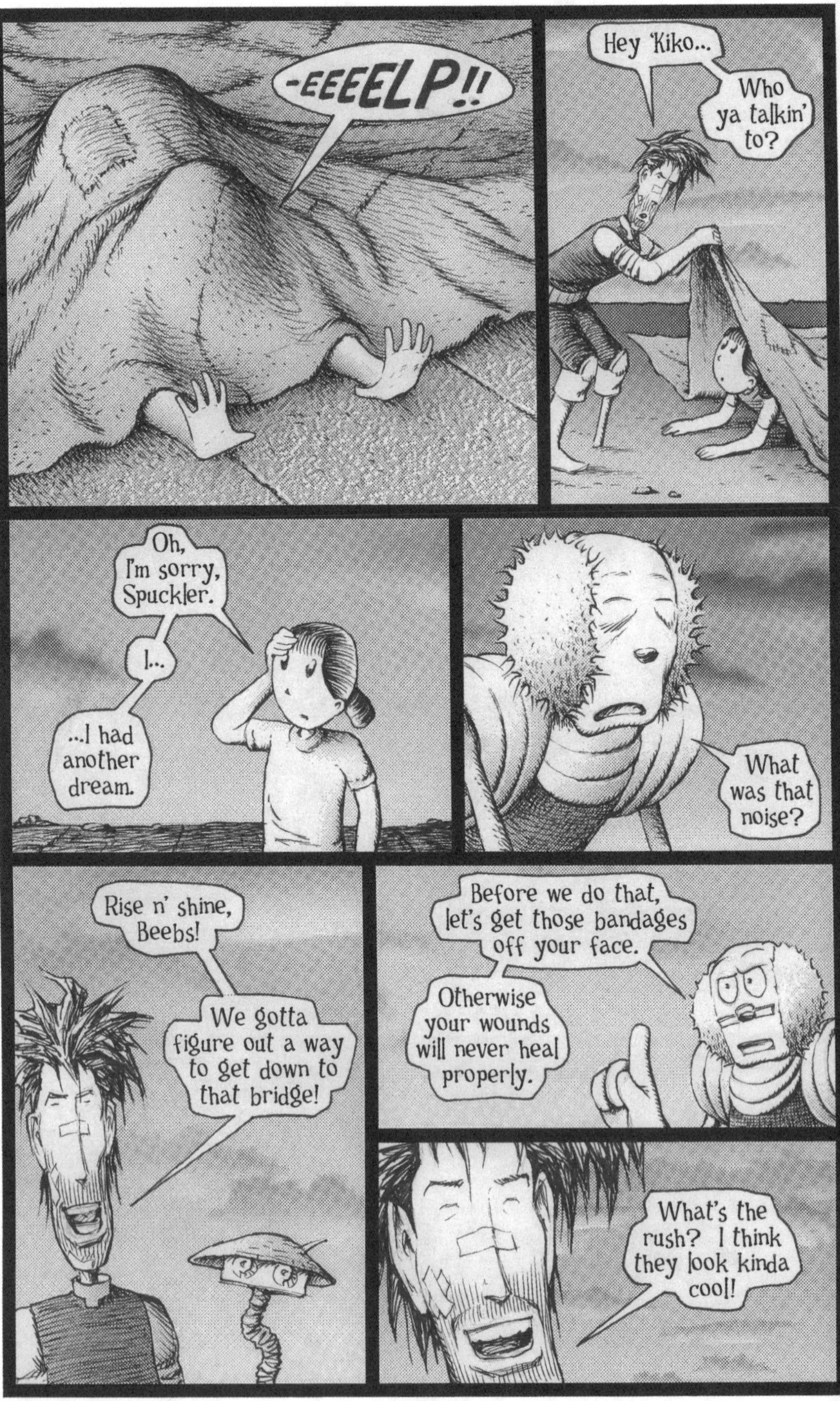
-EEEELP!!
Hey 'Kiko...
Who ya talkin' to?
Oh, I'm sorry, Spuckler.
I...
...I had another dream.
What was that noise?
Rise n' shine, Beebs!
We gotta figure out a way to get down to that bridge!
Before we do that, let's get those bandages off your face.
Otherwise your wounds will never heal properly.
What's the rush? I think they look kinda cool!

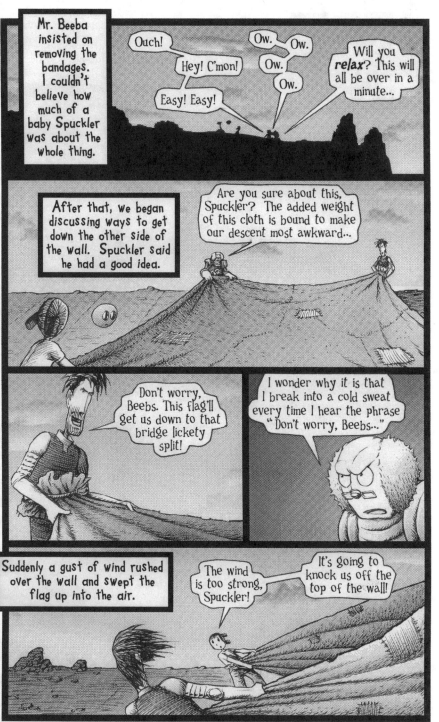

Mr. Beeba *insisted* on removing the bandages. I couldn't *believe* how much of a baby Spuckler was about the whole thing.

Ouch!

Hey! C'mon!

Easy! Easy!

Ow.   Ow.

Ow.

Ow.

Will you *relax*? This will all be over in a minute...

After that, we began discussing ways to get down the other side of the wall. Spuckler said he had a good idea.

Are you sure about this, Spuckler? The added weight of this cloth is bound to make our descent most awkward...

Don't worry, Beebs. This flag'll get us down to that bridge lickety split!

I wonder why it is that I break into a cold sweat every time I hear the phrase "Don't worry, Beebs..."

Suddenly a gust of wind rushed over the wall and swept the flag up into the air.

The wind is too strong, Spuckler!

It's going to knock us off the top of the wall!

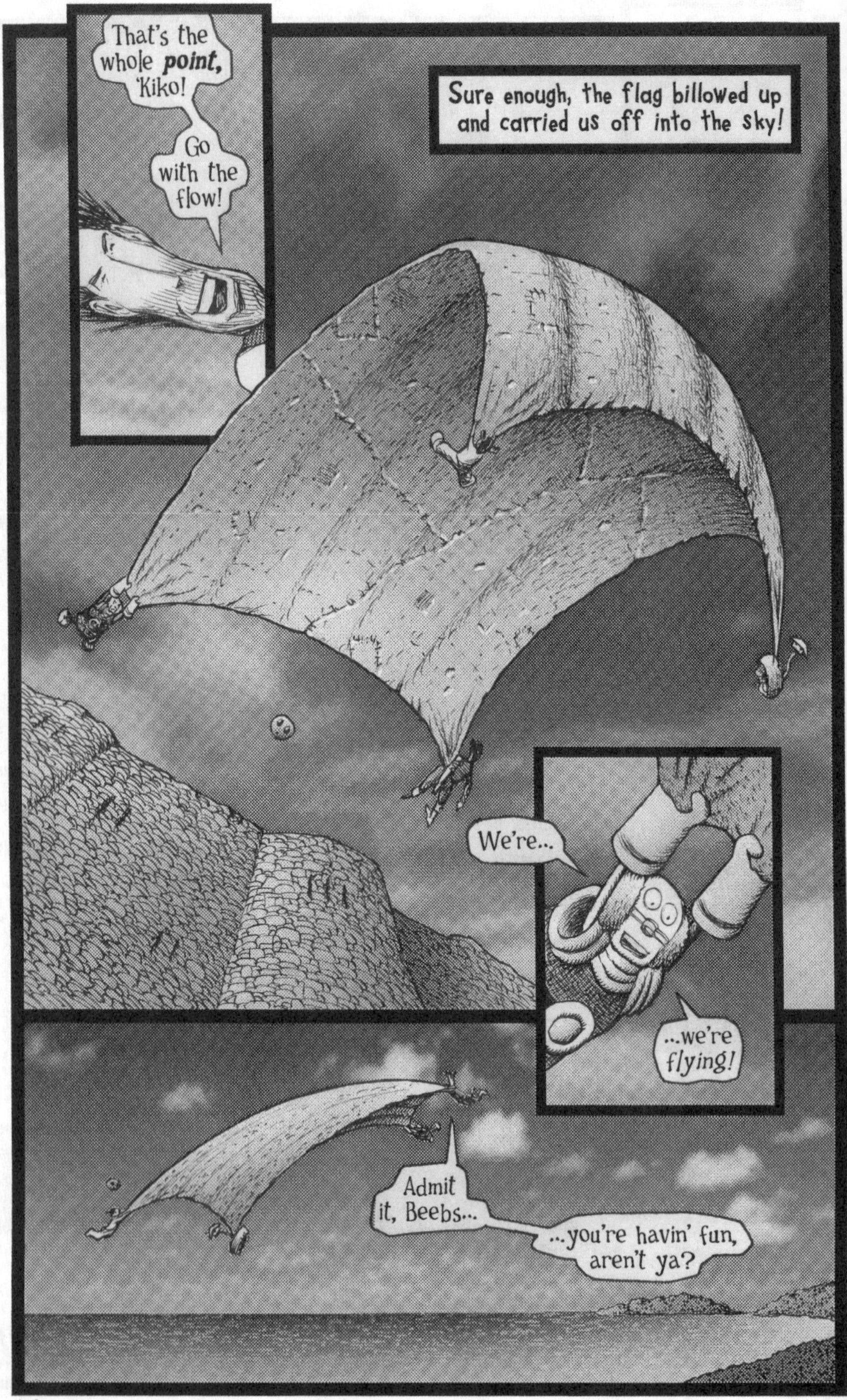
That's the whole **point,** 'Kiko!
Go with the flow!
Sure enough, the flag billowed up and carried us off into the sky!
We're...
...we're *flying!*
Admit it, Beebs...
...you're havin' fun, aren't ya?

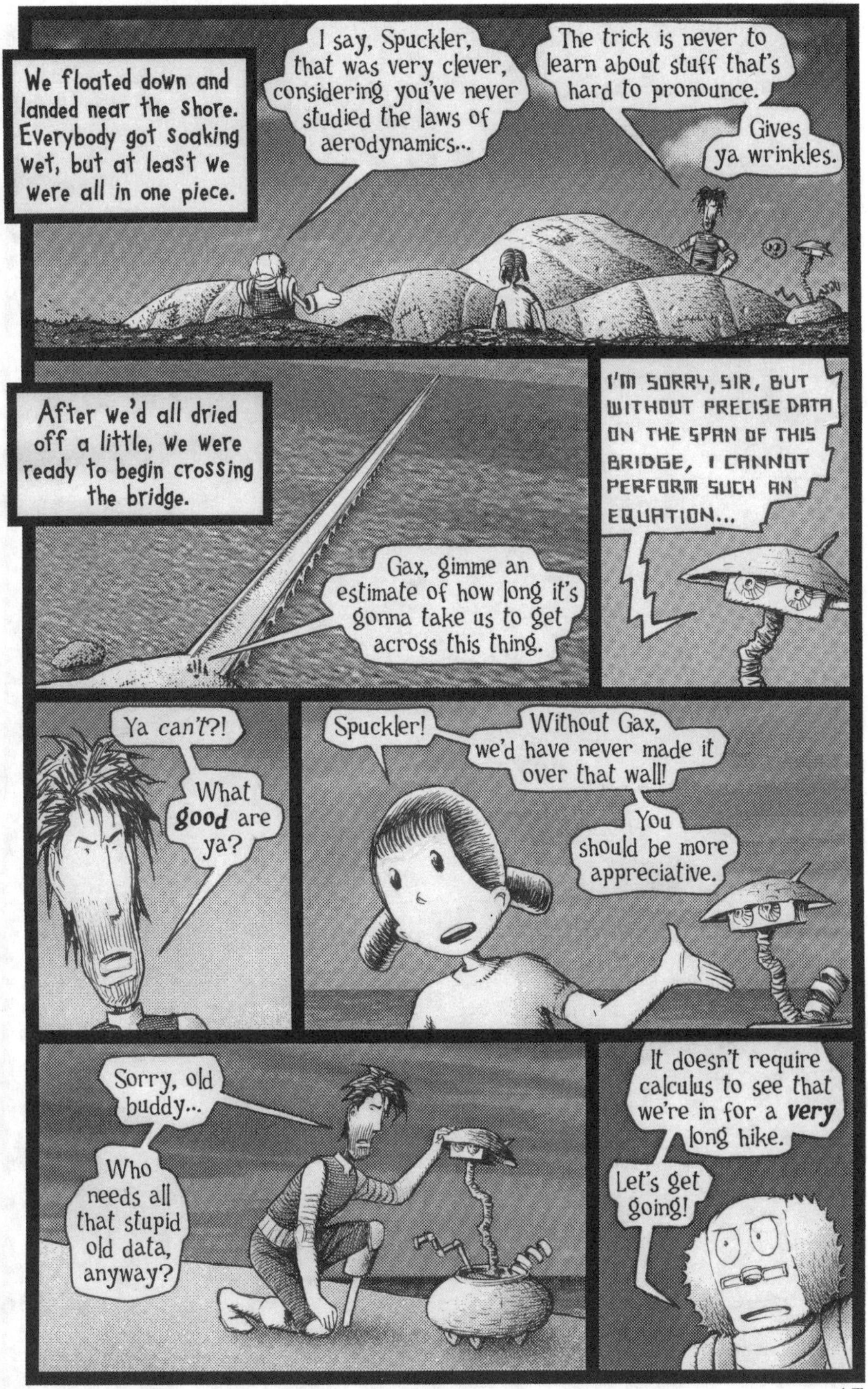

We floated down and landed near the shore. Everybody got soaking wet, but at least we were all in one piece.
I say, Spuckler, that was very clever, considering you've never studied the laws of aerodynamics...
The trick is never to learn about stuff that's hard to pronounce.
Gives ya wrinkles.
After we'd all dried off a little, we were ready to begin crossing the bridge.
Gax, gimme an estimate of how long it's gonna take us to get across this thing.
I'M SORRY, SIR, BUT WITHOUT PRECISE DATA ON THE SPAN OF THIS BRIDGE, I CANNOT PERFORM SUCH AN EQUATION...
Ya *can't*?!
What **good** are ya?
Spuckler!
Without Gax, we'd have never made it over that wall!
You should be more appreciative.
Sorry, old buddy...
Who needs all that stupid old data, anyway?
It doesn't require calculus to see that we're in for a ***very*** long hike.
Let's get going!

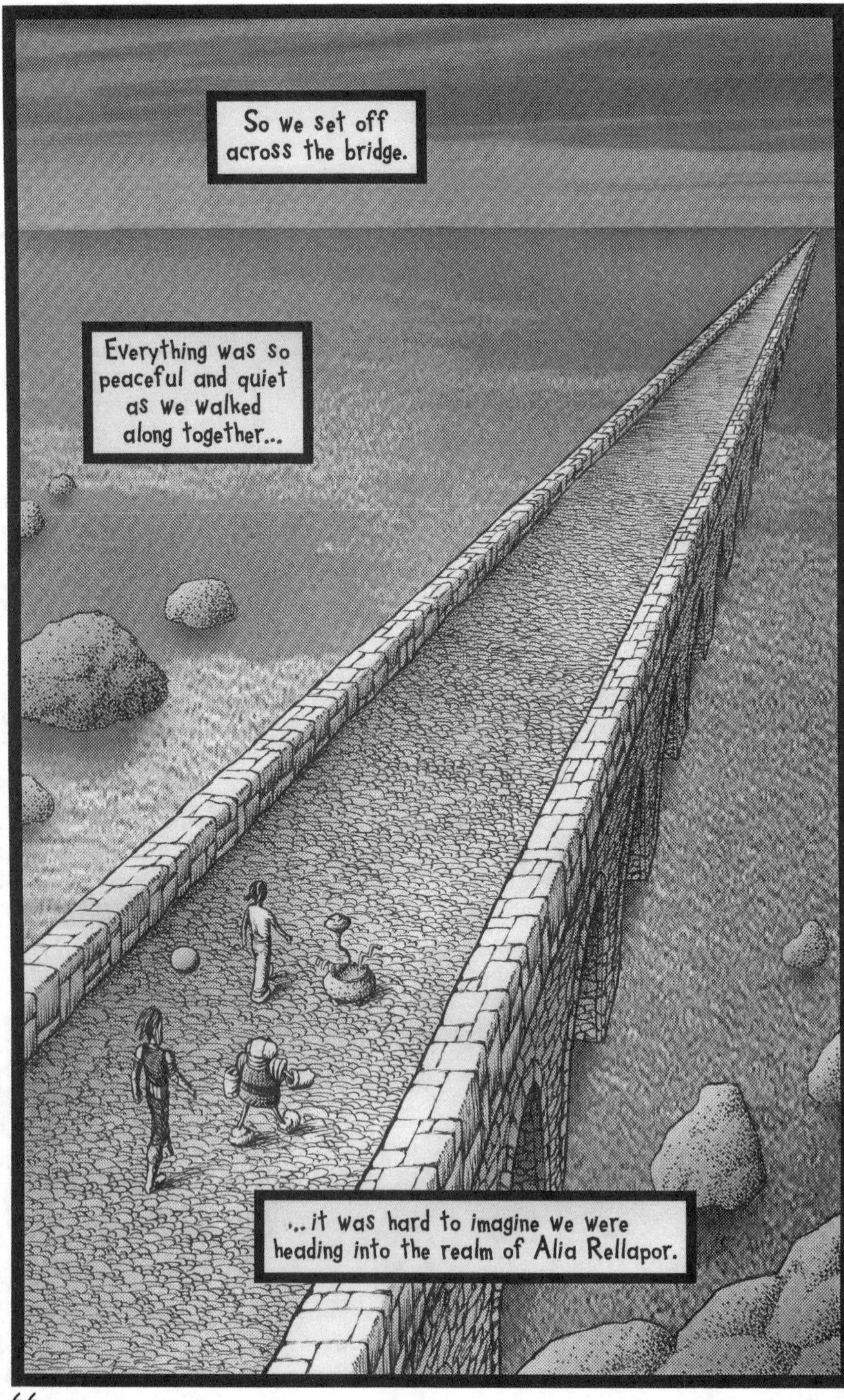
So we set off across the bridge.
Everything was so peaceful and quiet as we walked along together...
...it was hard to imagine we were heading into the realm of Alia Rellapor.

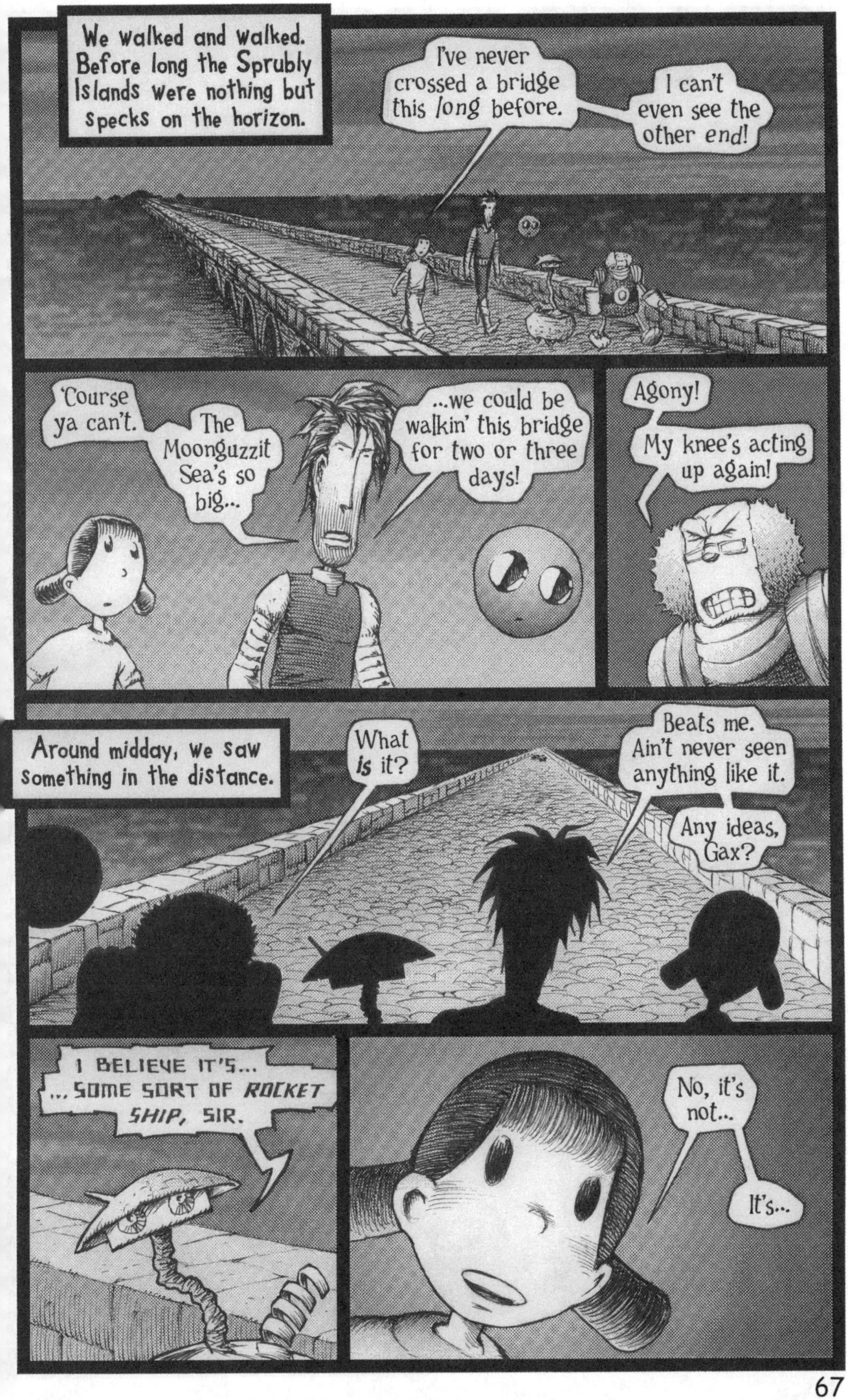

We walked and walked. Before long the Sprubly Islands were nothing but specks on the horizon.
I've never crossed a bridge this *long* before.
I can't even see the other *end*!
'Course ya can't.
The Moonguzzit Sea's so big...
...we could be walkin' this bridge for two or three days!
Agony!
My knee's acting up again!
Around midday, we saw something in the distance.
What *is* it?
Beats me. Ain't never seen anything like it.
Any ideas, Gax?
I BELIEVE IT'S...
...SOME SORT OF *ROCKET SHIP,* SIR.
No, it's not...
It's...

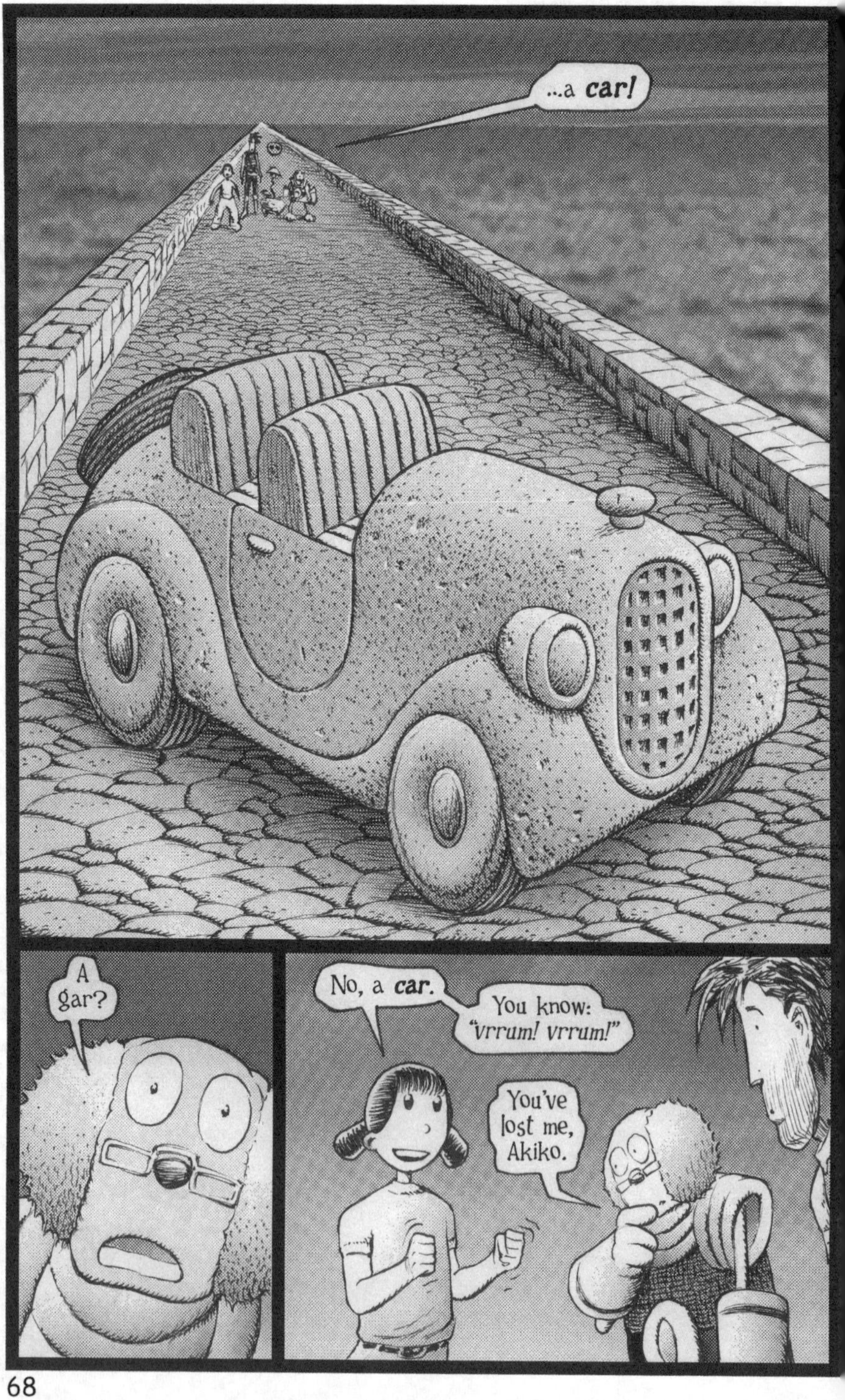
...a **car!**
A gar?
No, a **car.**
You know: "vrrum! vrrum!"
You've lost me, Akiko.

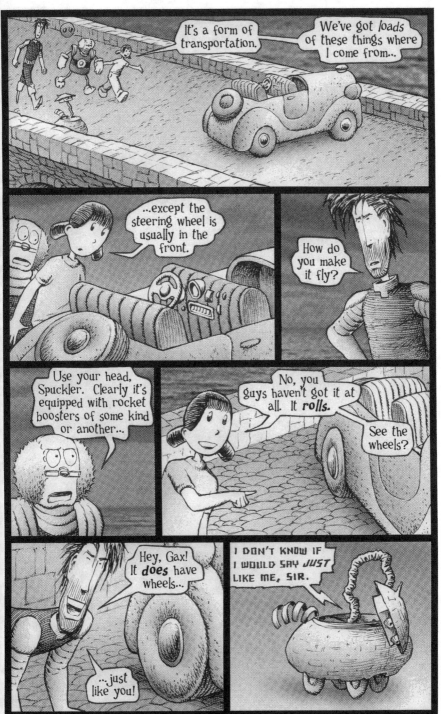

It's a form of transportation.

We've got *loads* of these things where I come from...

...except the steering wheel is usually in the front.

How do you make it fly?

Use your head, Spuckler. Clearly it's equipped with rocket boosters of some kind or another...

No, you guys haven't got it at all. It *rolls*.

See the wheels?

Hey, Gax! It *does* have wheels...

...just like you!

I DON'T KNOW IF I WOULD SAY *JUST* LIKE ME, SIR.

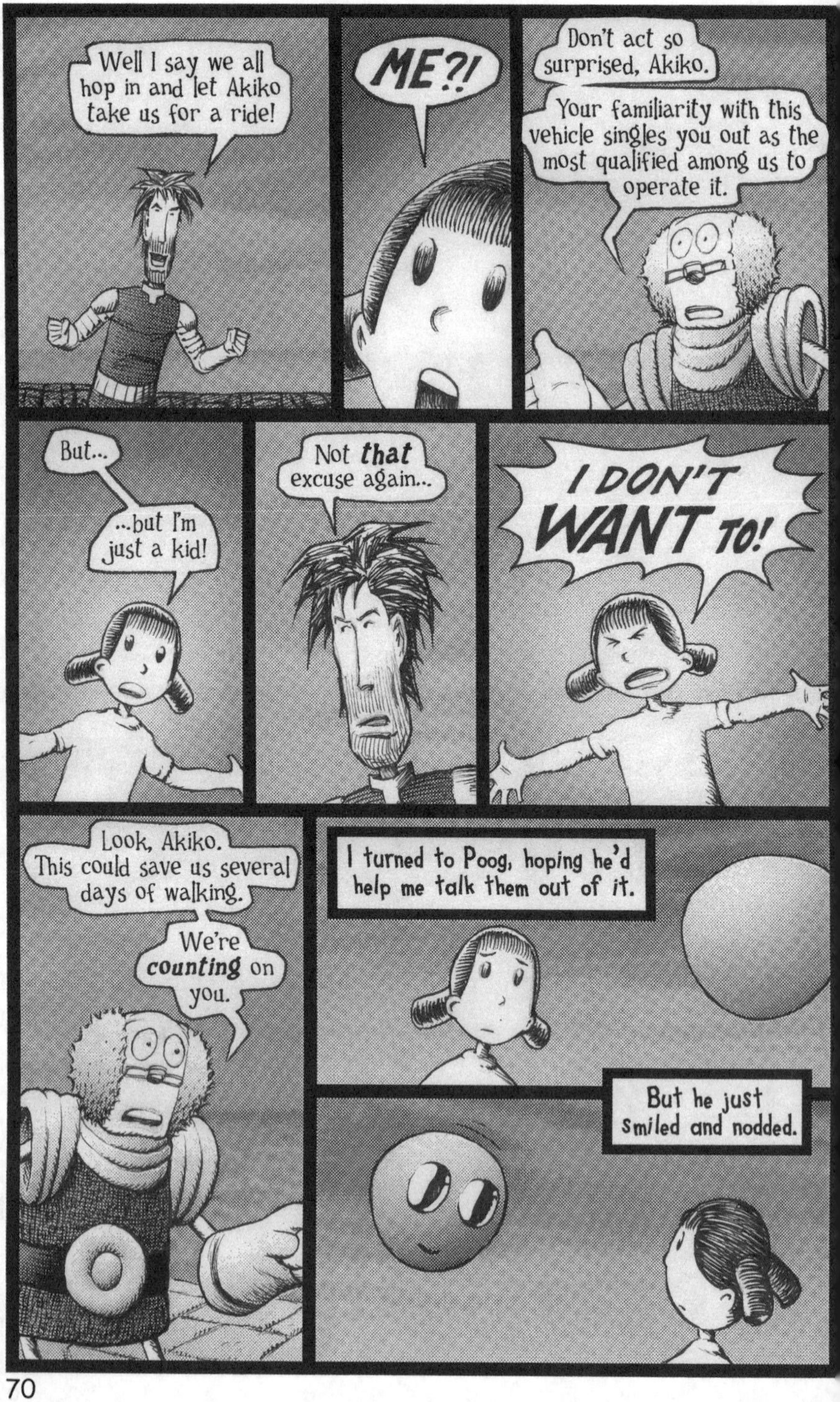
Well I say we all hop in and let Akiko take us for a ride!
ME?!
Don't act so surprised, Akiko.
Your familiarity with this vehicle singles you out as the most qualified among us to operate it.
But...
...but I'm just a kid!
Not **that** excuse again...
I DON'T WANT TO!
Look, Akiko. This could save us several days of walking.
We're **counting** on you.
I turned to Poog, hoping he'd help me talk them out of it.
But he just smiled and nodded.

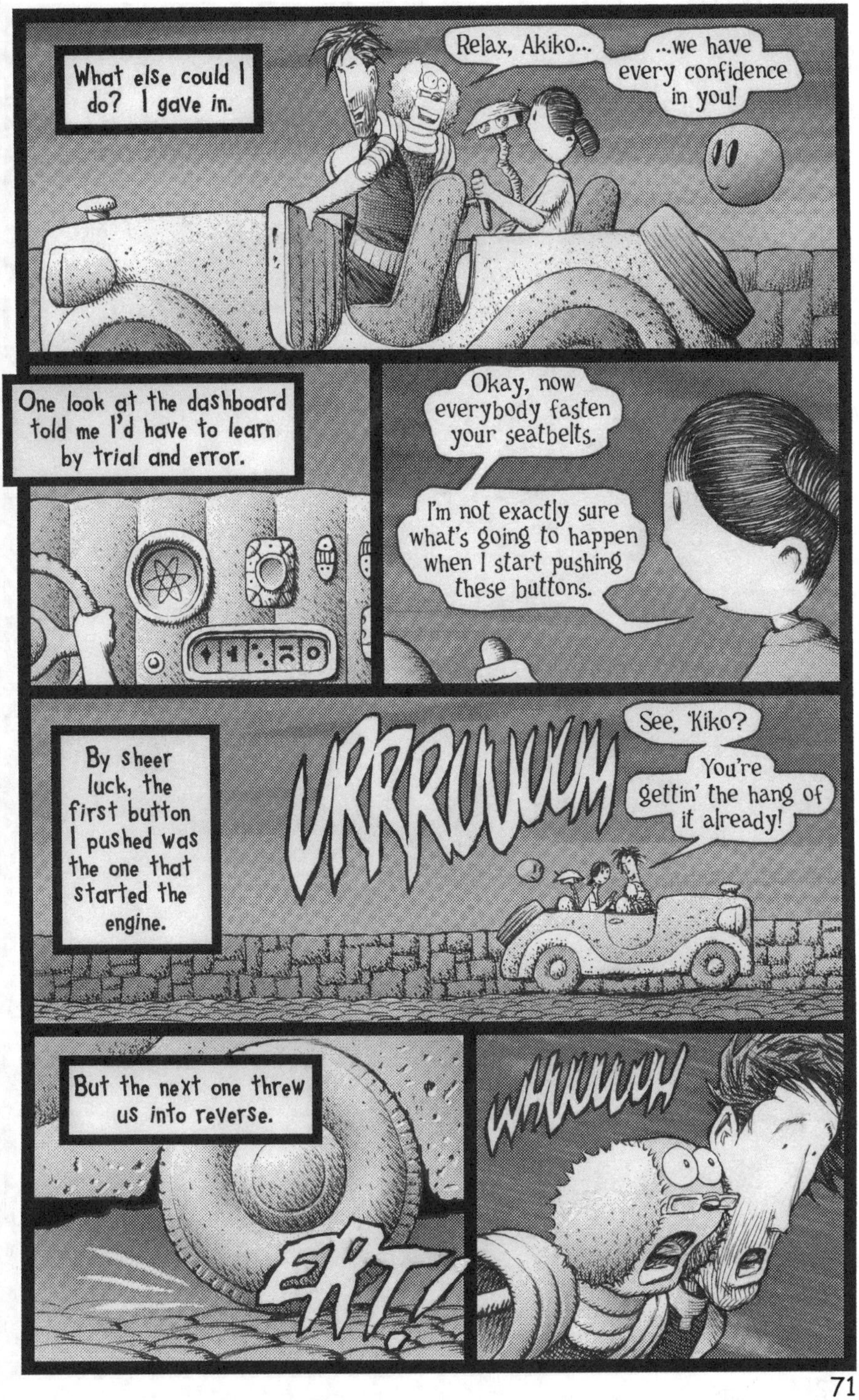
What else could I do? I gave in.
Relax, Akiko...
...we have every confidence in you!
One look at the dashboard told me I'd have to learn by trial and error.
Okay, now everybody fasten your seatbelts.
I'm not exactly sure what's going to happen when I start pushing these buttons.
By sheer luck, the first button I pushed was the one that started the engine.
URRRUUUUM
See, 'Kiko?
You're gettin' the hang of it already!
But the next one threw us into reverse.
ERT!
WHUUUUH

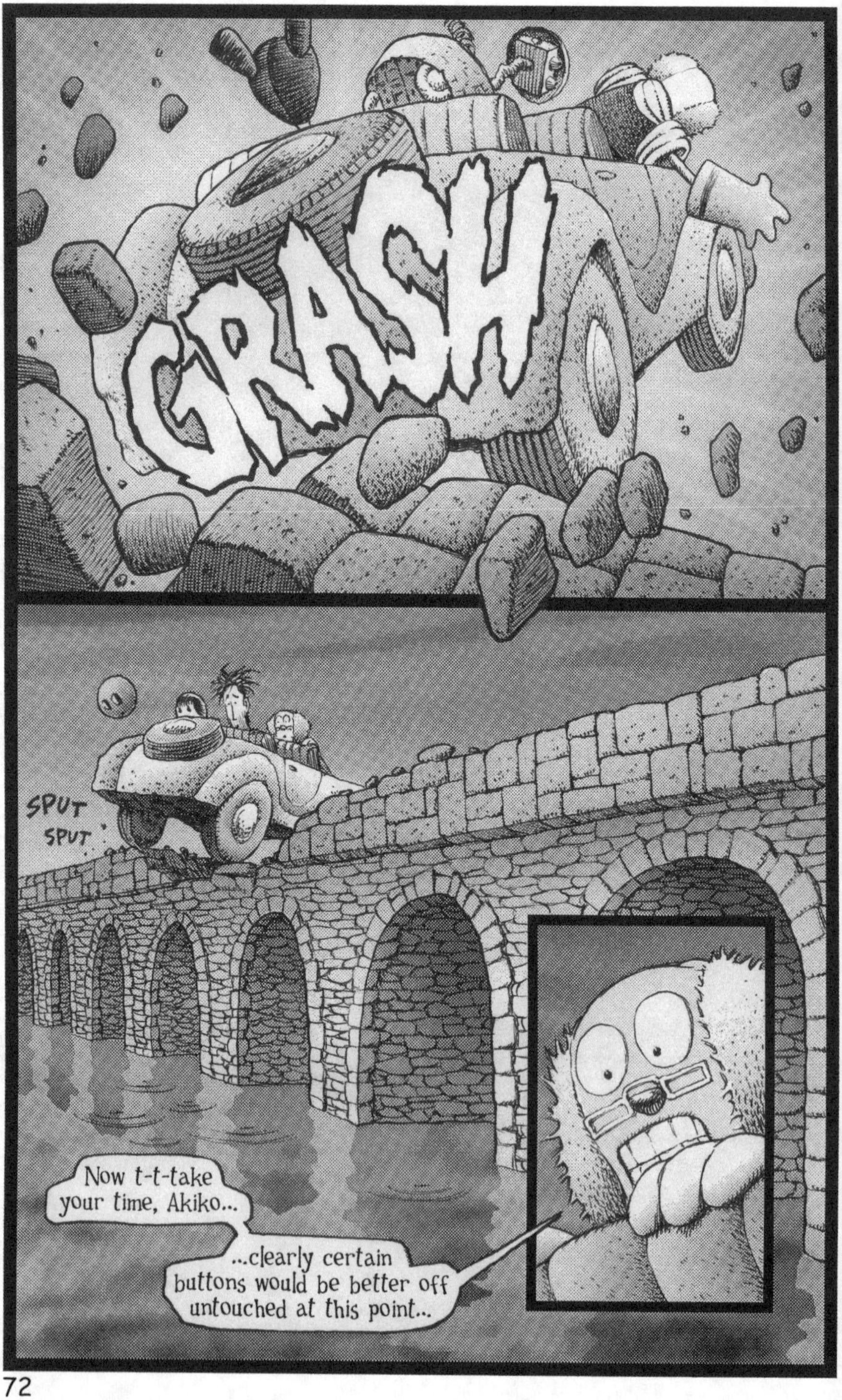
CRASH
SPUT SPUT
Now t-t-take your time, Akiko...
...clearly certain buttons would be better off untouched at this point...

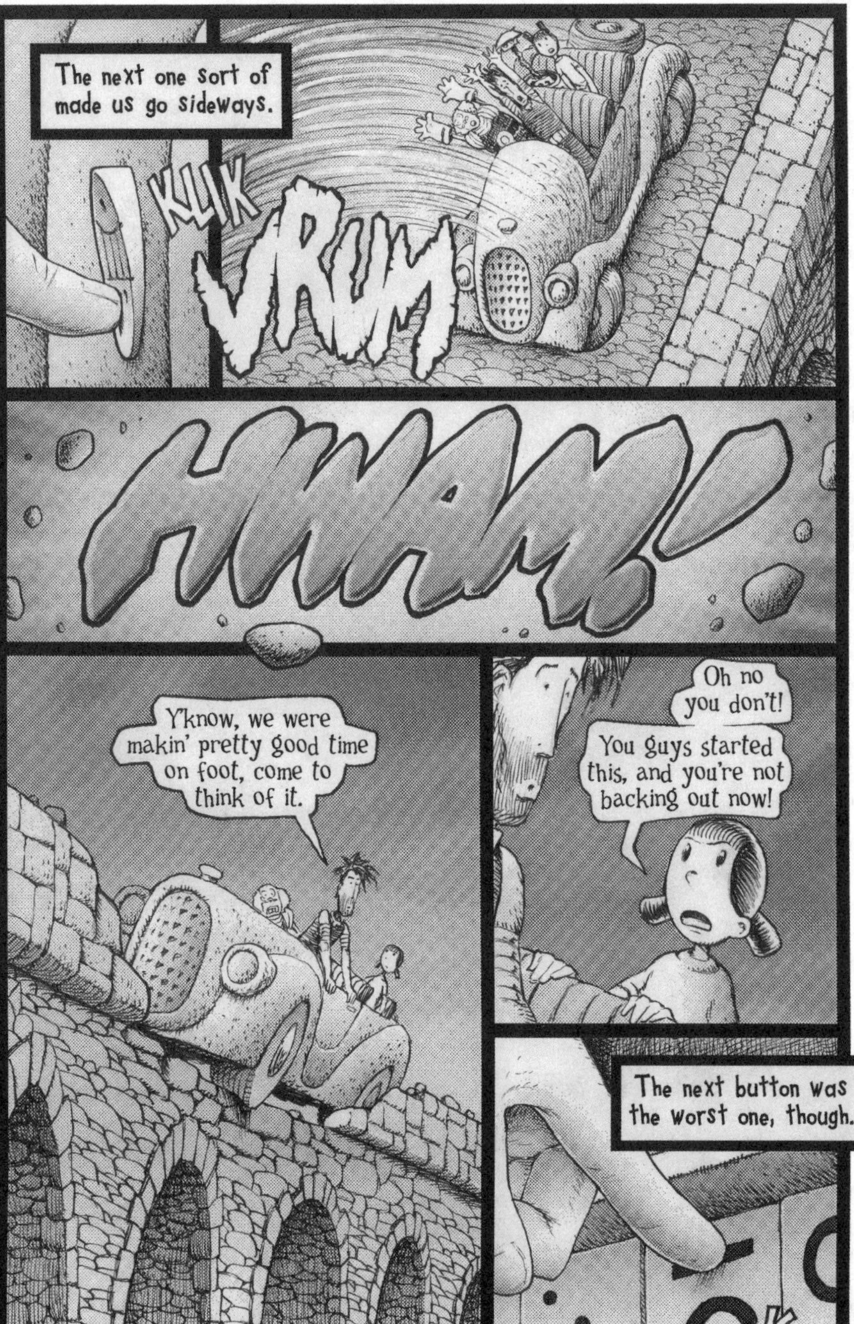
The next one sort of made us go sideways.
KLIK
VRUM
WHAM!
Y'know, we were makin' pretty good time on foot, come to think of it.
Oh no you don't!
You guys started this, and you're not backing out now!
The next button was the worst one, though.
KLIK

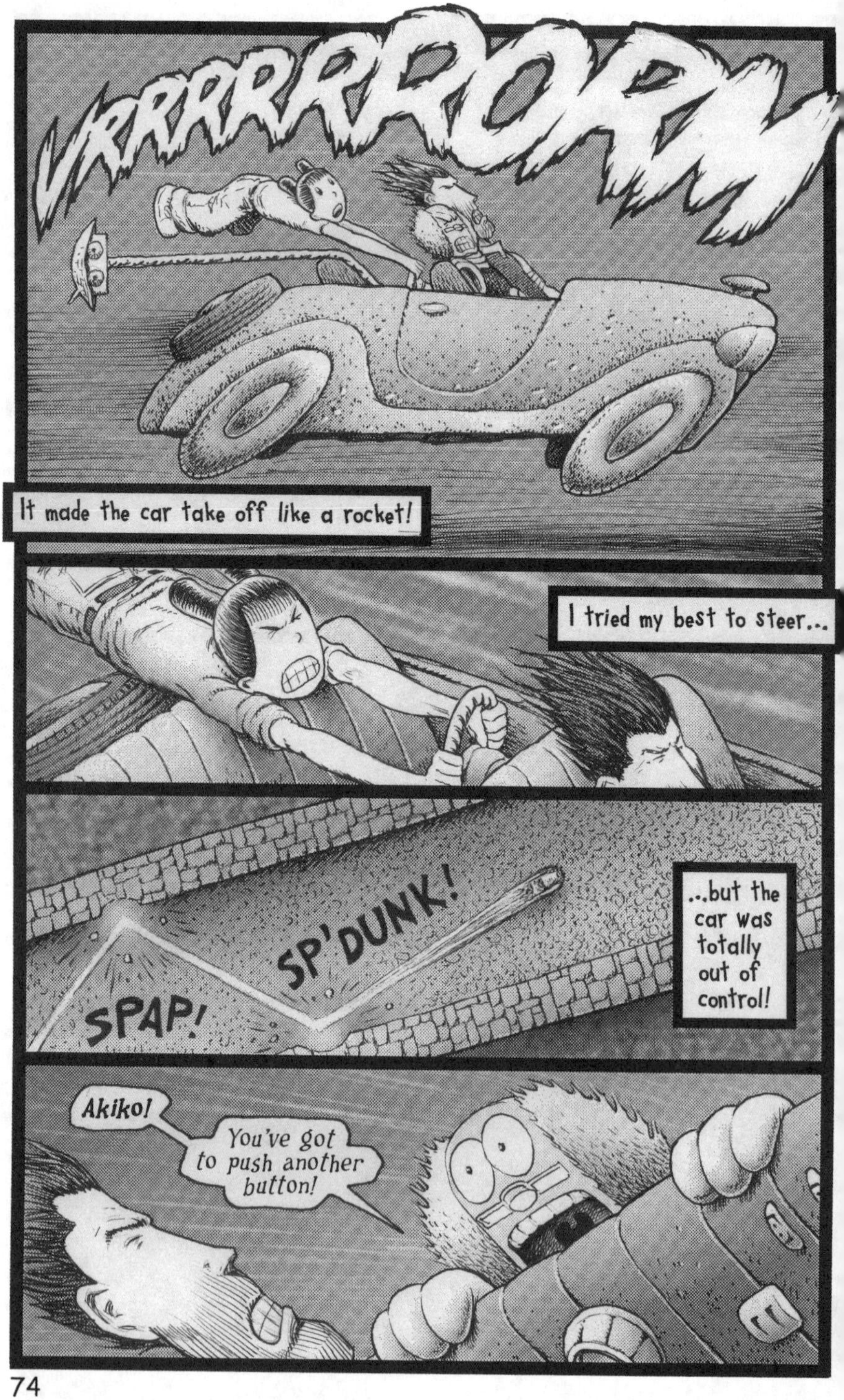
VRRRRRROOM
It made the car take off like a rocket!
I tried my best to steer...
...but the car was totally out of control!
SP'DUNK!
SPAP!
Akiko!
You've got to push another button!

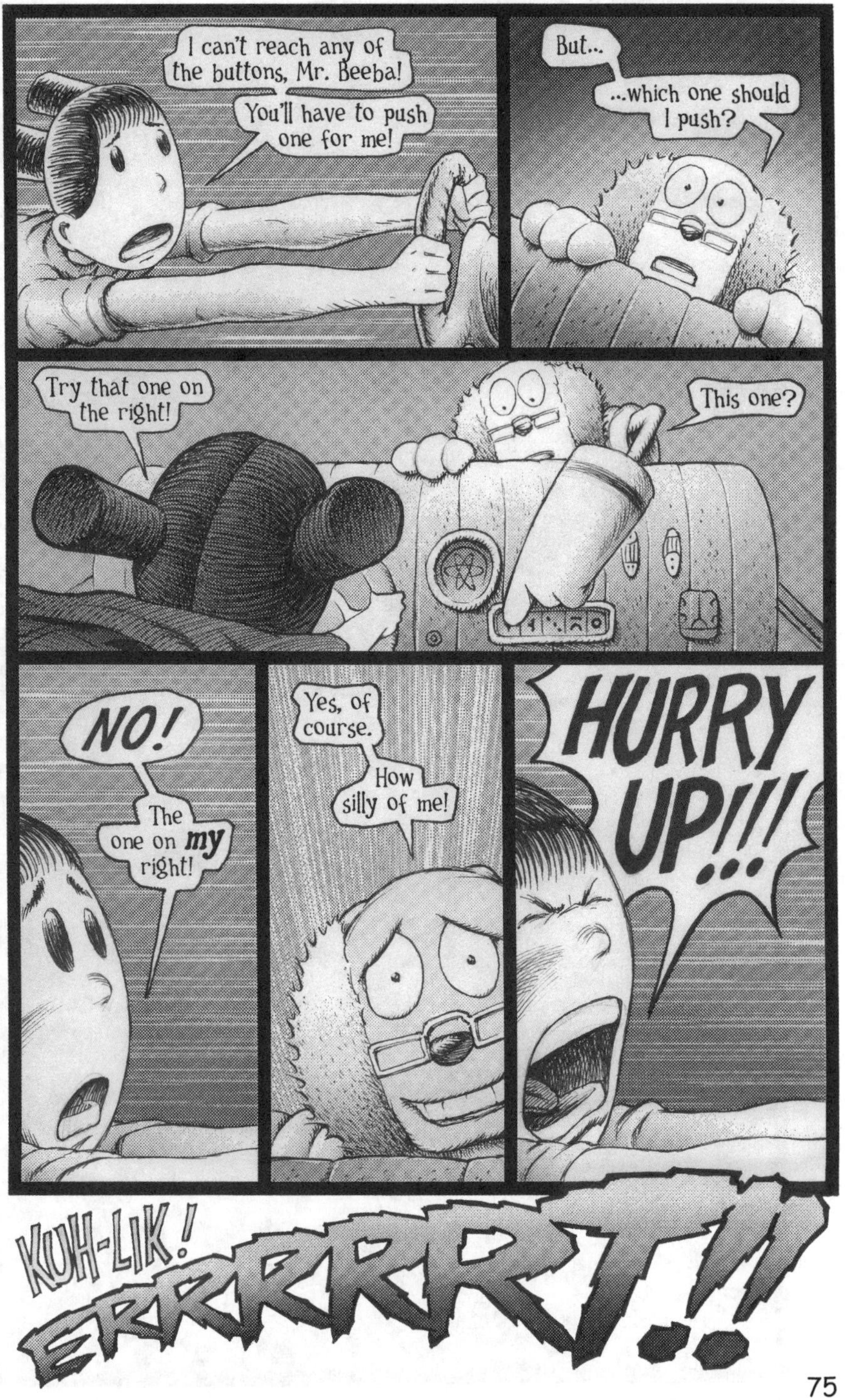
I can't reach any of the buttons, Mr. Beeba!
You'll have to push one for me!
But...
...which one should I push?
Try that one on the right!
This one?
NO!
The one on *my* right!
Yes, of course.
How silly of me!
HURRY UP!!!
KUH-LIK!
ERRRRRT!!

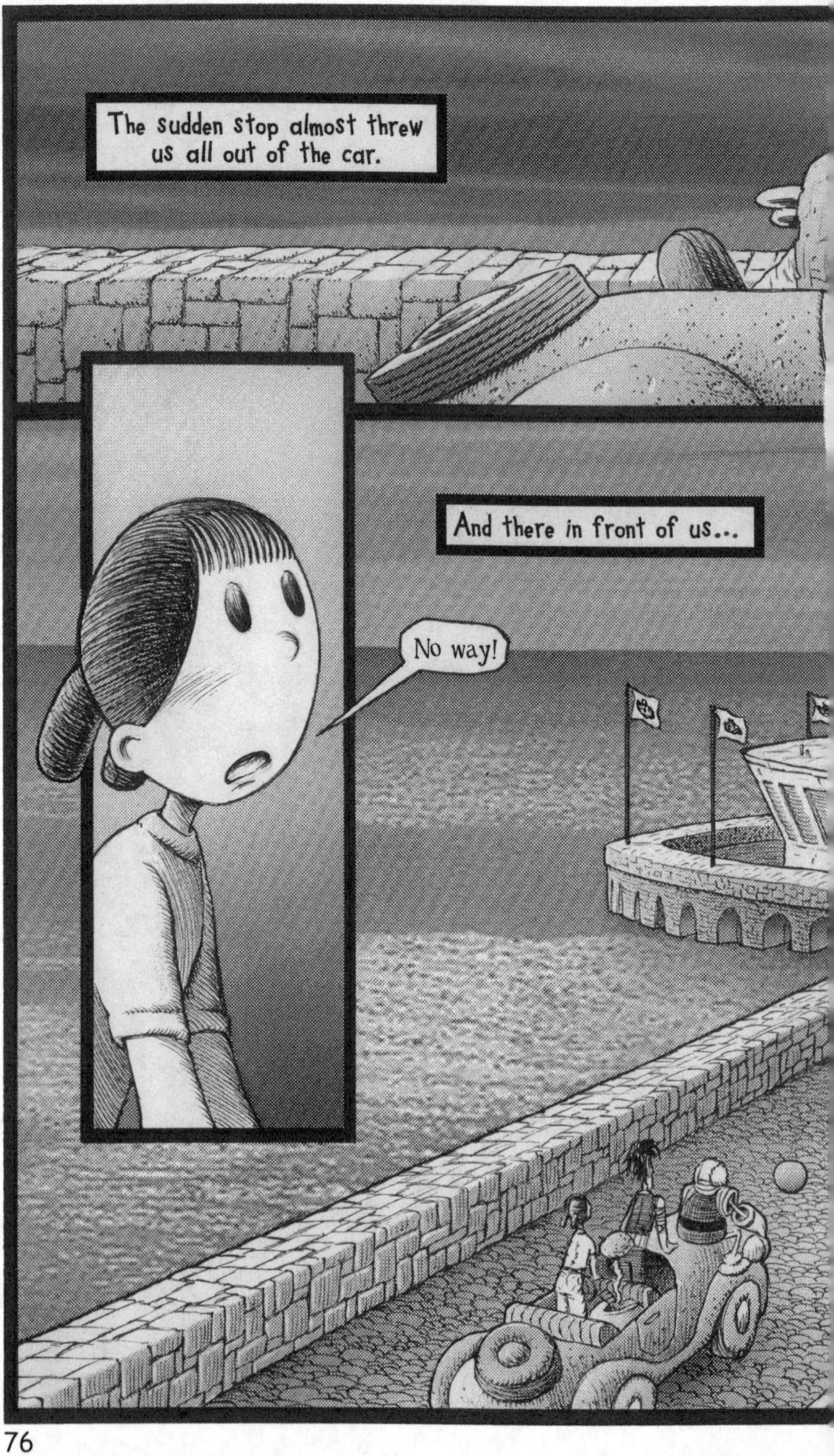
The sudden stop almost threw us all out of the car.
And there in front of us...
No way!

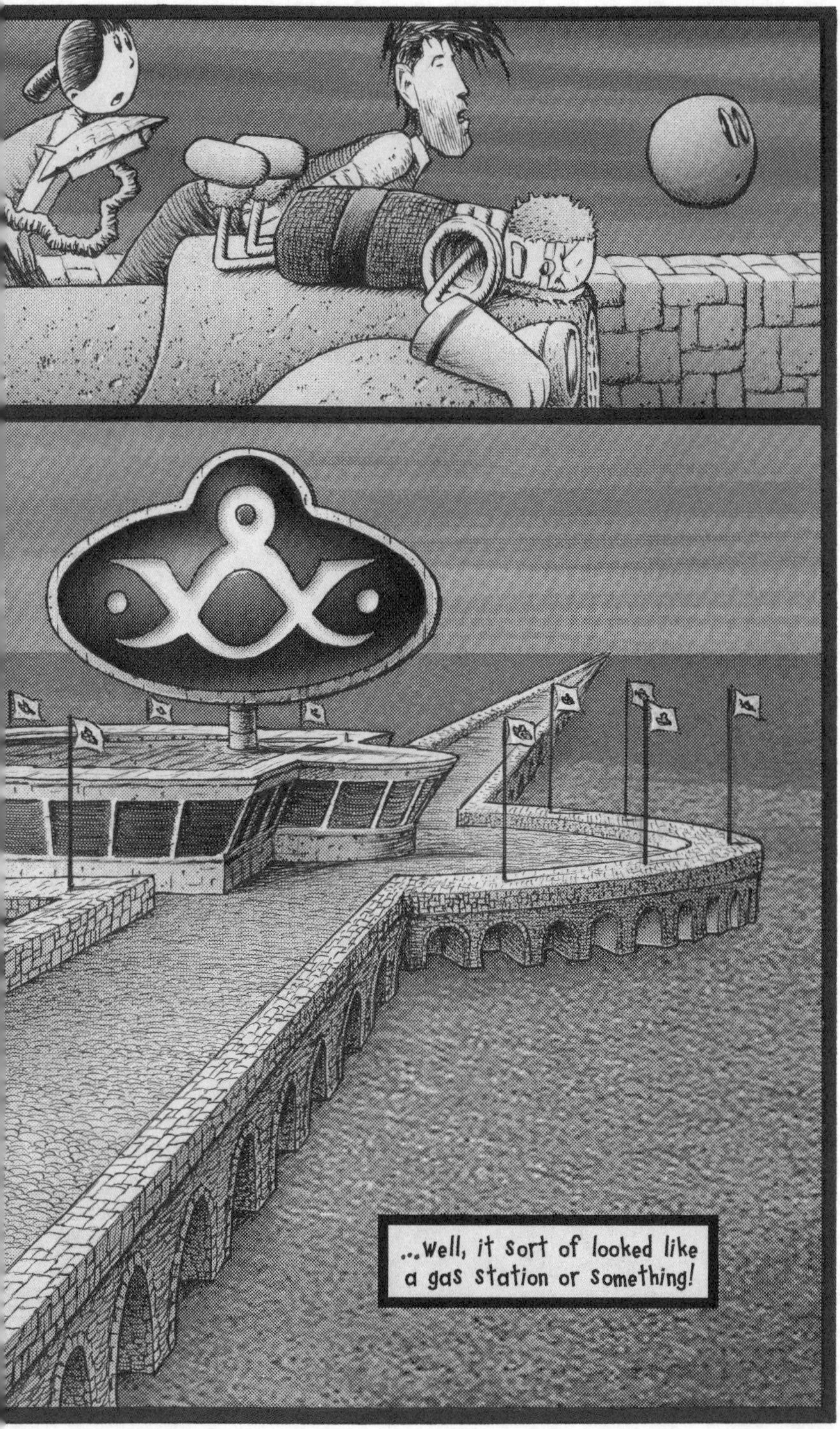
...well, it sort of looked like
a gas station or something!

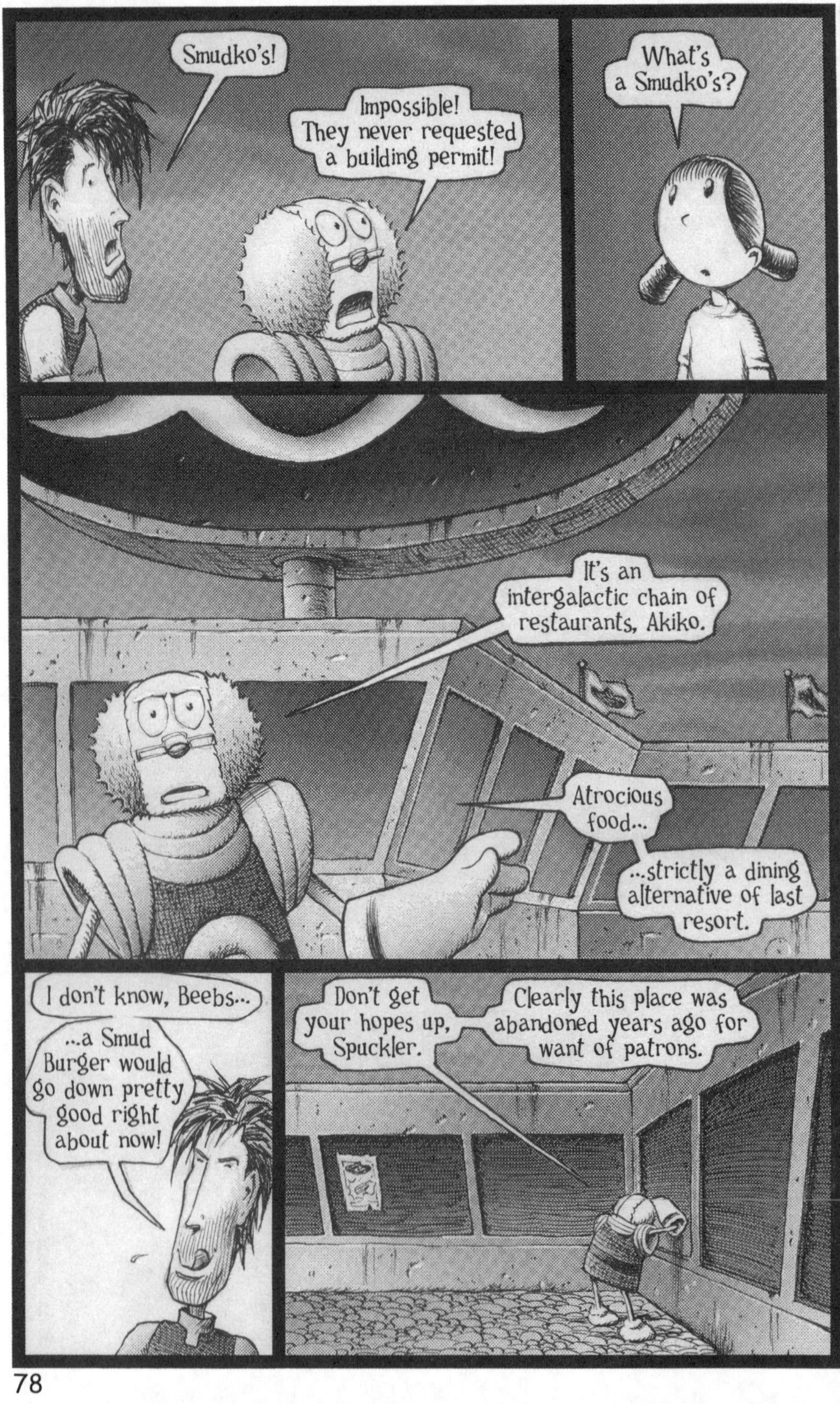

Smudko's!
Impossible! They never requested a building permit!
What's a Smudko's?
It's an intergalactic chain of restaurants, Akiko.
Atrocious food...
...strictly a dining alternative of last resort.
I don't know, Beebs...
...a Smud Burger would go down pretty good right about now!
Don't get your hopes up, Spuckler.
Clearly this place was abandoned years ago for want of patrons.

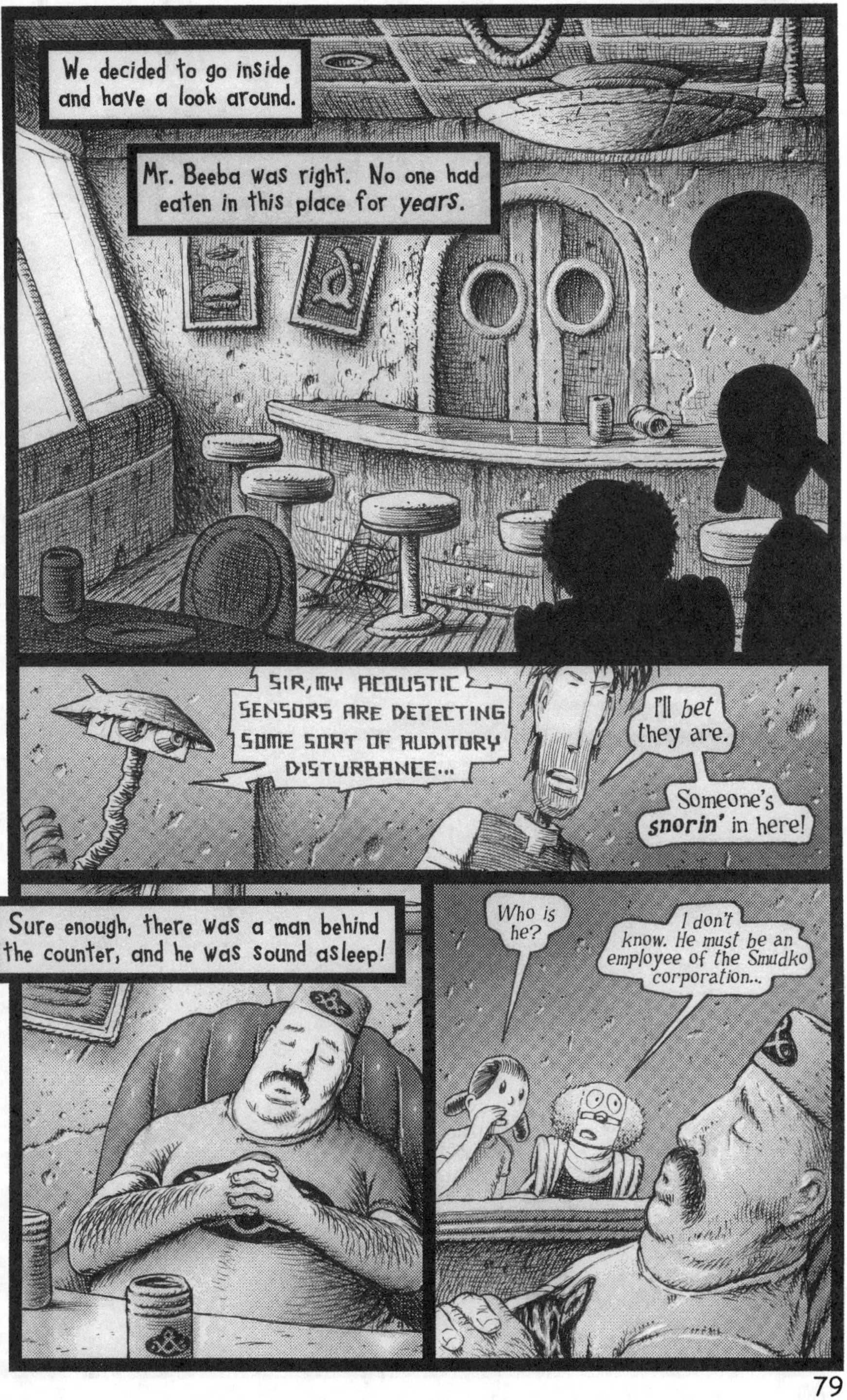

We decided to go inside and have a look around.
Mr. Beeba was right. No one had eaten in this place for *years*.
SIR, MY ACOUSTIC SENSORS ARE DETECTING SOME SORT OF AUDITORY DISTURBANCE...
I'll *bet* they are.
Someone's **snorin'** in here!
Sure enough, there was a man behind the counter, and he was sound asleep!
Who is he?
I don't know. He must be an employee of the Smudko corporation...

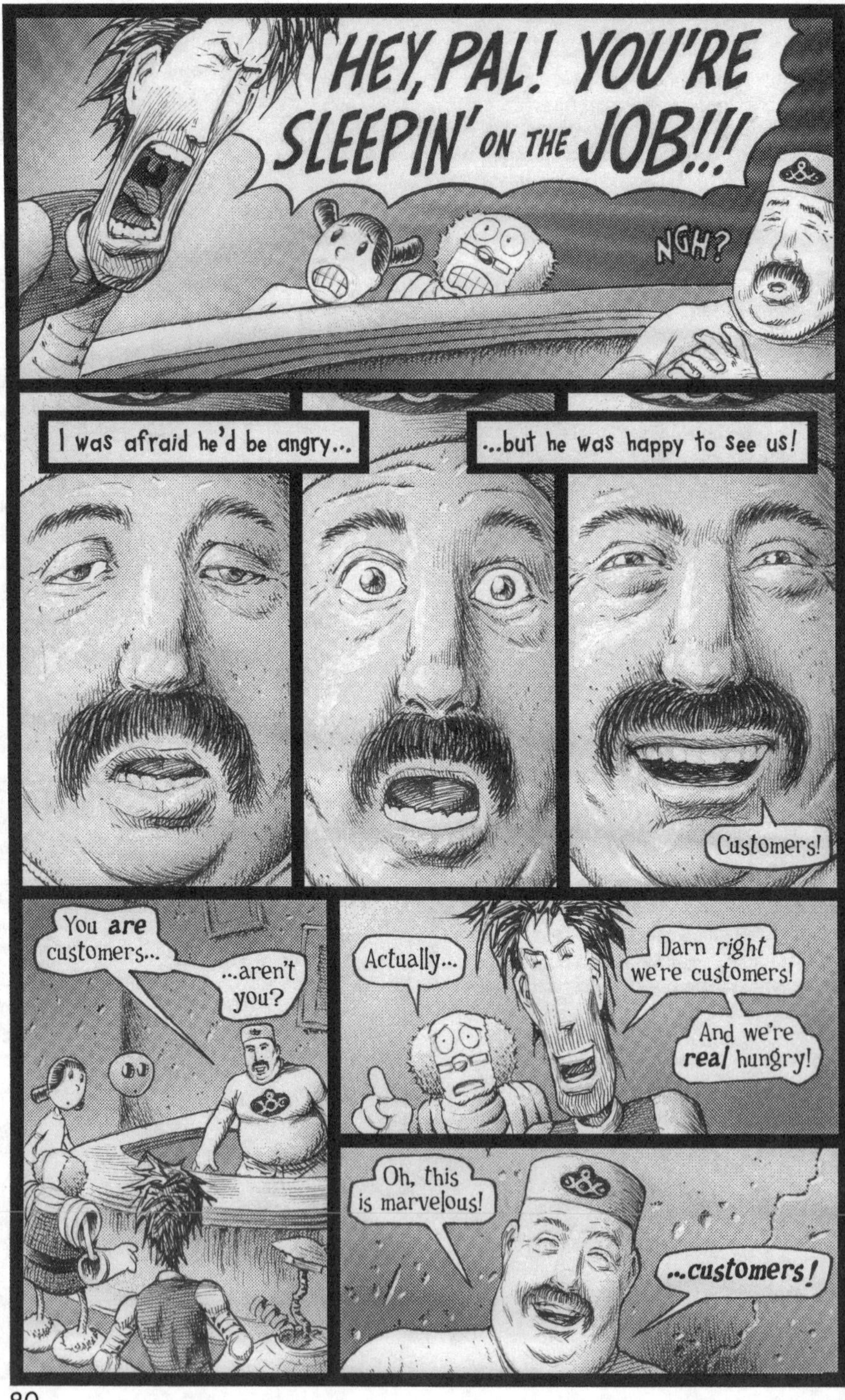

HEY, PAL! YOU'RE SLEEPIN' ON THE JOB!!!
NGH?
I was afraid he'd be angry...
...but he was happy to see us!
Customers!
You **are** customers...
...aren't you?
Actually...
Darn *right* we're customers!
And we're **real** hungry!
Oh, this is marvelous!
...customers!

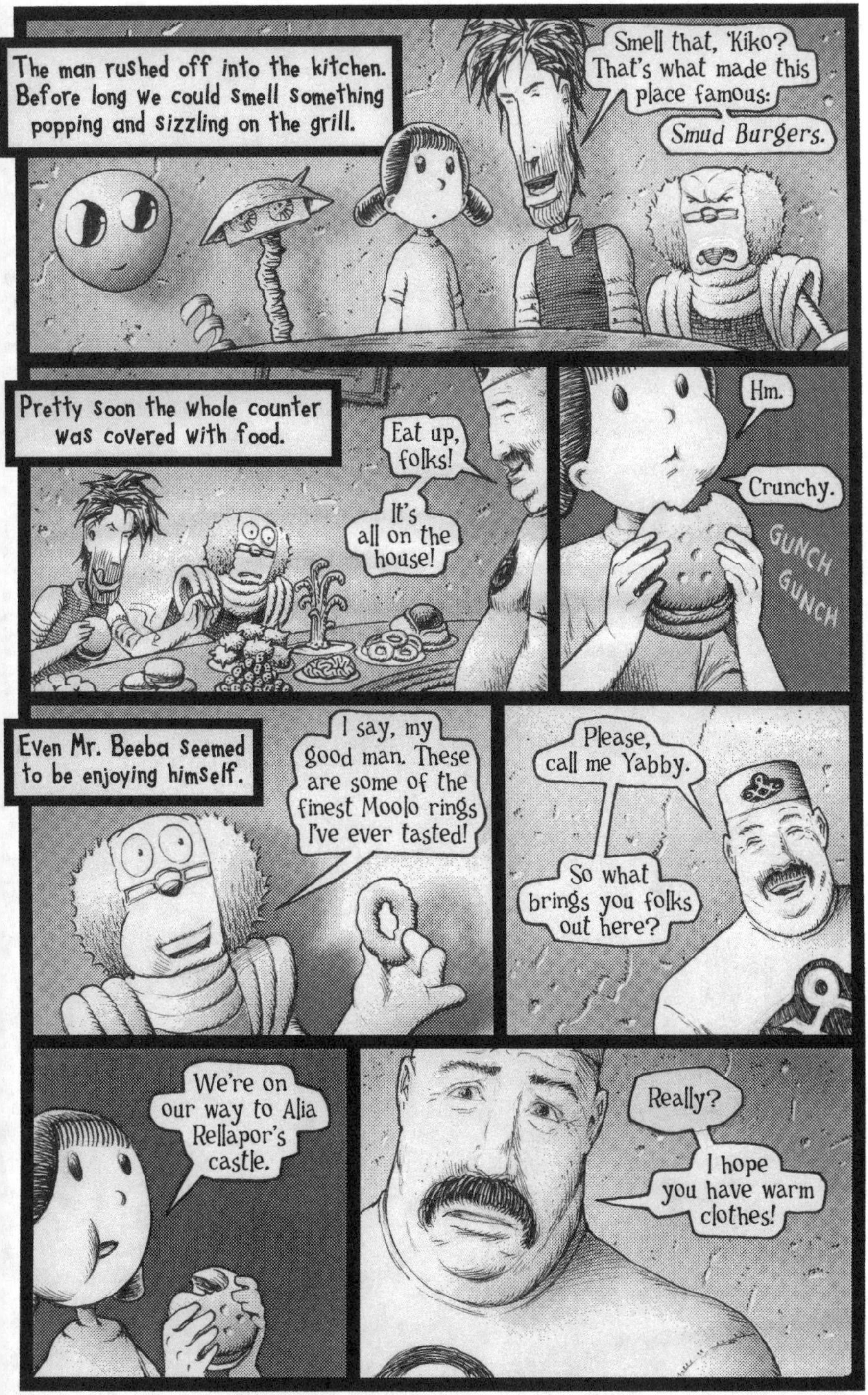
The man rushed off into the kitchen. Before long we could smell something popping and sizzling on the grill.
Smell that, 'Kiko? That's what made this place famous:
Smud Burgers.
Pretty soon the whole counter was covered with food.
Eat up, folks!
It's all on the house!
Hm.
Crunchy.
GUNCH GUNCH
Even Mr. Beeba seemed to be enjoying himself.
I say, my good man. These are some of the finest Moolo rings I've ever tasted!
Please, call me Yabby.
So what brings you folks out here?
We're on our way to Alia Rellapor's castle.
Really?
I hope you have warm clothes!

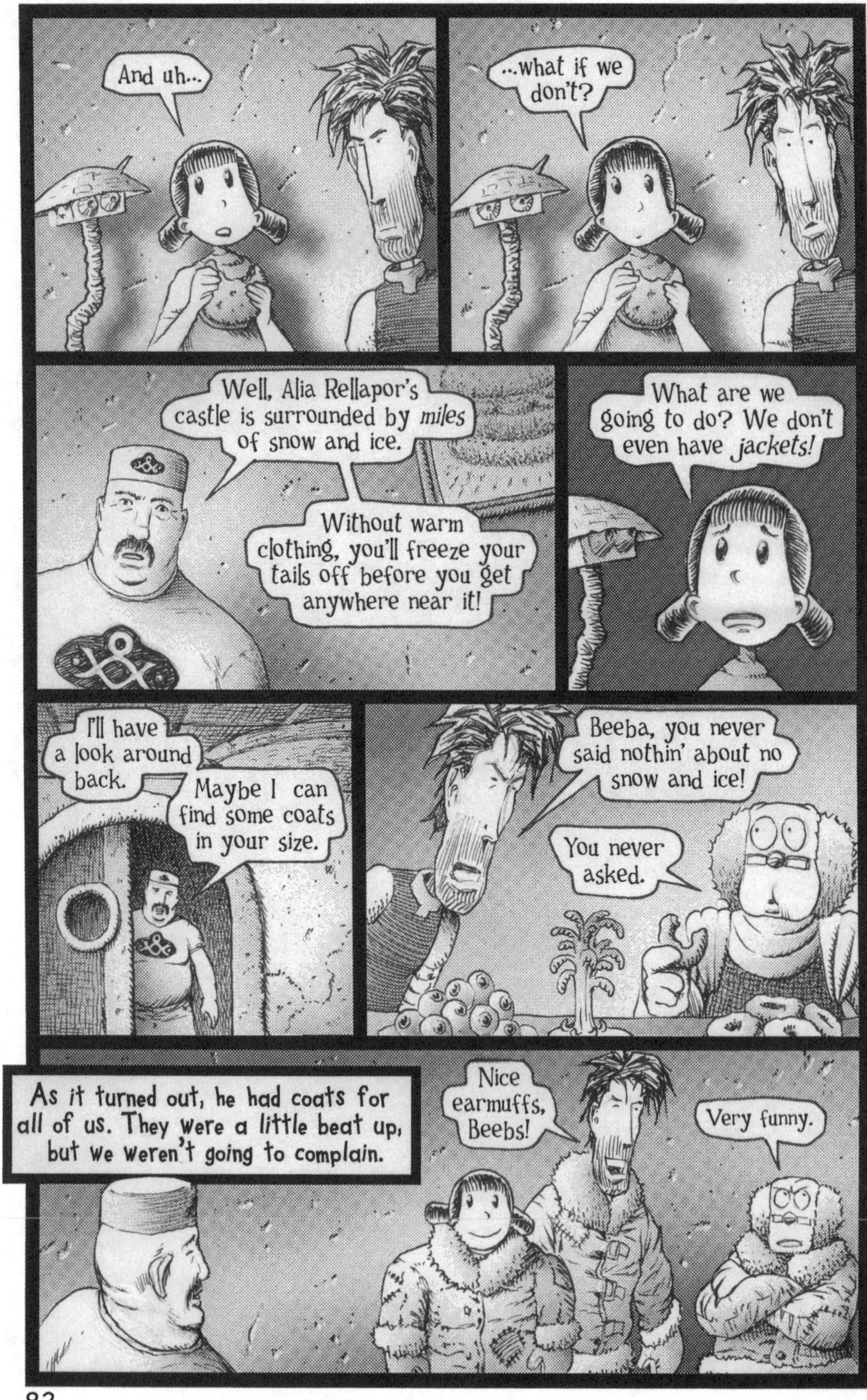
And uh...
...what if we don't?
Well, Alia Rellapor's castle is surrounded by *miles* of snow and ice.
Without warm clothing, you'll freeze your tails off before you get anywhere near it!
What are we going to do? We don't even have *jackets!*
I'll have a look around back.
Maybe I can find some coats in your size.
Beeba, you never said nothin' about no snow and ice!
You never asked.
As *it* turned out, he had coats for all of us. They were a *little* beat up, but we weren't going to complain.
Nice earmuffs, Beebs!
Very funny.

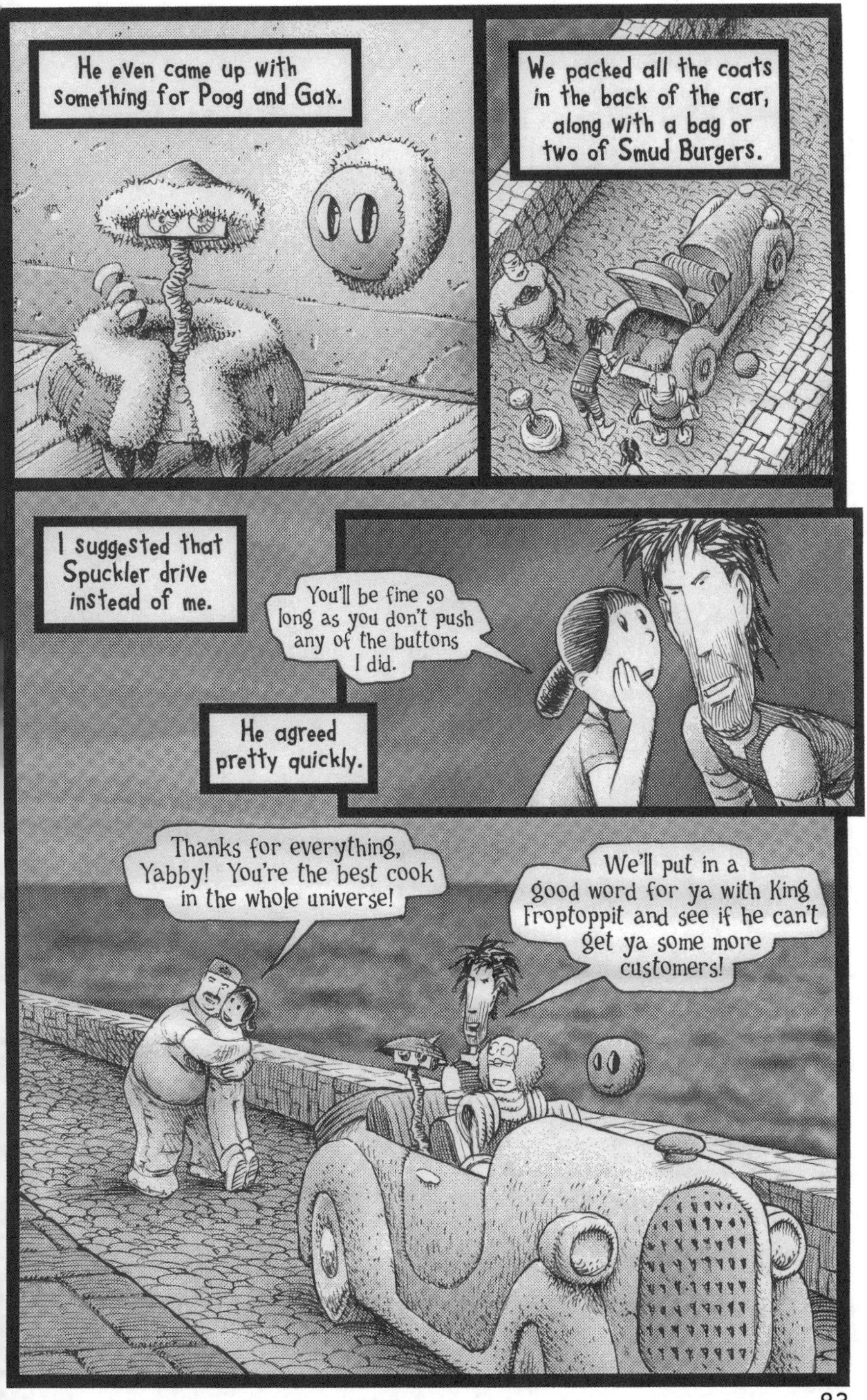
He even came up with something for Poog and Gax.
We packed all the coats in the back of the car, along with a bag or two of Smud Burgers.
I suggested that Spuckler drive instead of me.
You'll be fine so long as you don't push any of the buttons I did.
He agreed pretty quickly.
Thanks for everything, Yabby! You're the best cook in the whole universe!
We'll put in a good word for ya with King Froptoppit and see if he can't get ya some more customers!

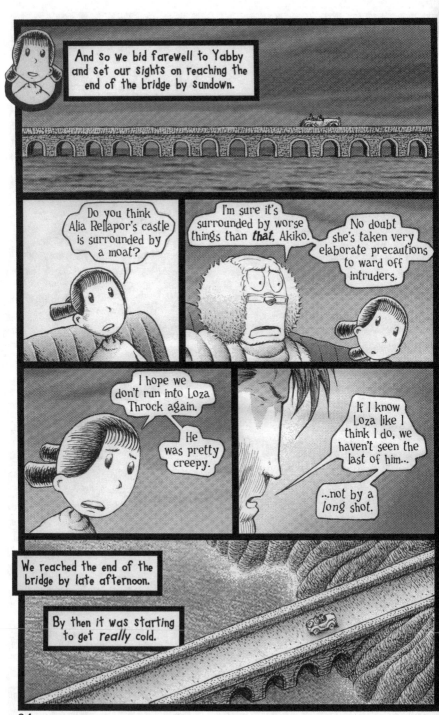

And so we bid farewell to Yabby and set our sights on reaching the end of the bridge by sundown.

Do you think Alia Rellapor's castle is surrounded by a moat?

I'm sure it's surrounded by worse things than *that*, Akiko.

No doubt she's taken very elaborate precautions to ward off intruders.

I hope we don't run into Loza Throck again.

He was pretty creepy.

If I know Loza like I think I do, we haven't seen the last of him...

...not by a *long* shot.

We reached the end of the bridge by *late* afternoon.

By then it was starting to get *really* cold.

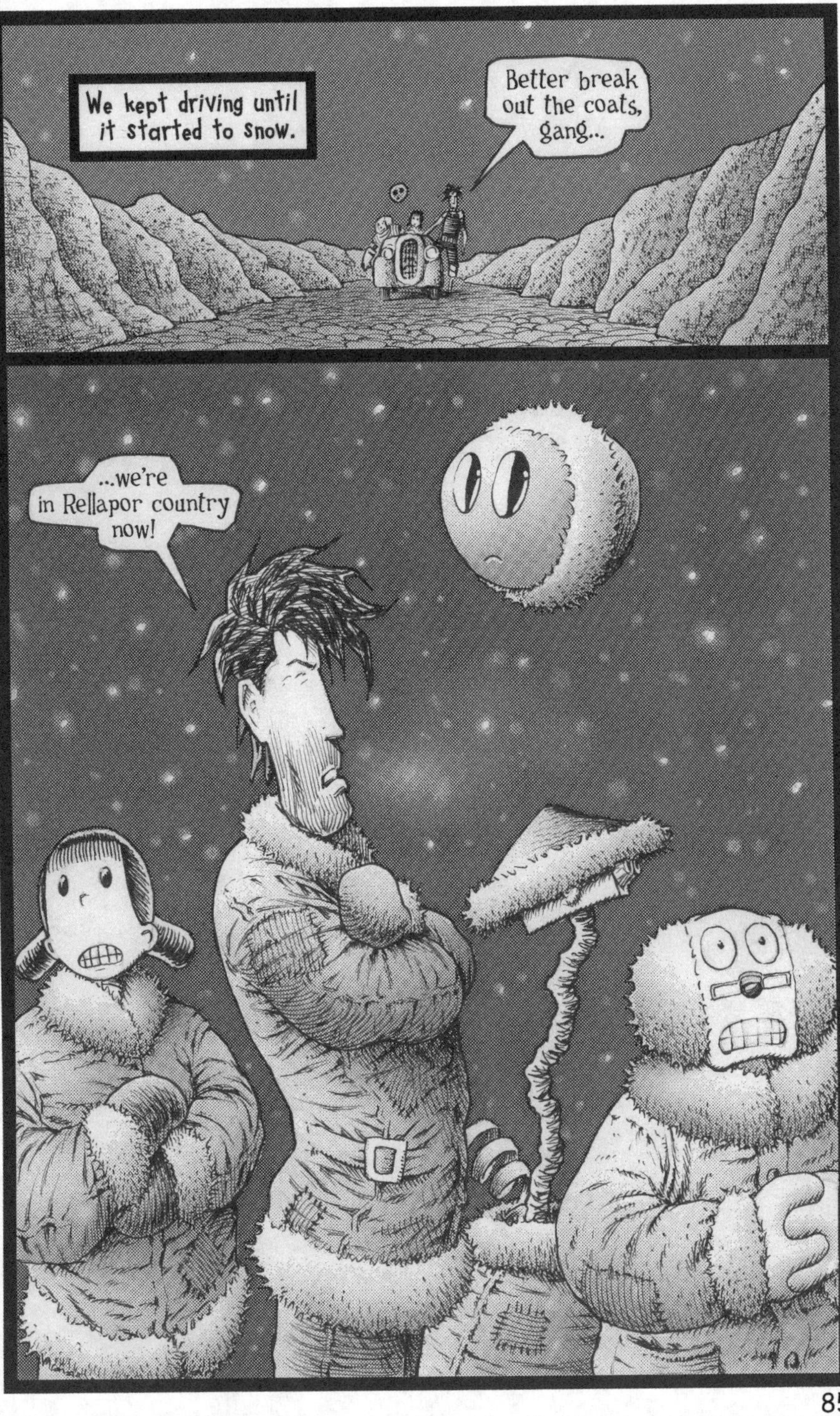
We kept driving until it started to snow.
Better break out the coats, gang...
...we're in Rellapor country now!

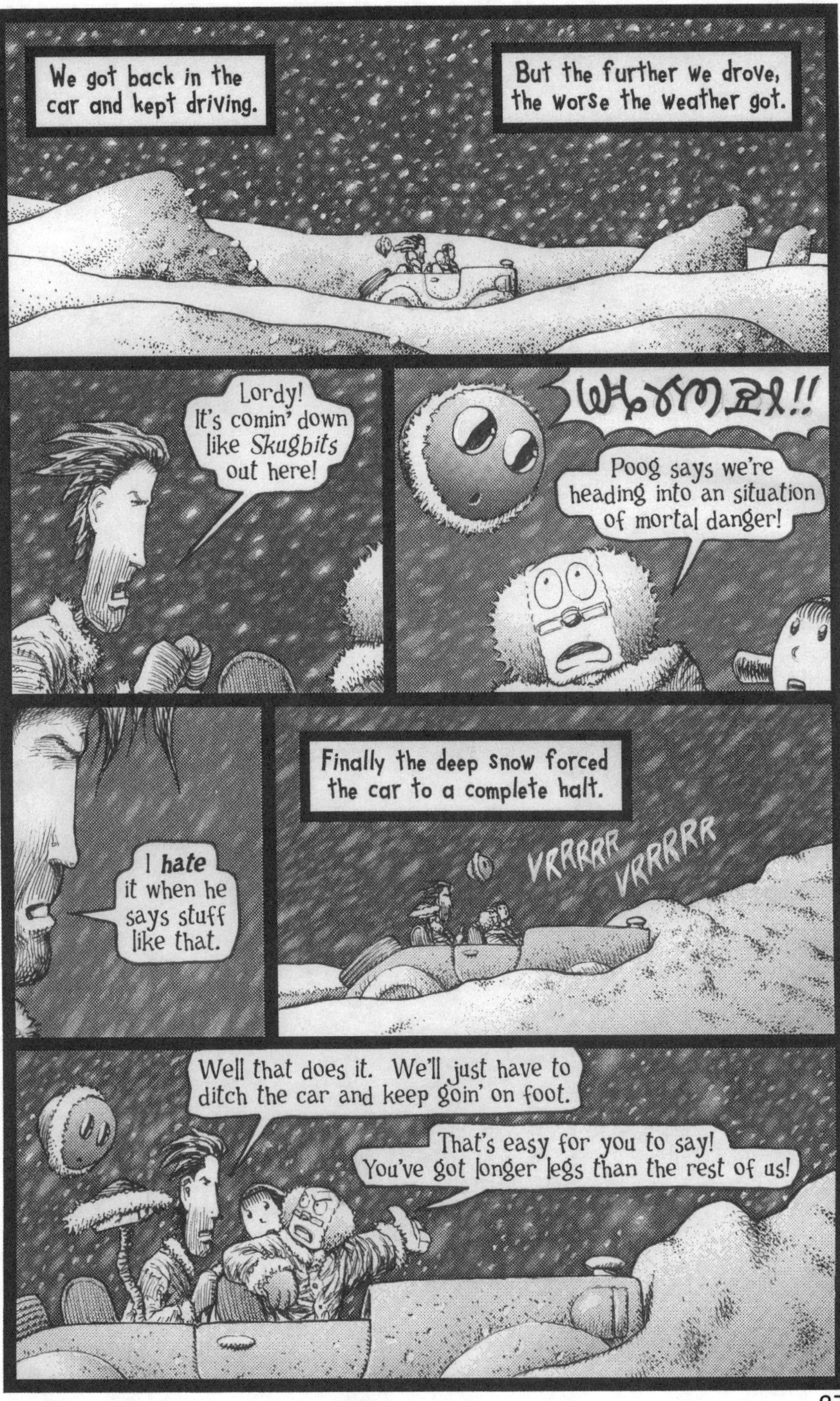
We got back in the car and kept driving.
But the further we drove, the worse the weather got.
Lordy! It's comin' down like *Skugbits* out here!
Poog says we're heading into an situation of mortal danger!
I **hate** it when he says stuff like that.
Finally the deep snow forced the car to a complete halt.
VRRRRR VRRRRR
Well that does it. We'll just have to ditch the car and keep goin' on foot.
That's easy for you to say! You've got longer legs than the rest of us!

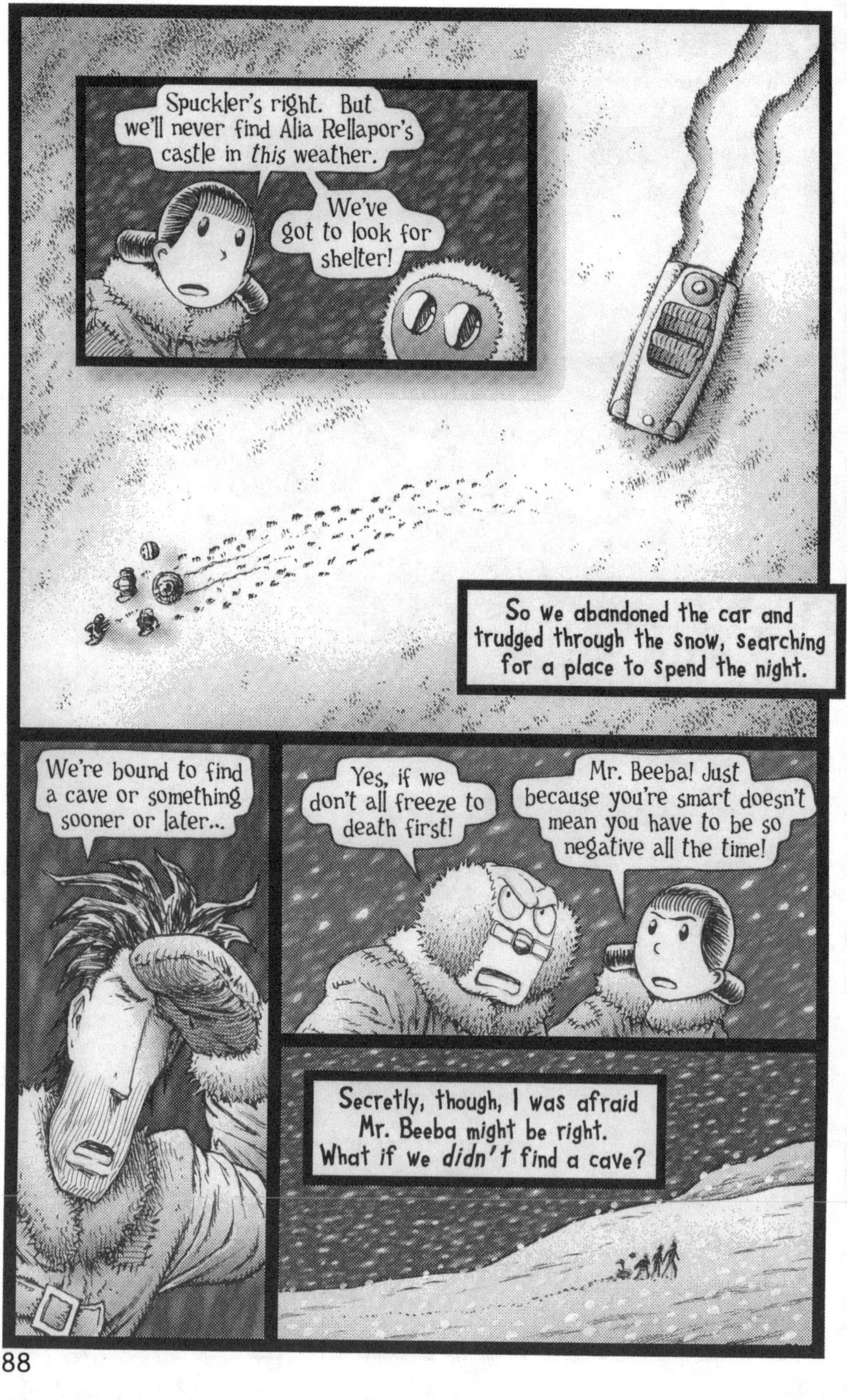
Spuckler's right. But we'll never find Alia Rellapor's castle in *this* weather.
We've got to look for shelter!
So we abandoned the car and trudged through the snow, searching for a place to spend the night.
We're bound to find a cave or something sooner or later...
Yes, if we don't all freeze to death first!
Mr. Beeba! Just because you're smart doesn't mean you have to be so negative all the time!
Secretly, though, I was afraid Mr. Beeba might be right. What if we *didn't* find a cave?

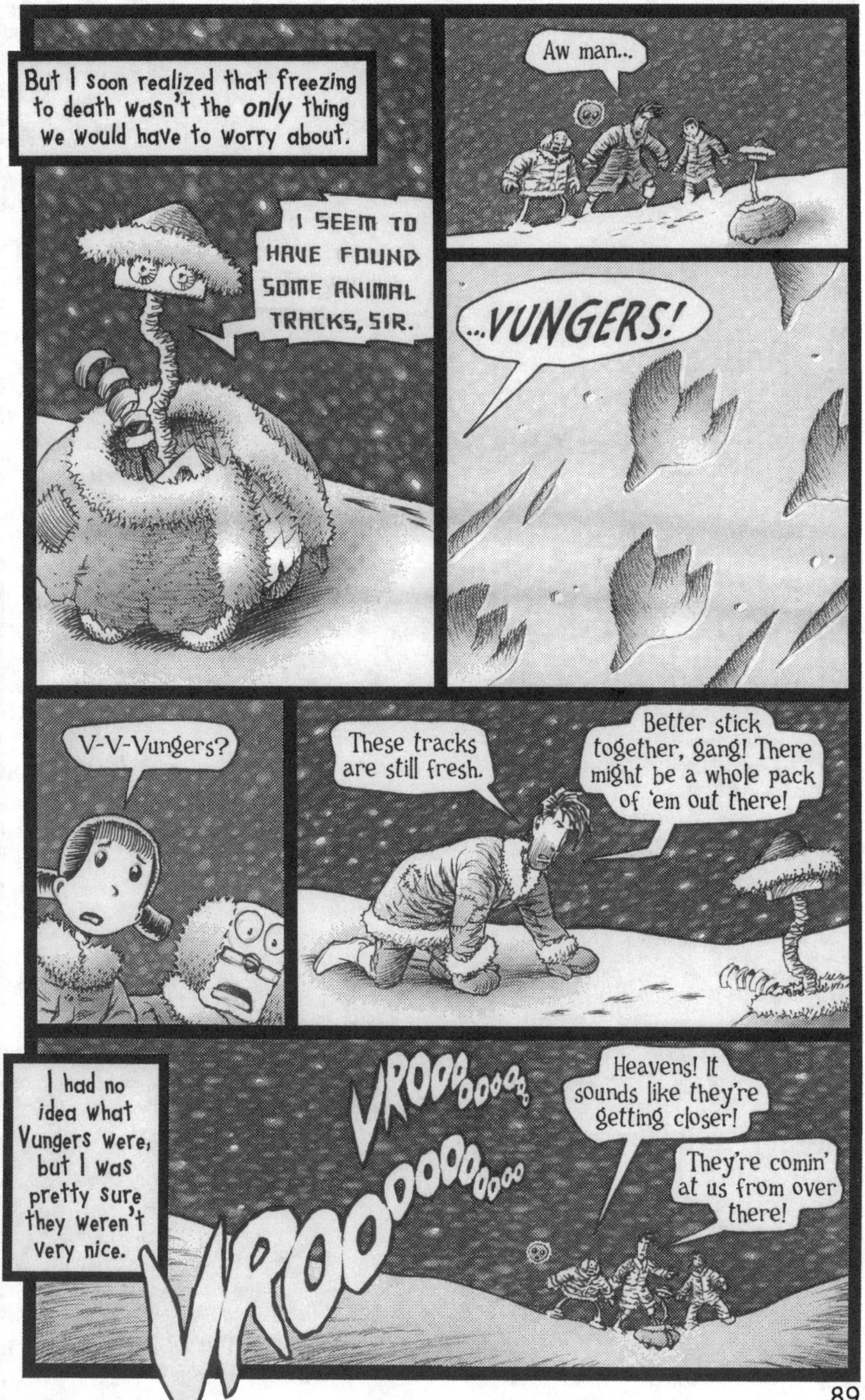
But I soon realized that freezing to death wasn't the *only* thing we would have to worry about.
I SEEM TO HAVE FOUND SOME ANIMAL TRACKS, SIR.
Aw man...
...VUNGERS!
V-V-Vungers?
These tracks are still fresh.
Better stick together, gang! There might be a whole pack of 'em out there!
I had no idea what Vungers were, but I was pretty sure they weren't very nice.
VROOooooooo
VROOOOOOOooooo
VROOOO
Heavens! It sounds like they're getting closer!
They're comin' at us from over there!

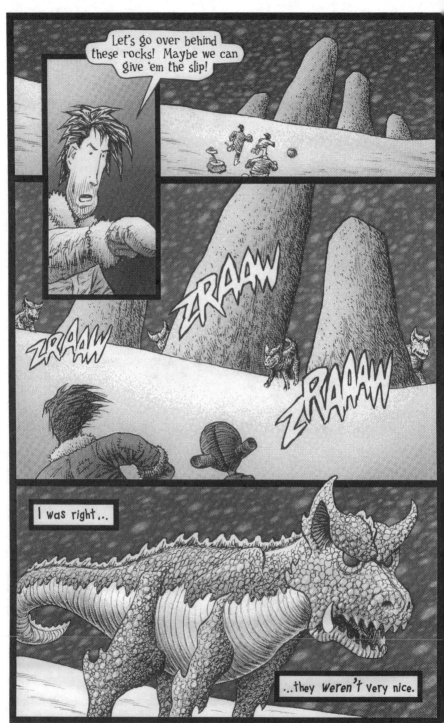

Let's go over behind these rocks! Maybe we can give 'em the slip!

ZRAAW

ZRAAW

ZRAAW

I was right...

...they *weren't* very nice.

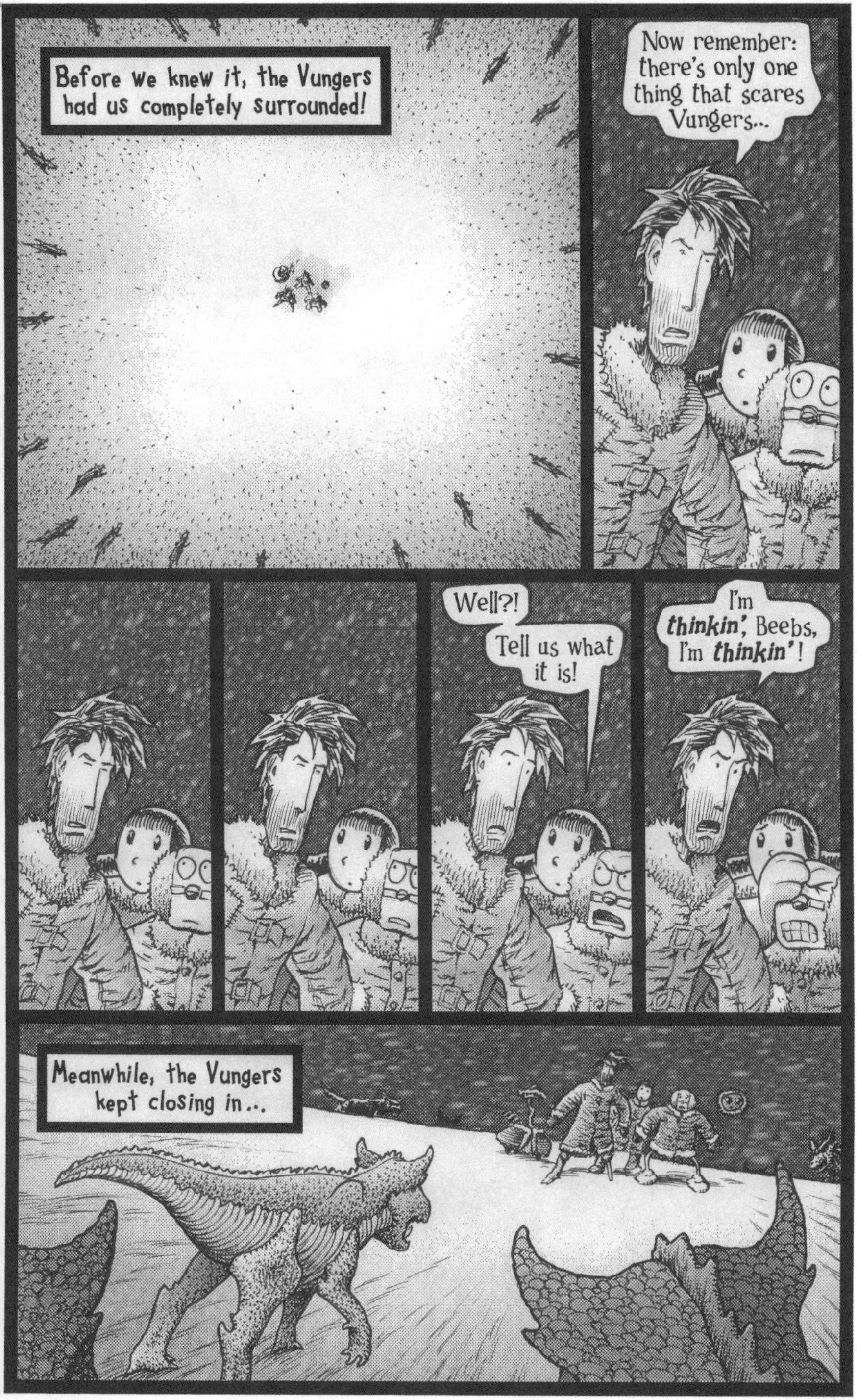
Before we knew it, the Vungers had us completely surrounded!
Now remember: there's only one thing that scares Vungers...
Well?!
Tell us what it is!
I'm *thinkin',* Beebs, I'm *thinkin'*!
Meanwhile, the Vungers kept closing in...

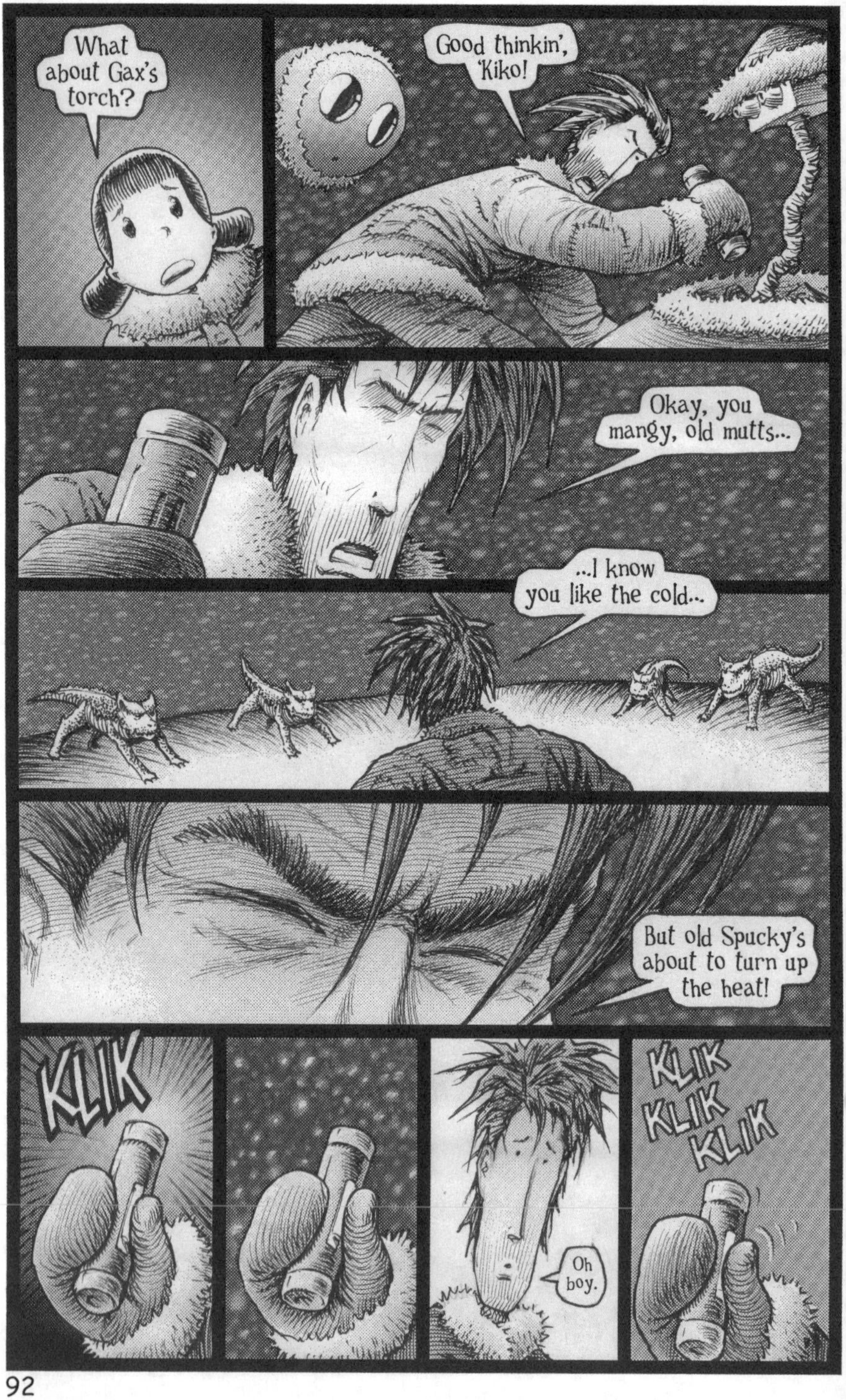
What about Gax's torch?
Good thinkin', 'Kiko!
Okay, you mangy, old mutts...
...I know you like the cold...
But old Spucky's about to turn up the heat!
KLIK
Oh boy.
KLIK KLIK KLIK

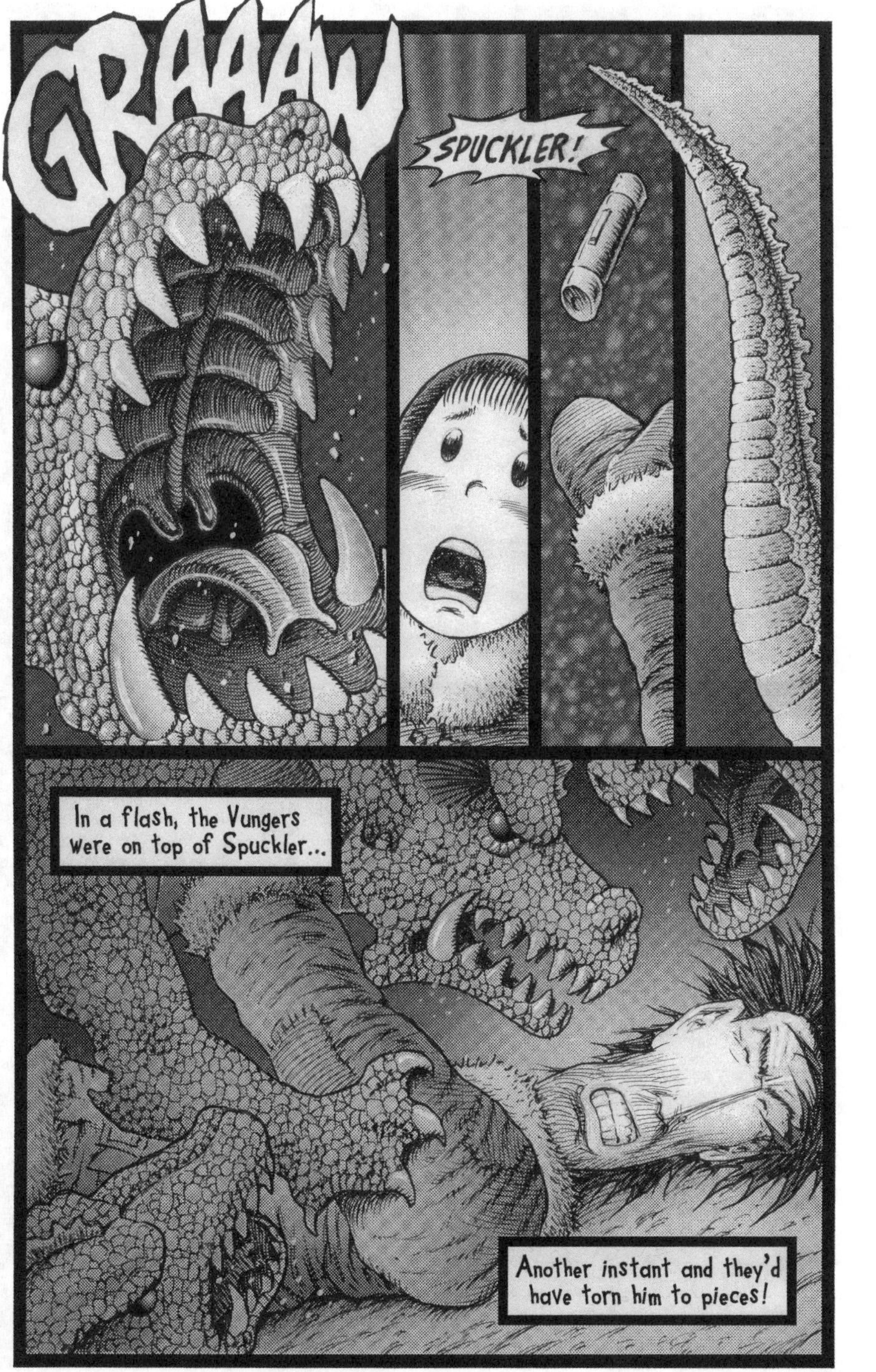
GRAAAW
SPUCKLER!
In a flash, the Vungers were on top of Spuckler...
Another instant and they'd have torn him to pieces!

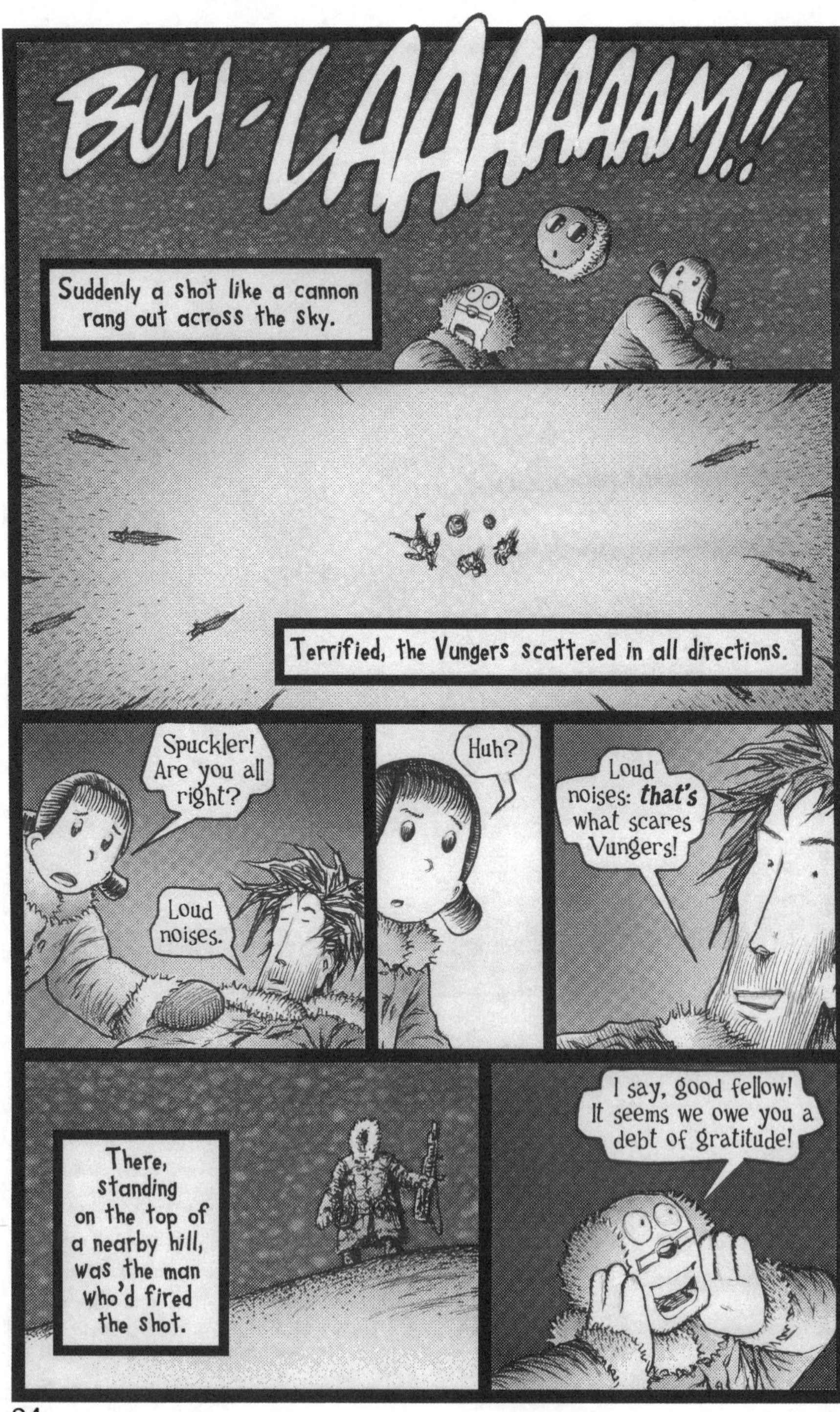
BUH-LAAAAAAM!!
Suddenly a shot like a cannon rang out across the sky.
Terrified, the Vungers scattered in all directions.
Spuckler! Are you all right?
Loud noises.
Huh?
Loud noises: *that's* what scares Vungers!
There, standing on the top of a nearby hill, was the man who'd fired the shot.
I say, good fellow! It seems we owe you a debt of gratitude!

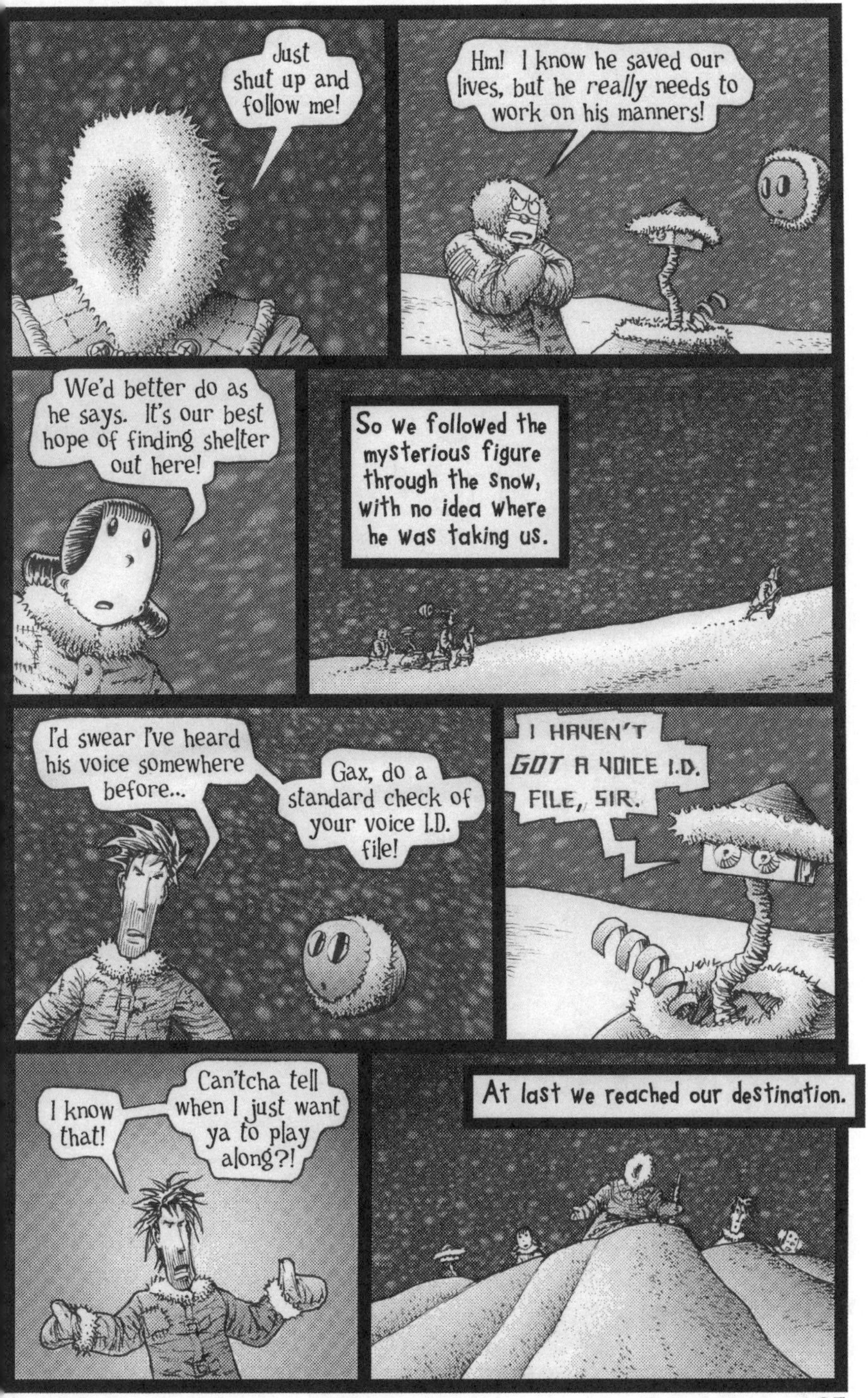
Just shut up and follow me!
Hm! I know he saved our lives, but he *really* needs to work on his manners!
We'd better do as he says. It's our best hope of finding shelter out here!
So we followed the mysterious figure through the snow, with no idea where he was taking us.
I'd swear I've heard his voice somewhere before...
Gax, do a standard check of your voice I.D. file!
I HAVEN'T *GOT* A VOICE I.D. FILE, SIR.
I know that!
Can'tcha tell when I just want ya to play along?!
At last we reached our destination.

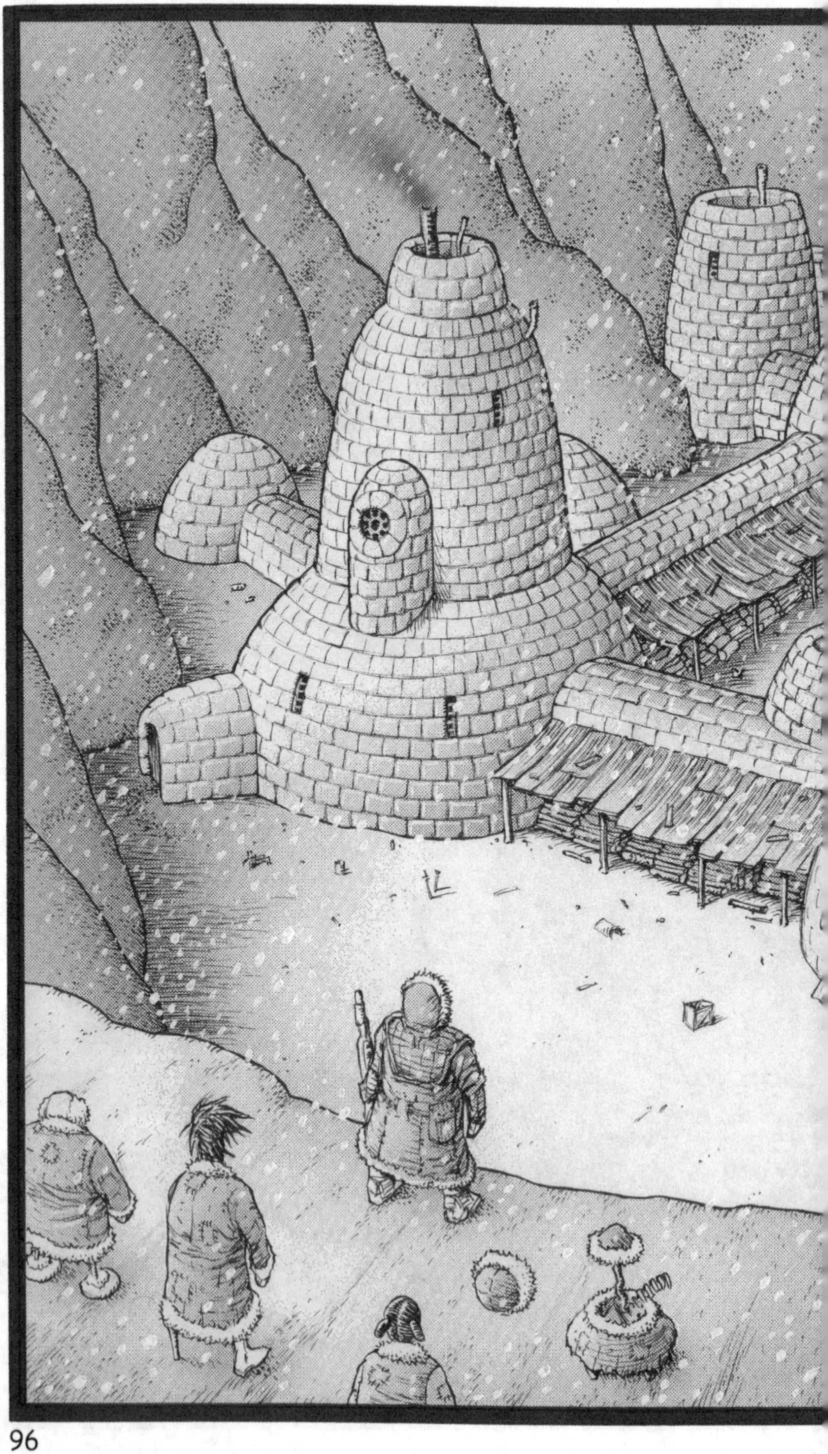

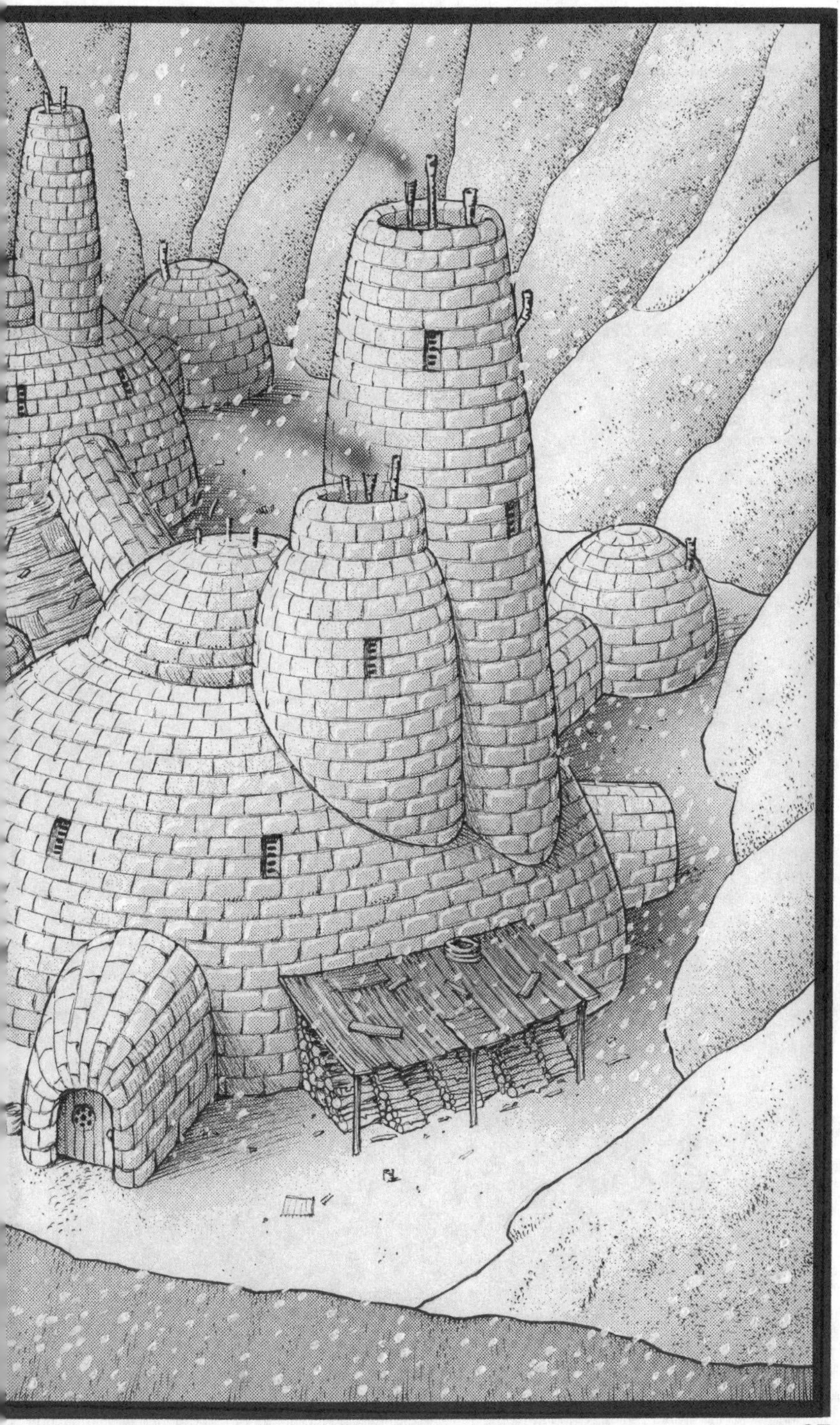

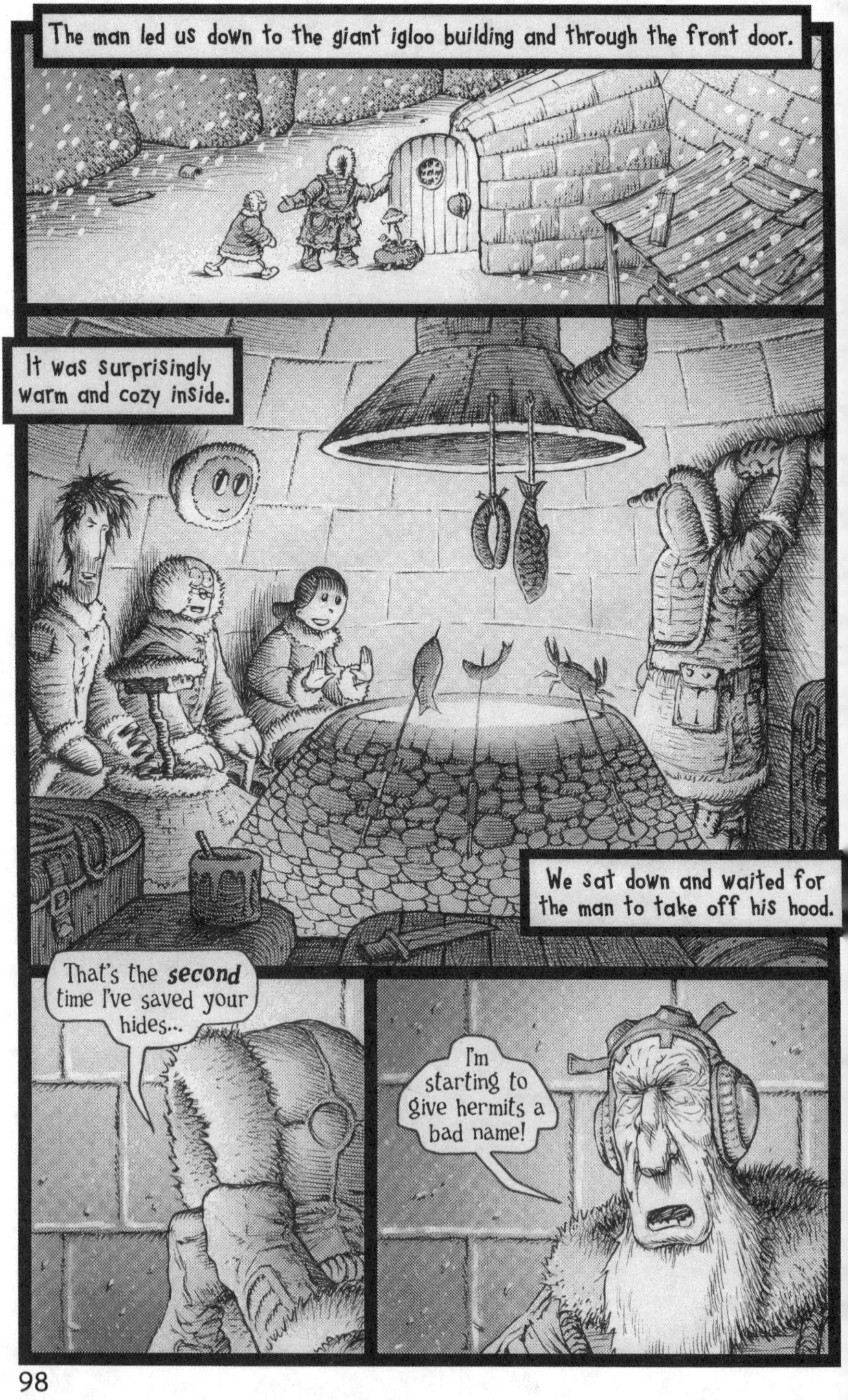
The man led us down to the giant igloo building and through the front door.
It was surprisingly warm and cozy inside.
We sat down and waited for the man to take off his hood.
That's the **second** time I've saved your hides...
I'm starting to give hermits a bad name!

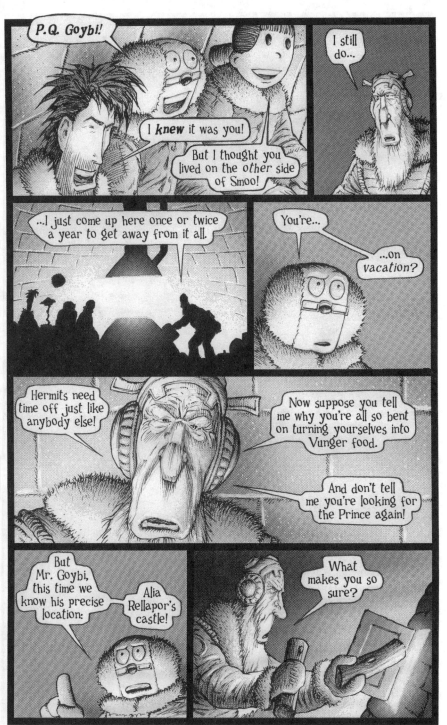

P.Q. Goybi!

I **knew** it was you!

But I thought you lived on the *other* side of Smoo!

I still do...

...I just come up here once or twice a year to get away from it all.

You're...

...on *vacation?*

Hermits need time off just like anybody else!

Now suppose you tell me why you're all so bent on turning yourselves into Vunger food.

And don't tell me you're looking for the Prince again!

But Mr. Goybi, this time we know his precise location: Alia Rellapor's castle!

What makes you so sure?

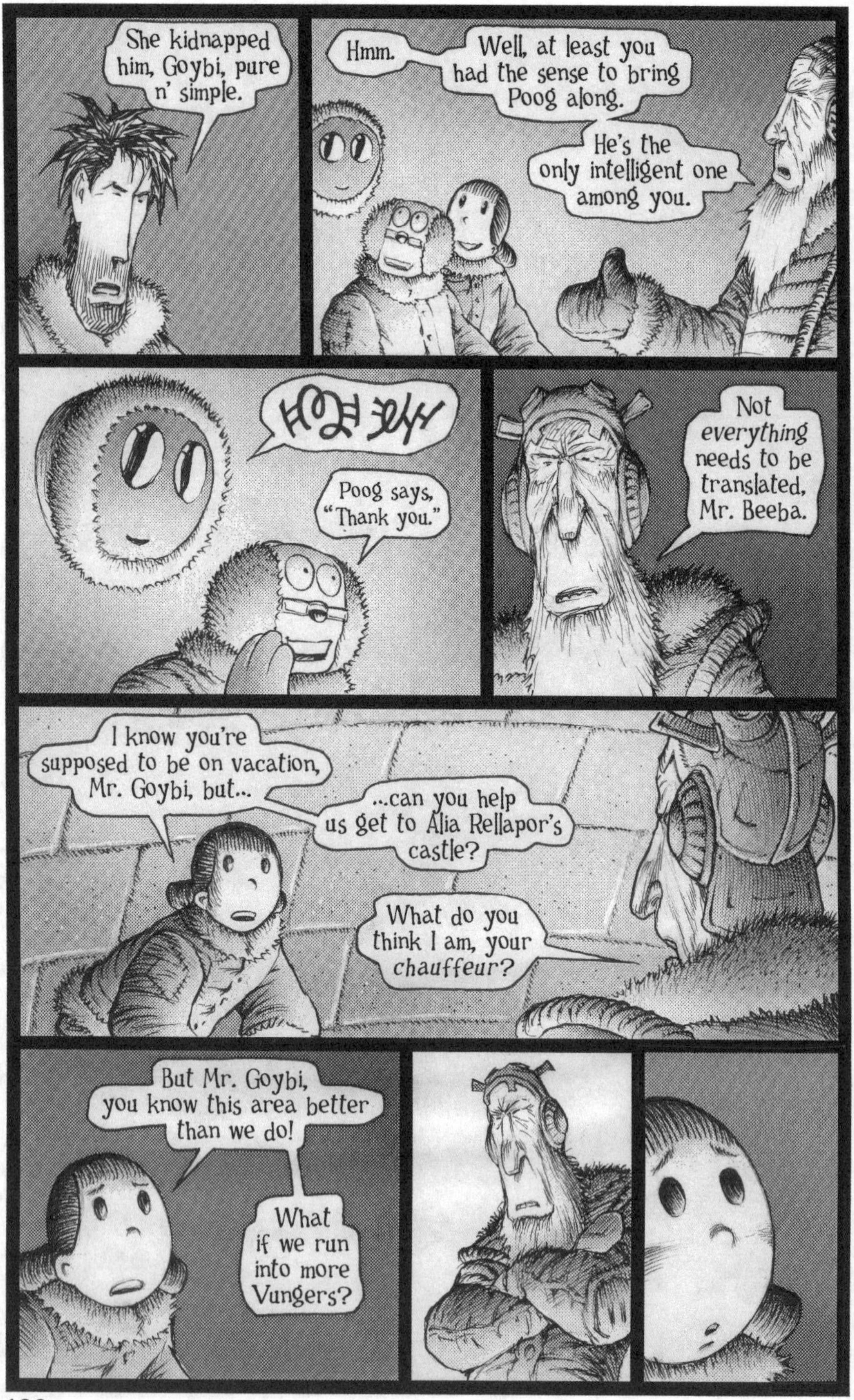
She kidnapped him, Goybi, pure n' simple.
Hmm.
Well, at least you had the sense to bring Poog along.
He's the only intelligent one among you.
Poog says, "Thank you."
Not *everything* needs to be translated, Mr. Beeba.
I know you're supposed to be on vacation, Mr. Goybi, but...
...can you help us get to Alia Rellapor's castle?
What do you think I am, your *chauffeur*?
But Mr. Goybi, you know this area better than we do!
What if we run into more Vungers?

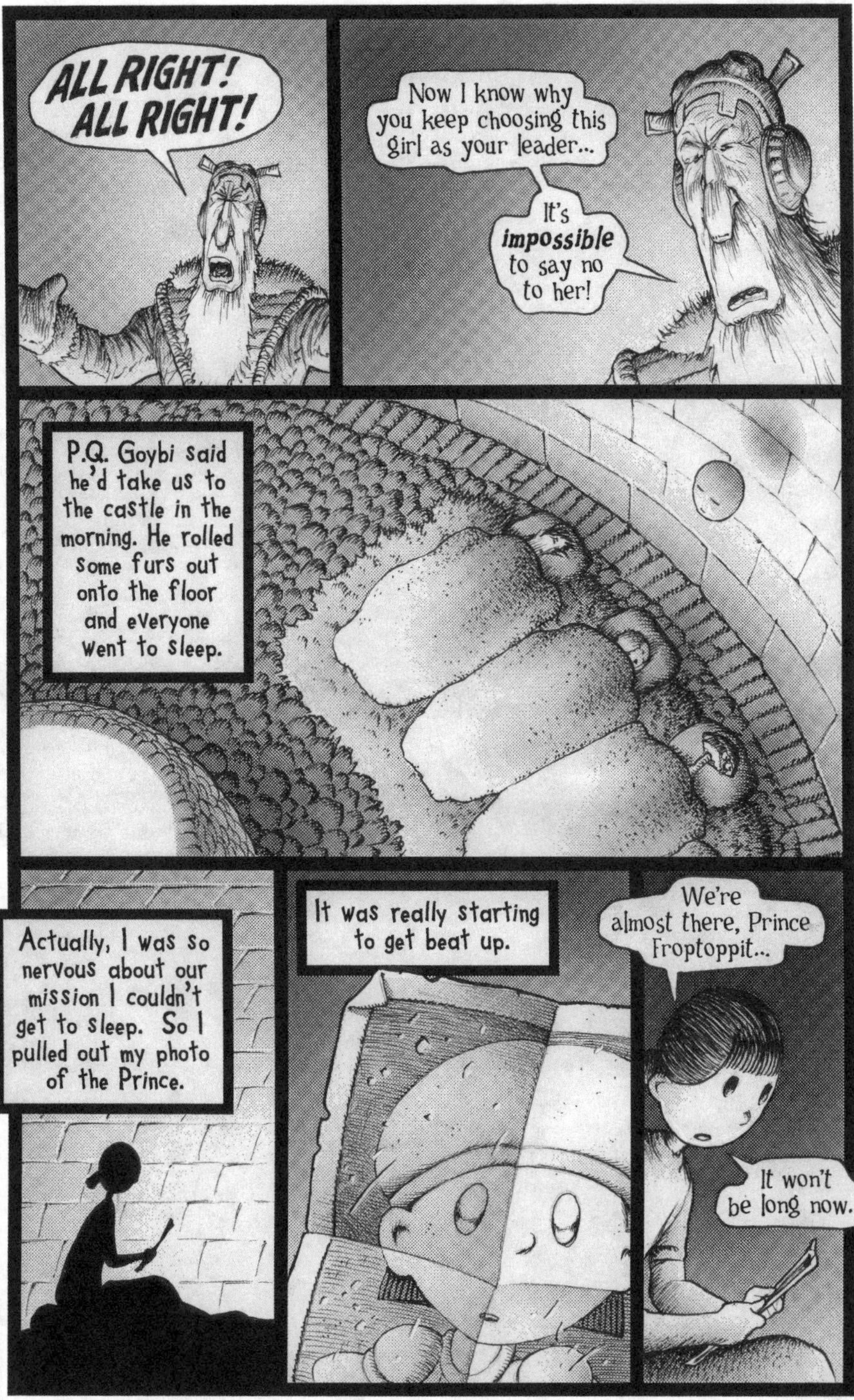
ALL RIGHT! ALL RIGHT!
Now I know why you keep choosing this girl as your leader...
It's ***impossible*** to say no to her!
P.Q. Goybi said he'd take us to the castle in the morning. He rolled some furs out onto the floor and everyone went to sleep.
Actually, I was so nervous about our mission I couldn't get to sleep. So I pulled out my photo of the Prince.
It was really starting to get beat up.
We're almost there, Prince Froptoppit...
It won't be long now...

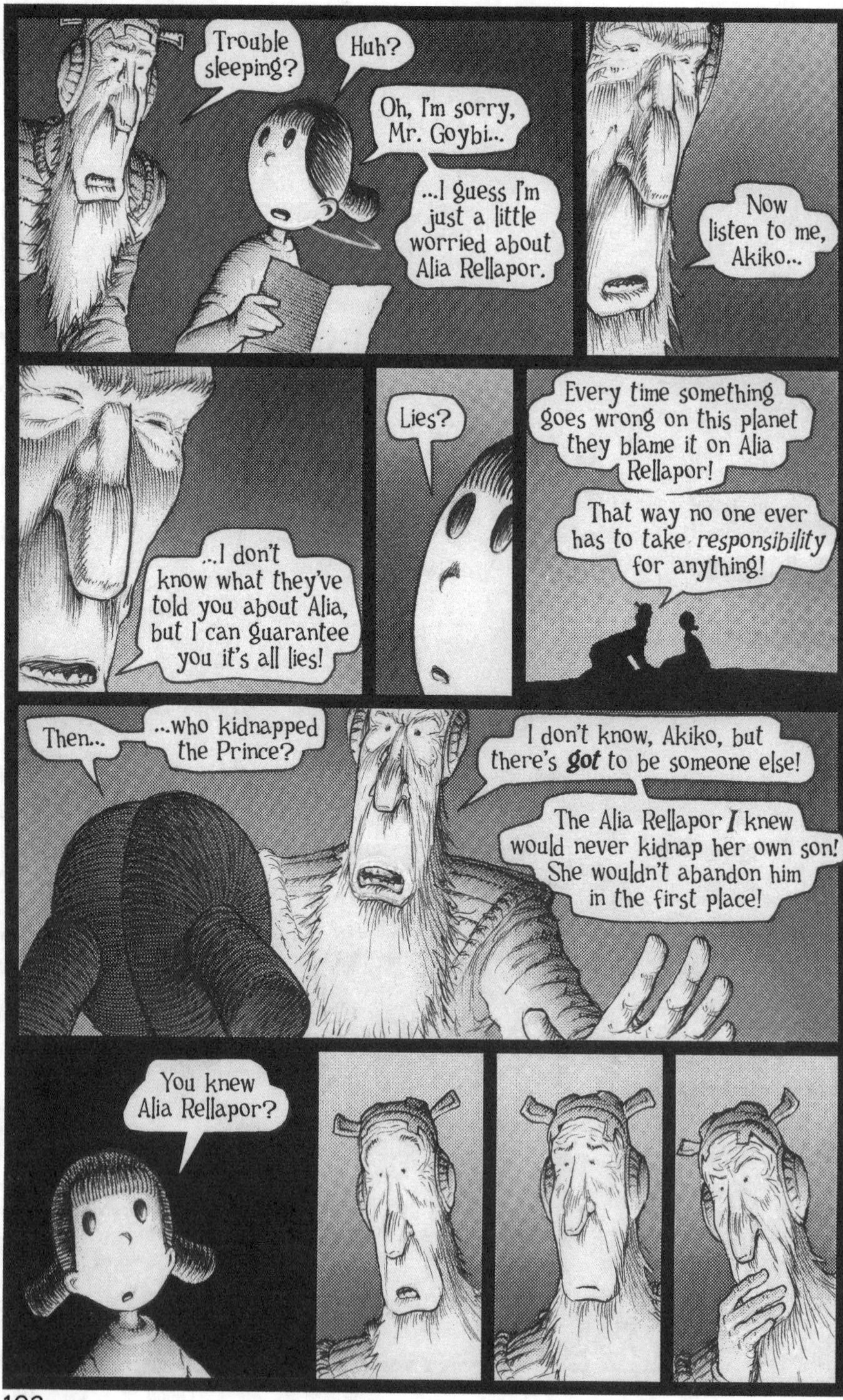
Trouble sleeping?
Huh?
Oh, I'm sorry, Mr. Goybi...
...I guess I'm just a little worried about Alia Rellapor.
Now listen to me, Akiko...
...I don't know what they've told you about Alia, but I can guarantee you it's all lies!
Lies?
Every time something goes wrong on this planet they blame it on Alia Rellapor!
That way no one ever has to take *responsibility* for anything!
Then...
...who kidnapped the Prince?
I don't know, Akiko, but there's ***got*** to be someone else!
The Alia Rellapor ***I*** knew would never kidnap her own son! She wouldn't abandon him in the first place!
You knew Alia Rellapor?

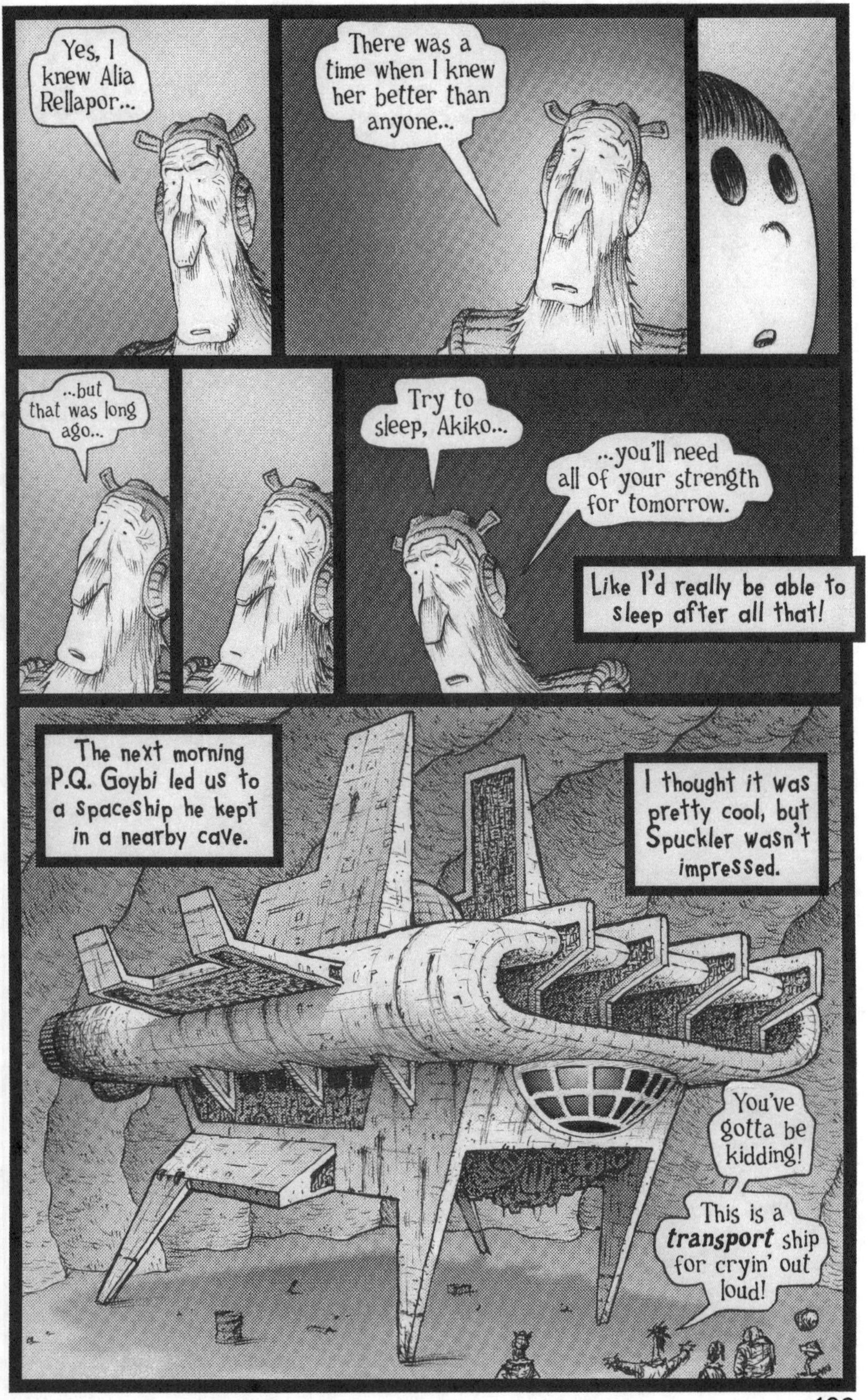
Yes, I knew Alia Rellapor...
There was a time when I knew her better than anyone...
...but that was long ago...
Try to sleep, Akiko...
...you'll need all of your strength for tomorrow.
Like I'd really be able to sleep after all that!
The next morning P.Q. Goybi led us to a spaceship he kept in a nearby cave.
I thought it was pretty cool, but Spuckler wasn't impressed.
You've gotta be kidding!
This is a ***transport*** ship for cryin' out loud!

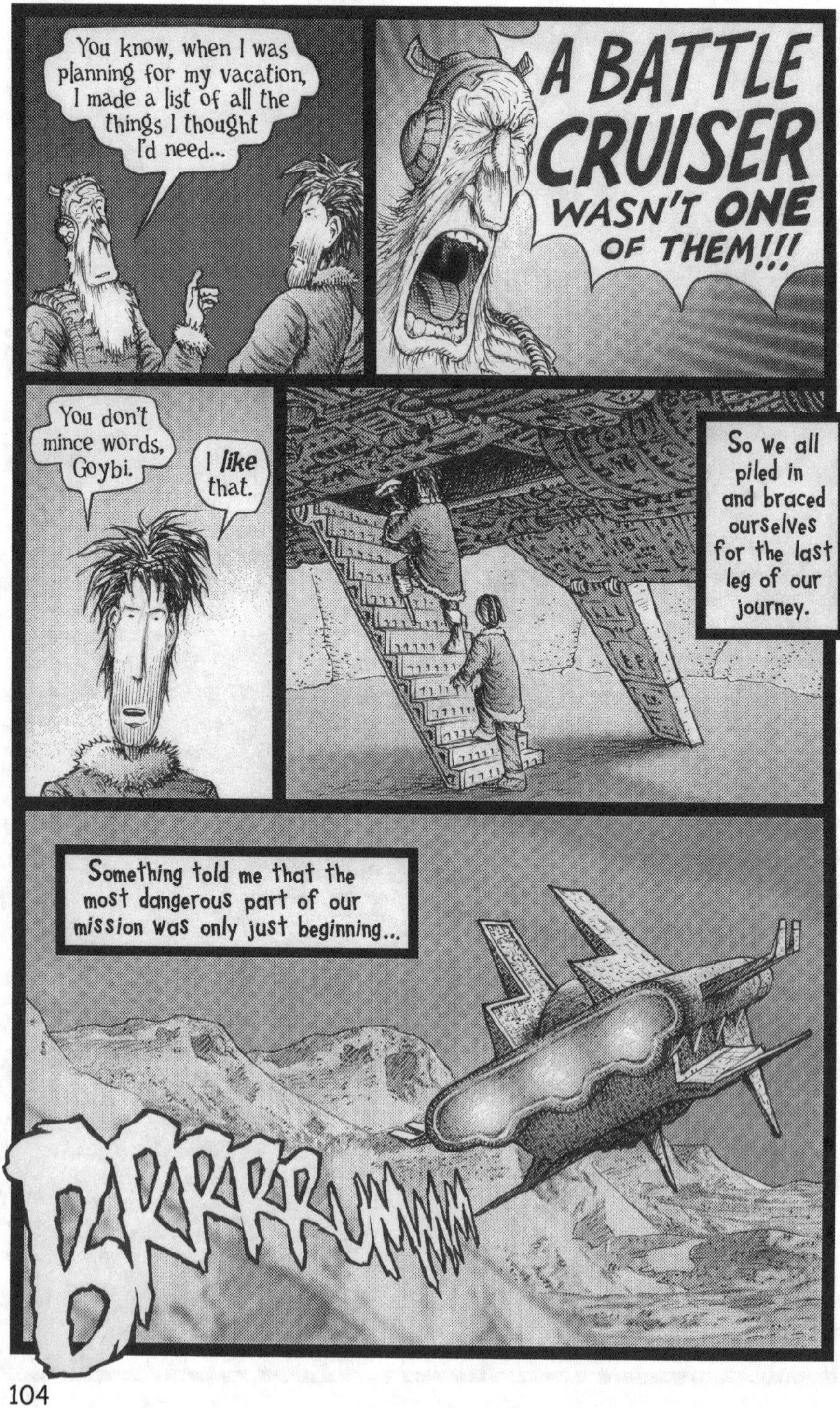

You know, when I was planning for my vacation, I made a list of all the things I thought I'd need...
A BATTLE CRUISER WASN'T ONE OF THEM!!!
You don't mince words, Goybi.
I like that.
So we all piled in and braced ourselves for the last leg of our journey.
Something told me that the most dangerous part of our mission was only just beginning...
BRRRRRUMMM

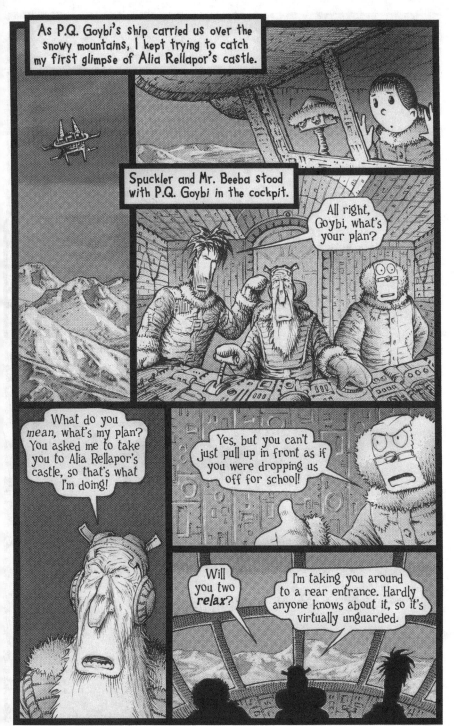

As P.Q. Goybi's ship carried us over the snowy mountains, I kept trying to catch my first glimpse of Alia Rellapor's castle.

Spuckler and Mr. Beeba stood with P.Q. Goybi in the cockpit.

All right, Goybi, what's your plan?

What do you *mean*, what's my plan? You asked me to take you to Alia Rellapor's castle, so that's what I'm doing!

Yes, but you can't just pull up in front as if you were dropping us off for school!

Will you two *relax*?

I'm taking you around to a rear entrance. Hardly anyone knows about it, so it's virtually unguarded.

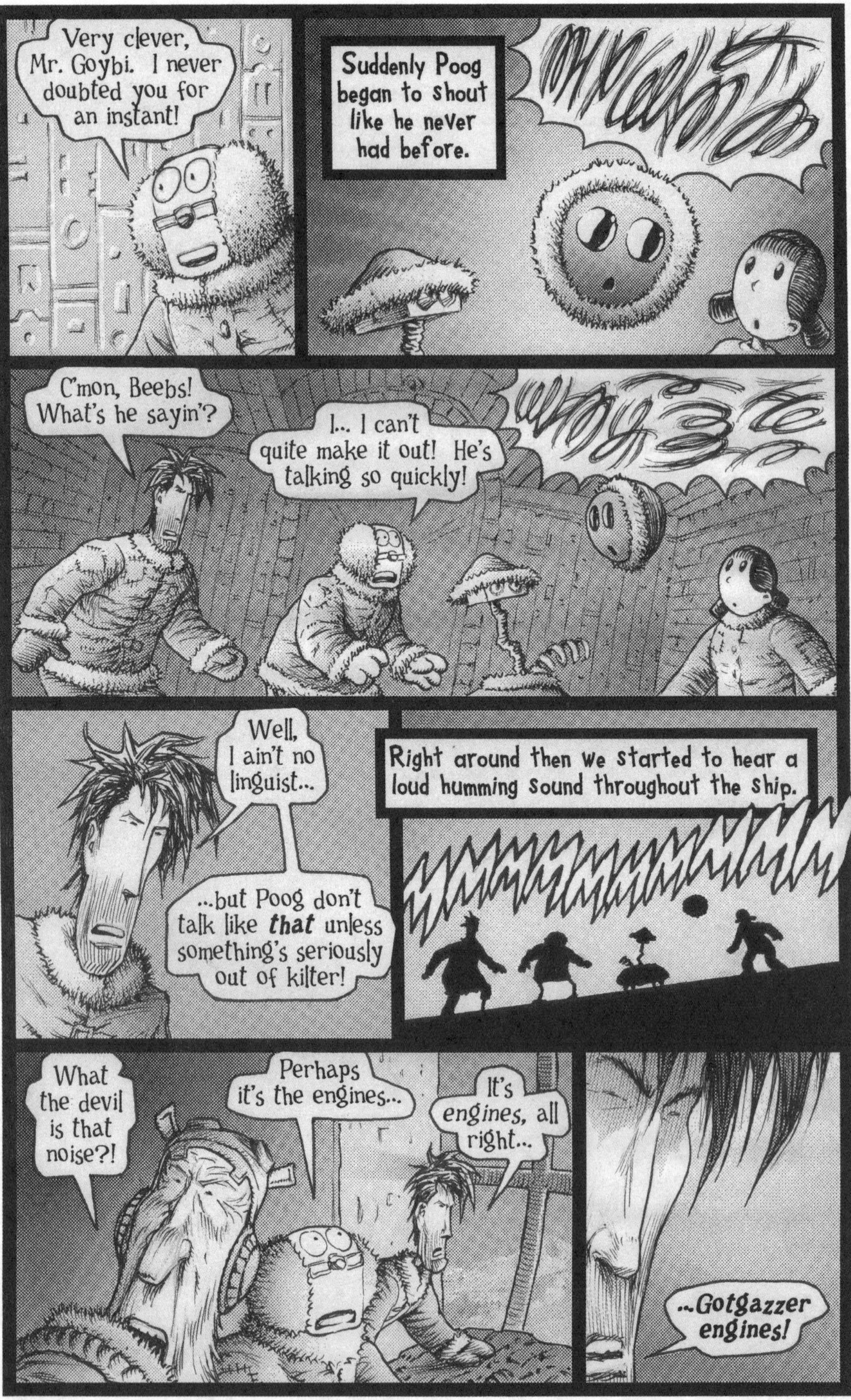
Very clever, Mr. Goybi. I never doubted you for an instant!
Suddenly Poog began to shout like he never had before.
C'mon, Beebs! What's he sayin'?
I... I can't quite make it out! He's talking so quickly!
Well, I ain't no linguist...
...but Poog don't talk like ***that*** unless something's seriously out of kilter!
Right around then we started to hear a loud humming sound throughout the ship.
What the devil is that noise?!
Perhaps it's the engines...
It's *engines*, all right...
...Gotgazzer engines!

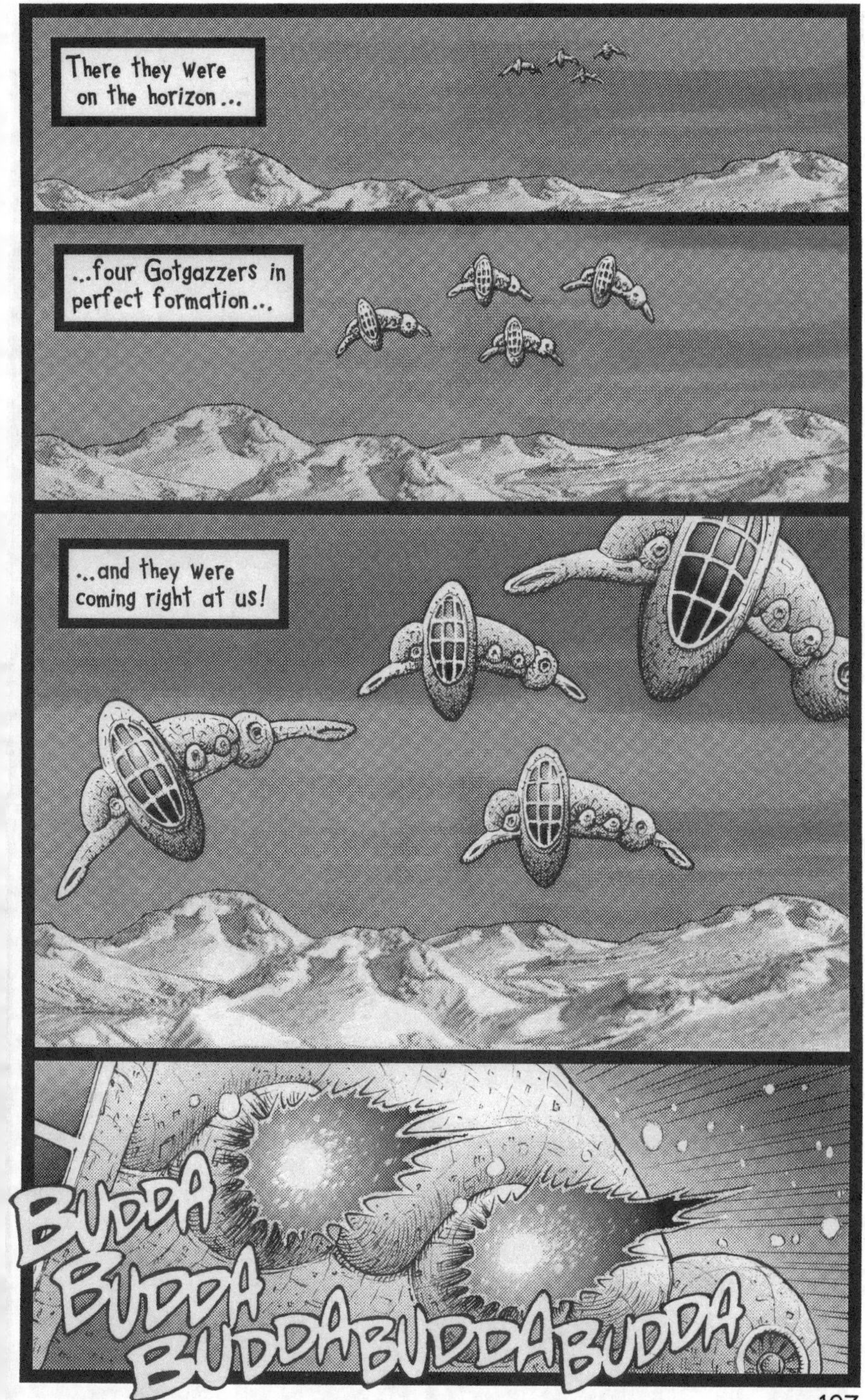

There they were on the horizon...
...four Gotgazzers in perfect formation...
...and they were coming right at us!
BUDDA BUDDA BUDDABUDDABUDDA

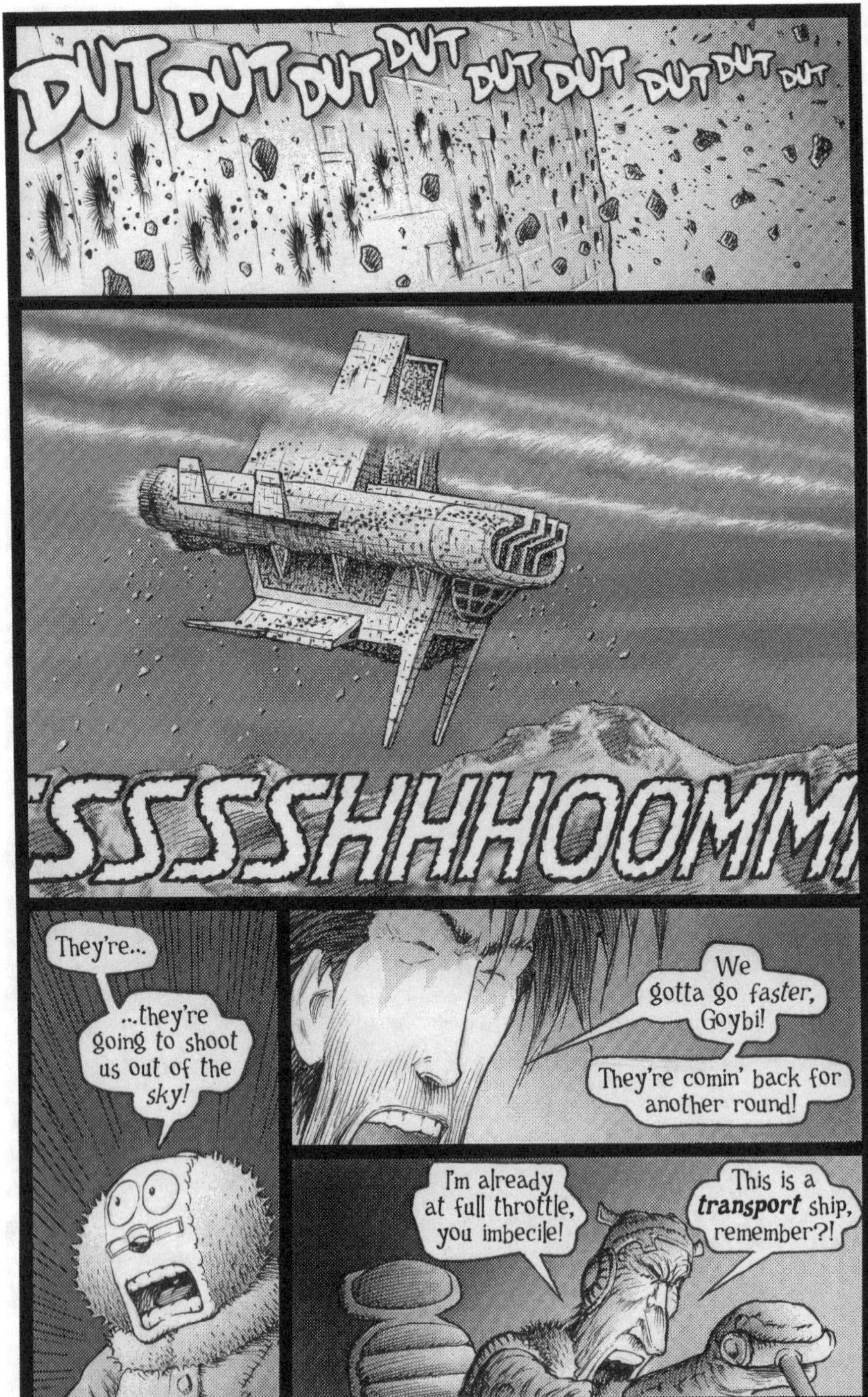
DUT DUT DUT DUT DUT DUT DUT DUT DUT
SSSSHHOOMM
They're...
...they're going to shoot us out of the sky!
We gotta go faster, Goybi!
They're comin' back for another round!
I'm already at full throttle, you imbecile!
This is a transport ship, remember?!

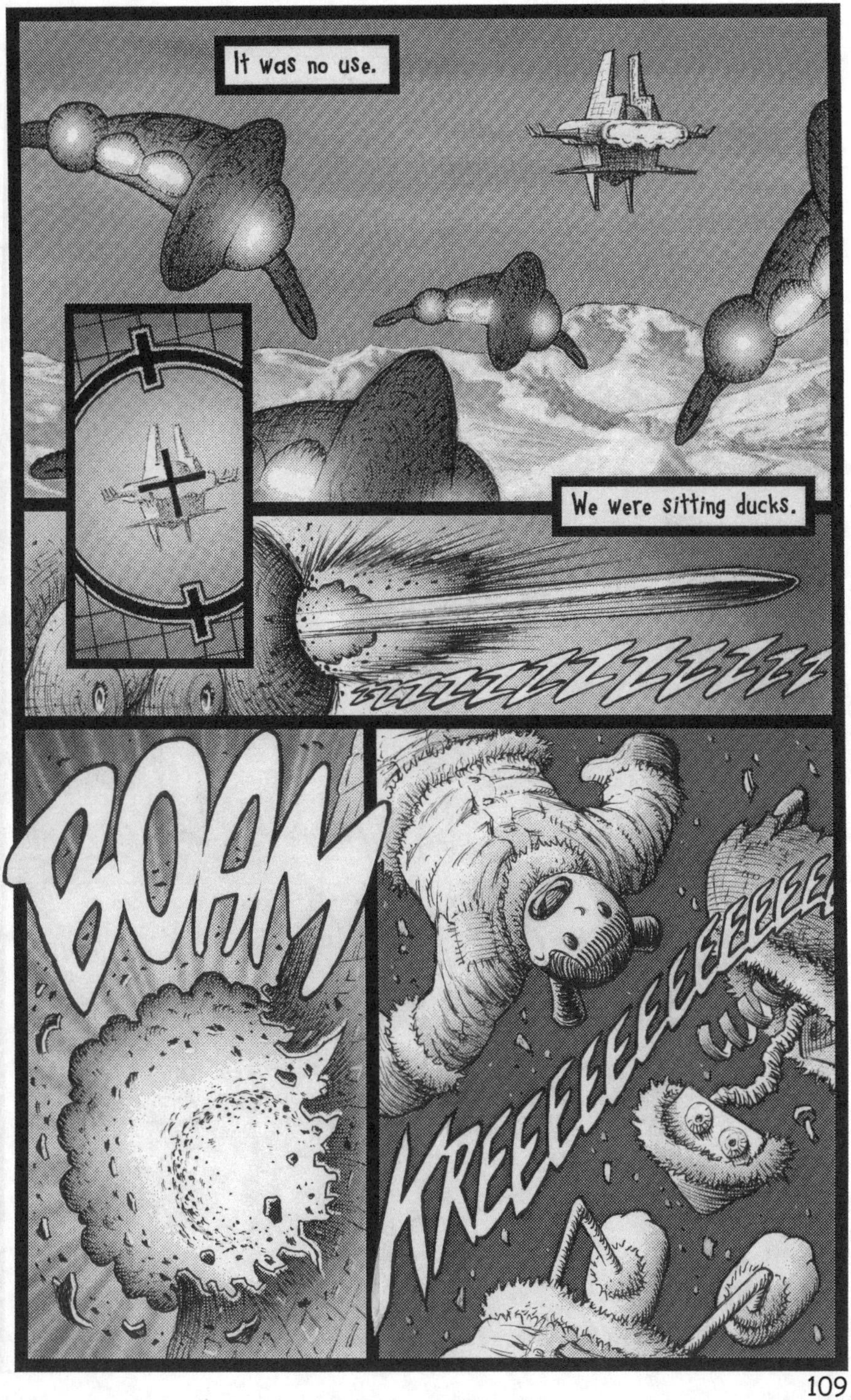
It was no use.
We were sitting ducks.
ZZZZZZZZZZZZZ
BOOM
KREEEEEEEEEEE

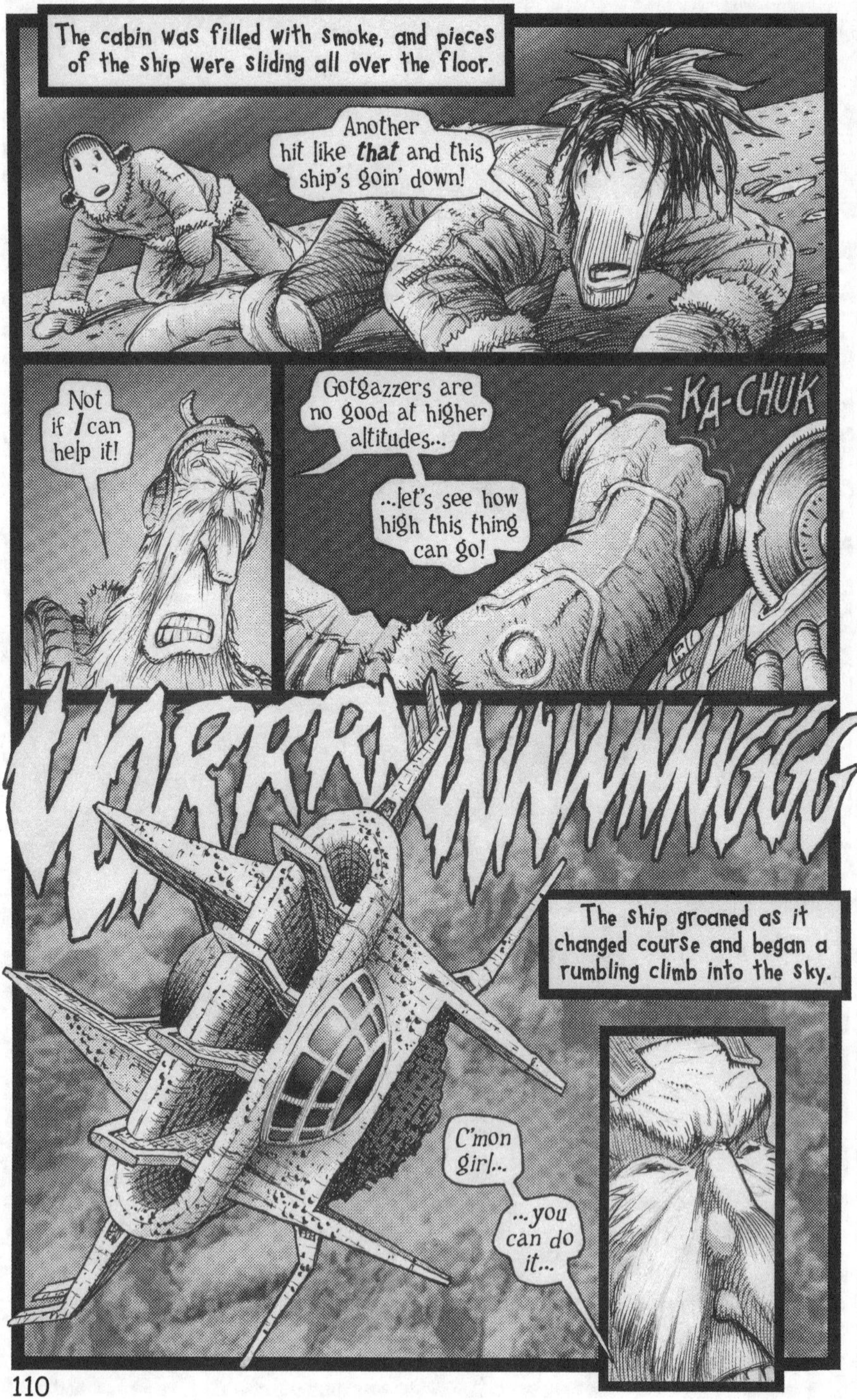

The cabin was filled with smoke, and pieces of the ship were sliding all over the floor.
Another hit like that and this ship's goin' down!
Not if I can help it!
Gotgazzers are no good at higher altitudes...
...let's see how high this thing can go!
KA-CHUK
The ship groaned as it changed course and began a rumbling climb into the sky.
C'mon girl...
...you can do it...

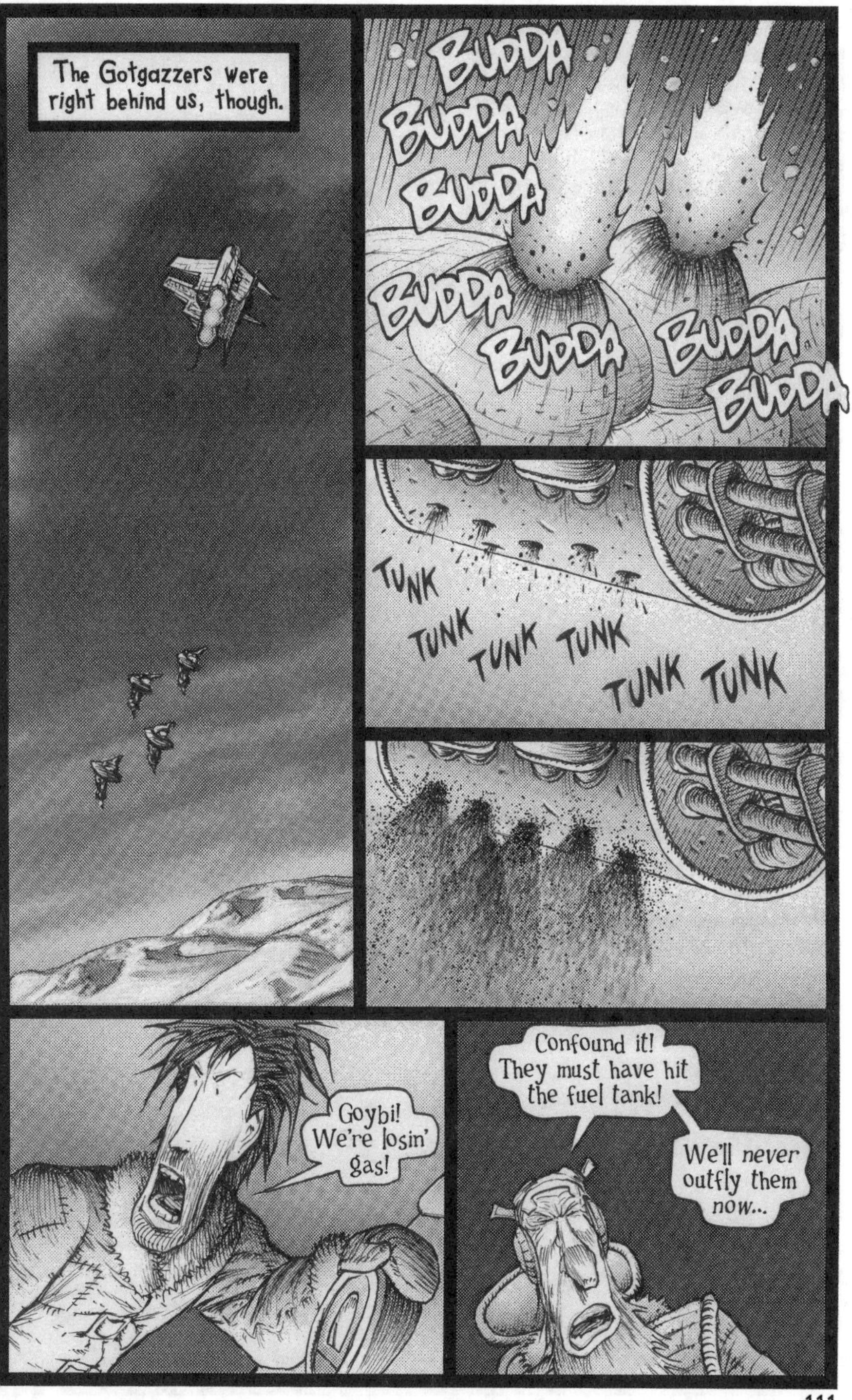
The Gotgazzers were right behind us, though.
BUDDA BUDDA BUDDA BUDDA BUDDA BUDDA BUDDA
TUNK TUNK TUNK TUNK TUNK TUNK
Goybi! We're losin' gas!
Confound it! They must have hit the fuel tank!
We'll *never* outfly them *now*...

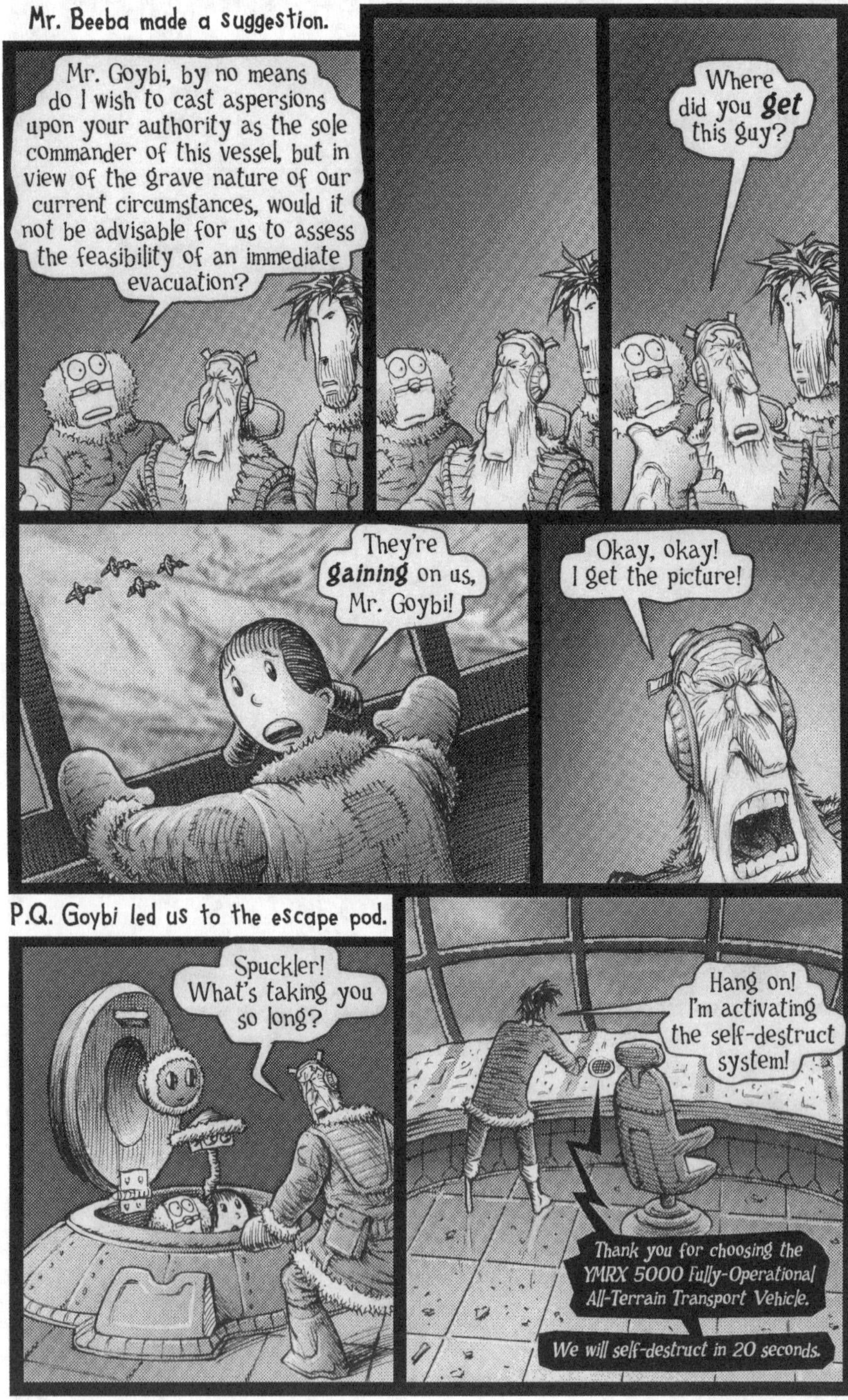
Mr. Beeba made a suggestion.
Mr. Goybi, by no means do I wish to cast aspersions upon your authority as the sole commander of this vessel, but in view of the grave nature of our current circumstances, would it not be advisable for us to assess the feasibility of an immediate evacuation?
Where did you **get** this guy?
They're **gaining** on us, Mr. Goybi!
Okay, okay! I get the picture!
P.Q. Goybi led us to the escape pod.
Spuckler! What's taking you so long?
Hang on! I'm activating the self-destruct system!
Thank you for choosing the YMRX 5000 Fully-Operational All-Terrain Transport Vehicle.
We will self-destruct in 20 seconds.

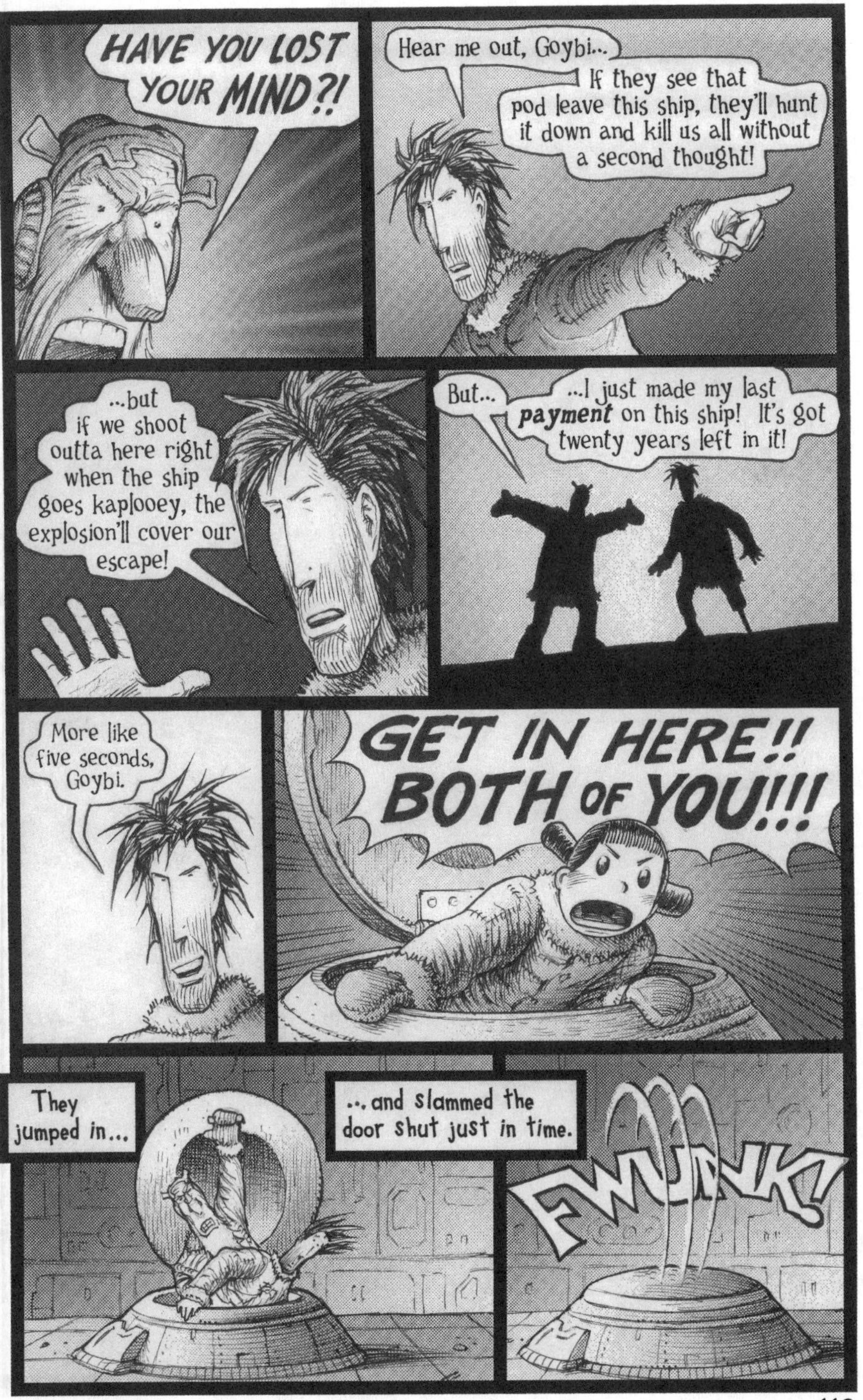
HAVE YOU LOST YOUR MIND?!
Hear me out, Goybi...
If they see that pod leave this ship, they'll hunt it down and kill us all without a second thought!
...but if we shoot outta here right when the ship goes kaplooey, the explosion'll cover our escape!
But...
...I just made my last payment on this ship! It's got twenty years left in it!
More like five seconds, Goybi.
GET IN HERE!! BOTH OF YOU!!!
They jumped in...
...and slammed the door shut just in time.
FWUNK!

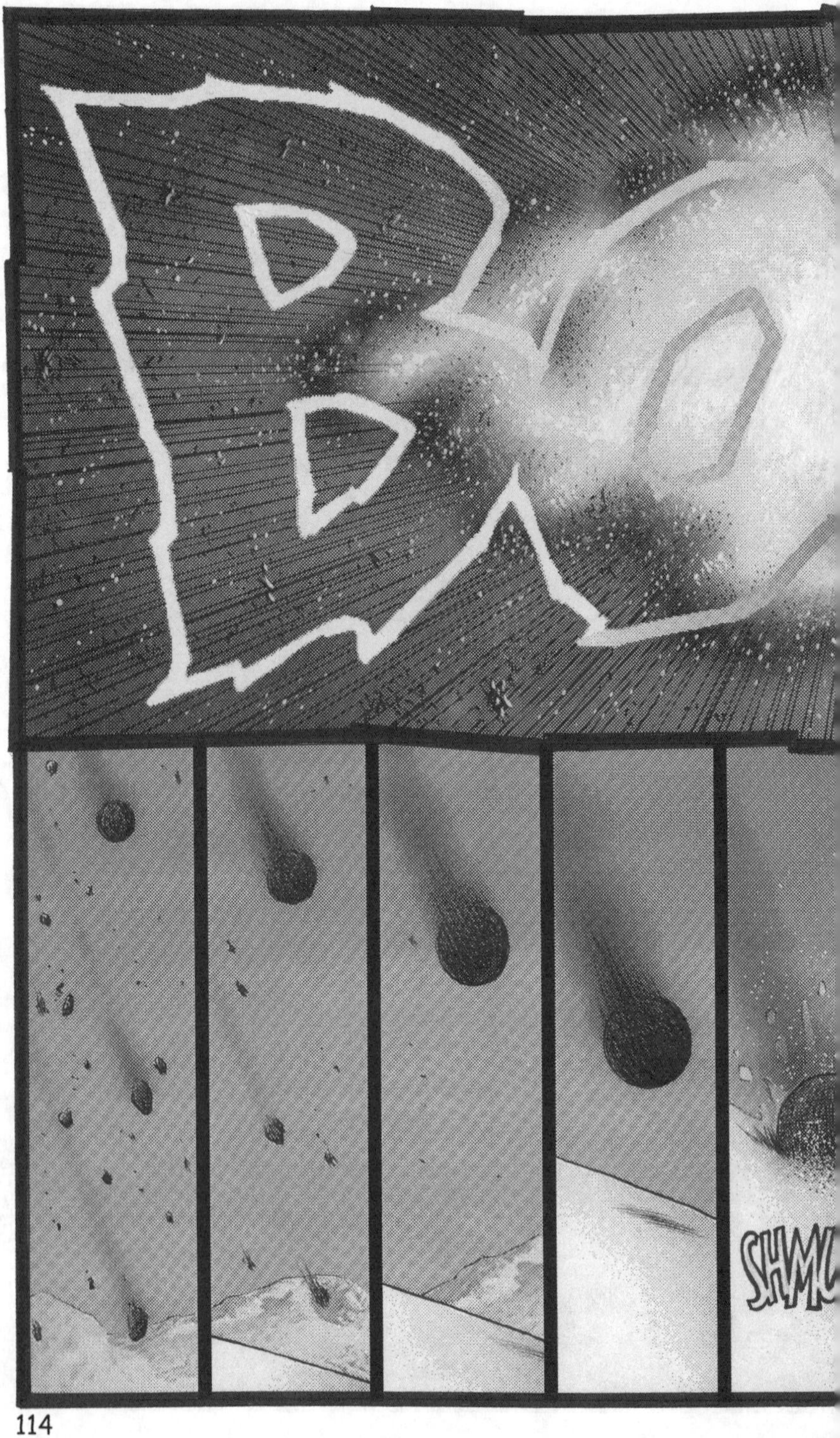
SHMU

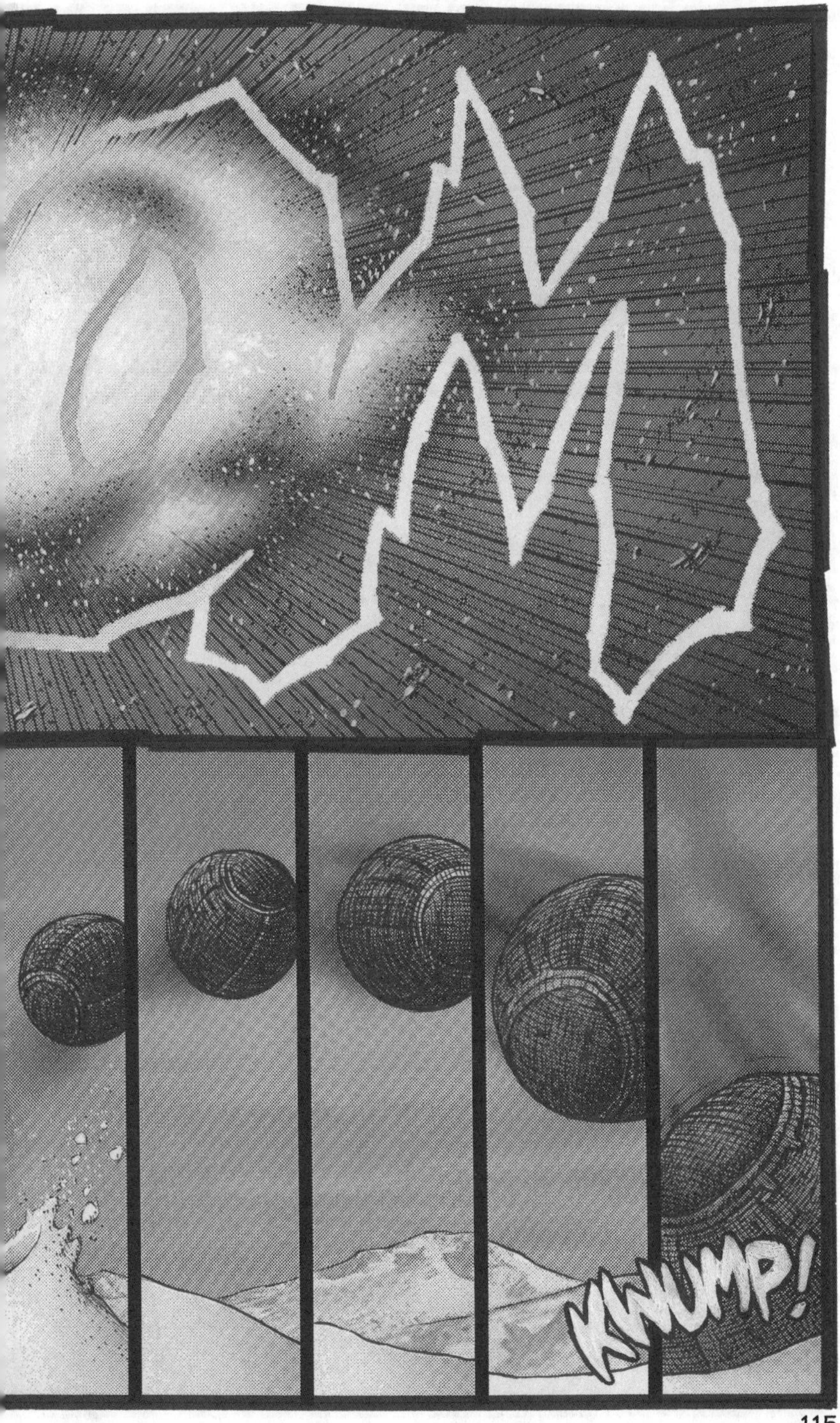
KWUMP!

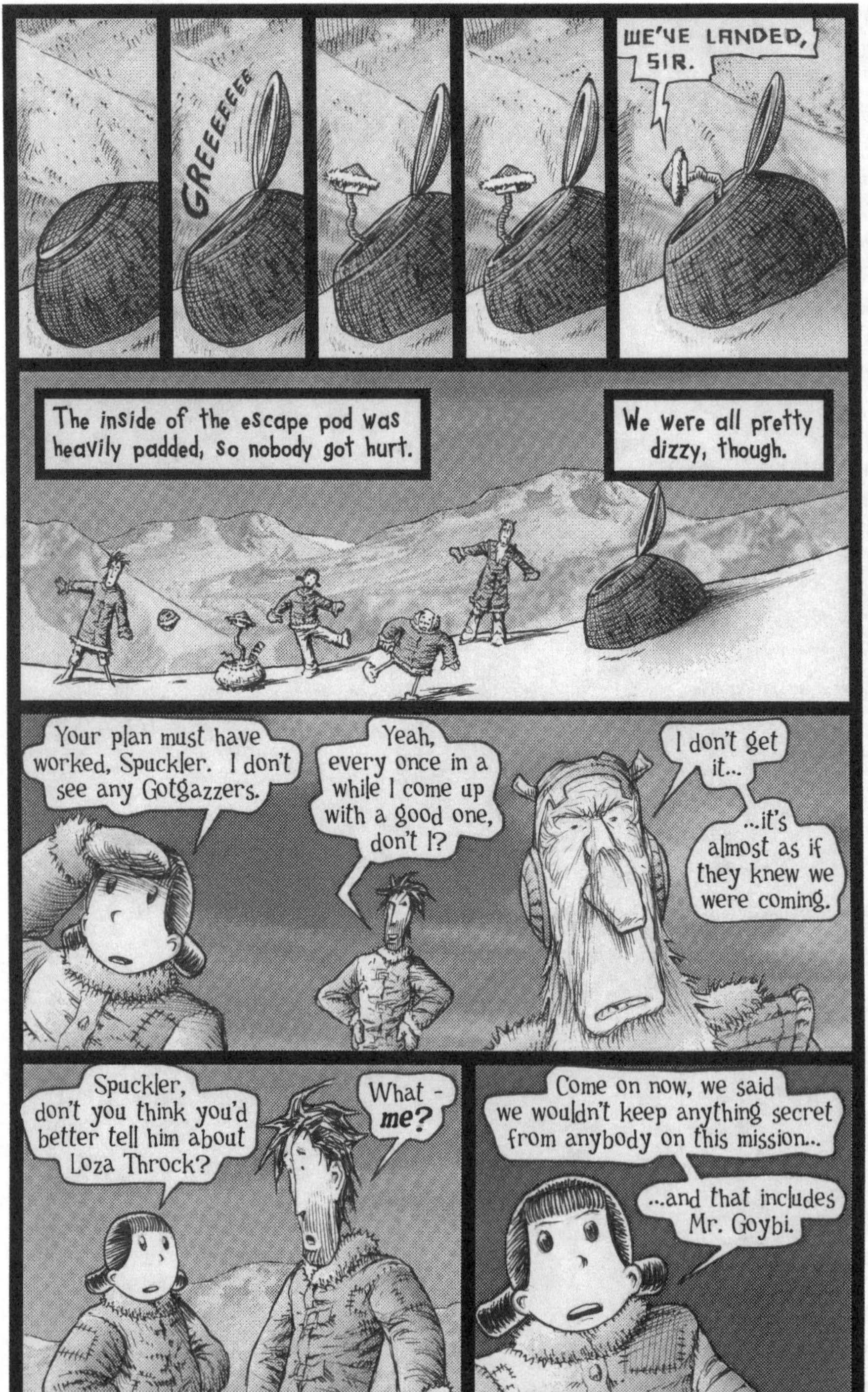
GREEEEEEE
WE'VE LANDED, SIR.
The inside of the escape pod was heavily padded, so nobody got hurt.
We were all pretty dizzy, though.
Your plan must have worked, Spuckler. I don't see any Gotgazzers.
Yeah, every once in a while I come up with a good one, don't I?
I don't get it...
...it's almost as if they knew we were coming.
Spuckler, don't you think you'd better tell him about Loza Throck?
What - *me?*
Come on now, we said we wouldn't keep anything secret from anybody on this mission...
...and that includes Mr. Goybi.

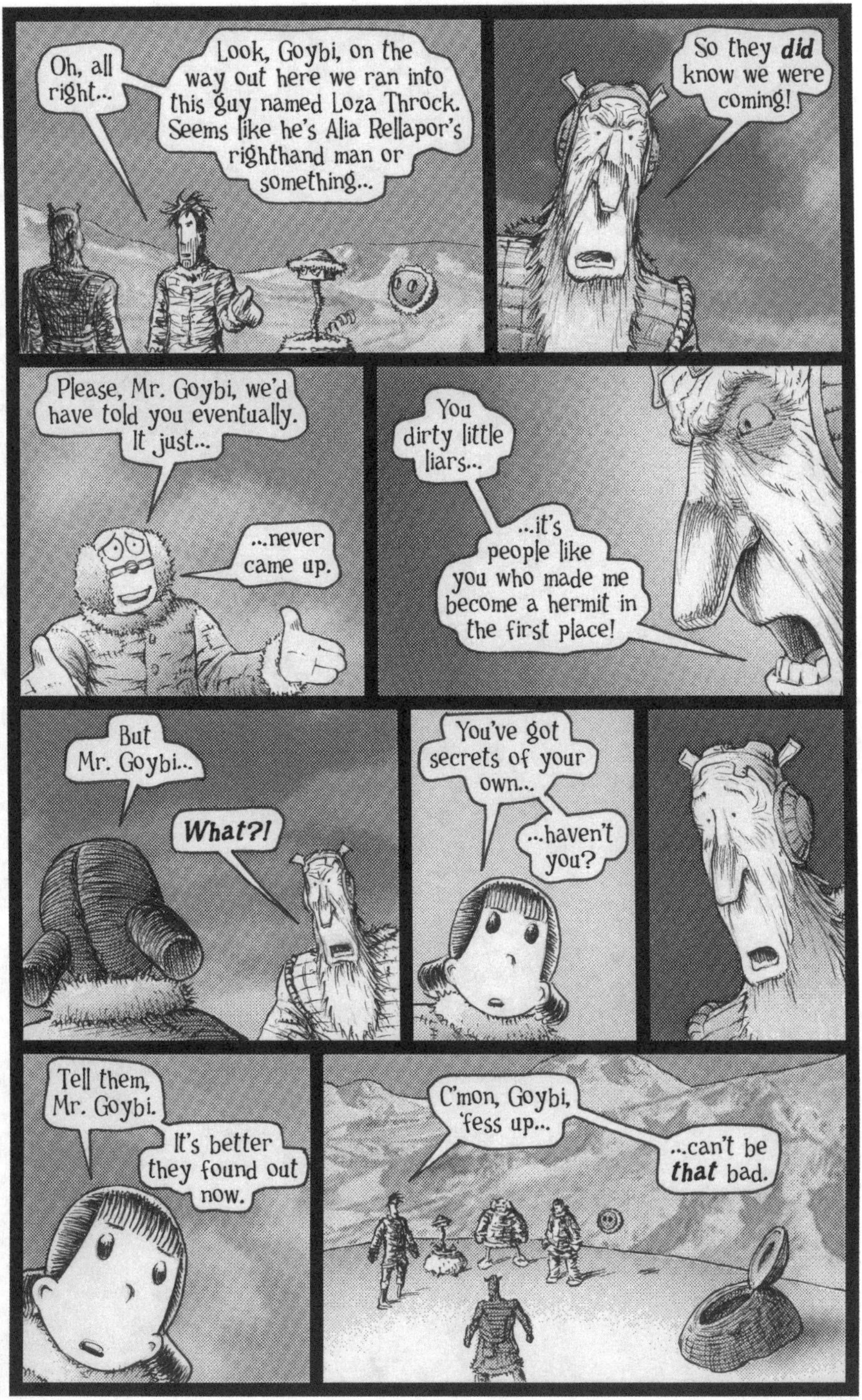
Oh, all right...
Look, Goybi, on the way out here we ran into this guy named Loza Throck. Seems like he's Alia Rellapor's righthand man or something...
So they *did* know we were coming!
Please, Mr. Goybi, we'd have told you eventually. It just...
...never came up.
You dirty little liars...
...it's people like you who made me become a hermit in the first place!
But Mr. Goybi...
What?!
You've got secrets of your own...
...haven't you?
Tell them, Mr. Goybi.
It's better they found out now.
C'mon, Goybi, 'fess up...
...can't be *that* bad.

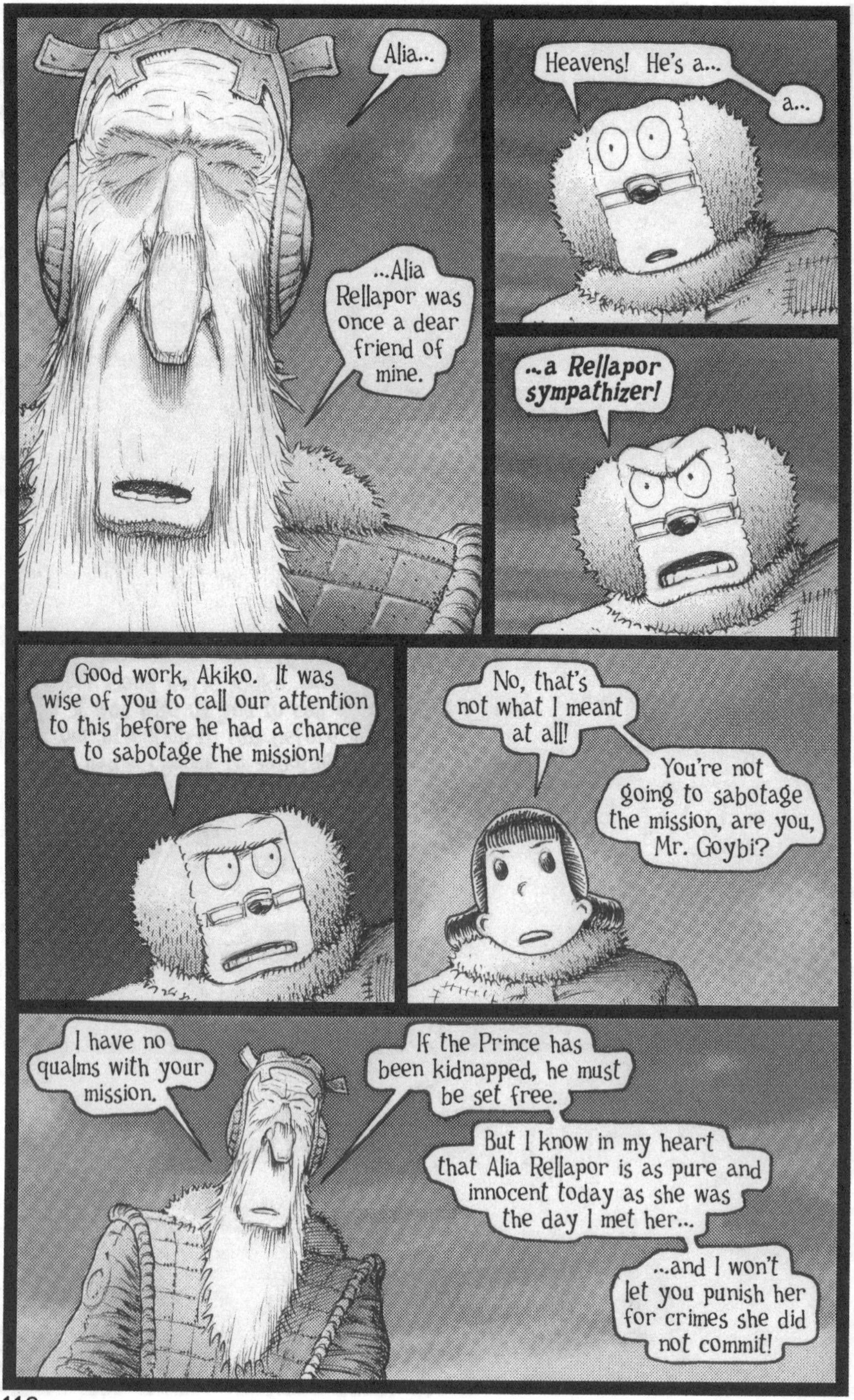
Alia...
...Alia Rellapor was once a dear friend of mine.
Heavens! He's a...
a...
...a Rellapor sympathizer!
Good work, Akiko. It was wise of you to call our attention to this before he had a chance to sabotage the mission!
No, that's not what I meant at all!
You're not going to sabotage the mission, are you, Mr. Goybi?
I have no qualms with your mission.
If the Prince has been kidnapped, he must be set free.
But I know in my heart that Alia Rellapor is as pure and innocent today as she was the day I met her...
...and I won't let you punish her for crimes she did not commit!

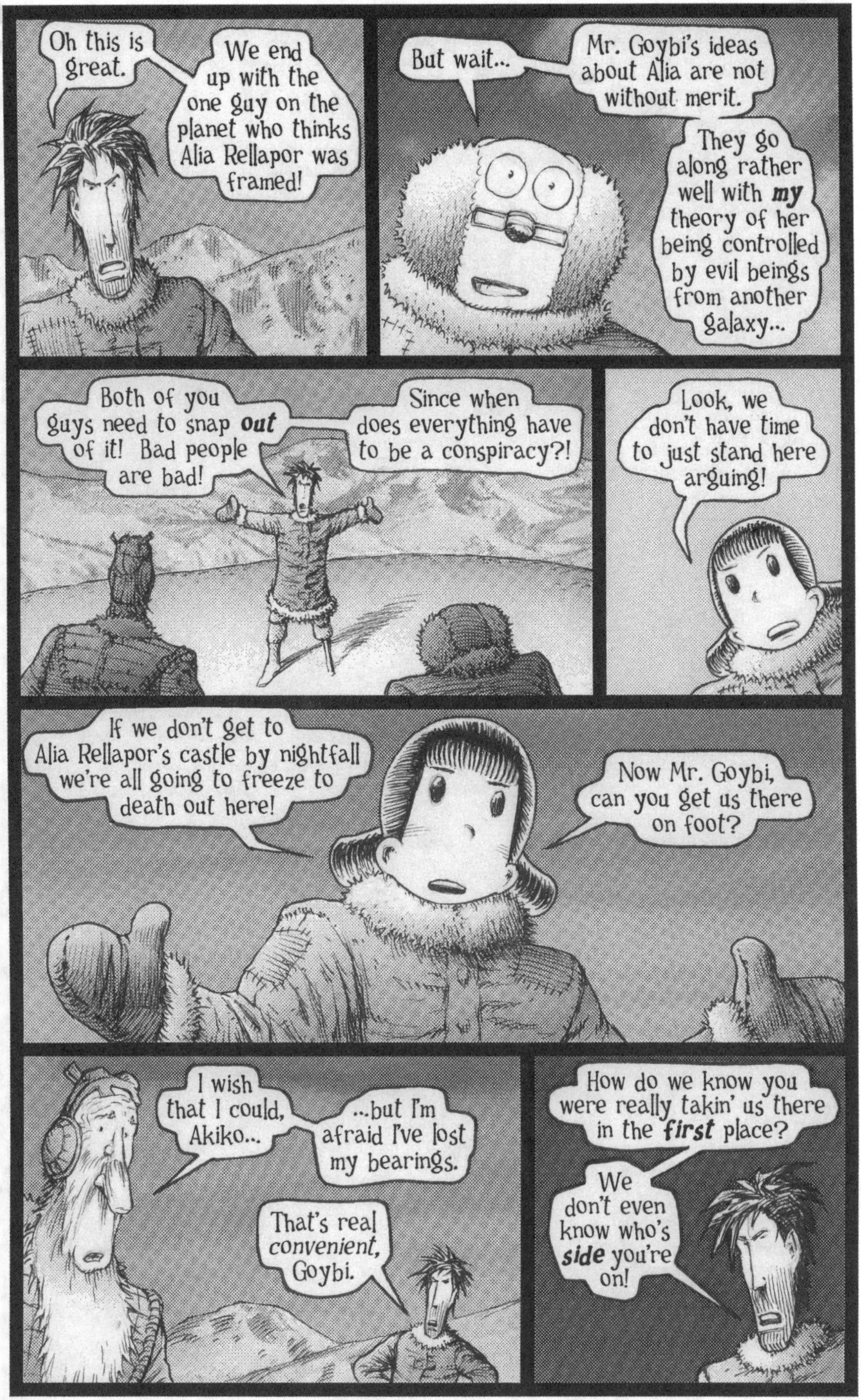
Oh this is great.
We end up with the one guy on the planet who thinks Alia Rellapor was framed!
But wait...
Mr. Goybi's ideas about Alia are not without merit.
They go along rather well with **my** theory of her being controlled by evil beings from another galaxy...
Both of you guys need to snap **out** of it! Bad people are bad!
Since when does everything have to be a conspiracy?!
Look, we don't have time to just stand here arguing!
If we don't get to Alia Rellapor's castle by nightfall we're all going to freeze to death out here!
Now Mr. Goybi, can you get us there on foot?
I wish that I could, Akiko...
...but I'm afraid I've lost my bearings.
That's real *convenient*, Goybi.
How do we know you were really takin' us there in the **first** place?
We don't even know who's **side** you're on!

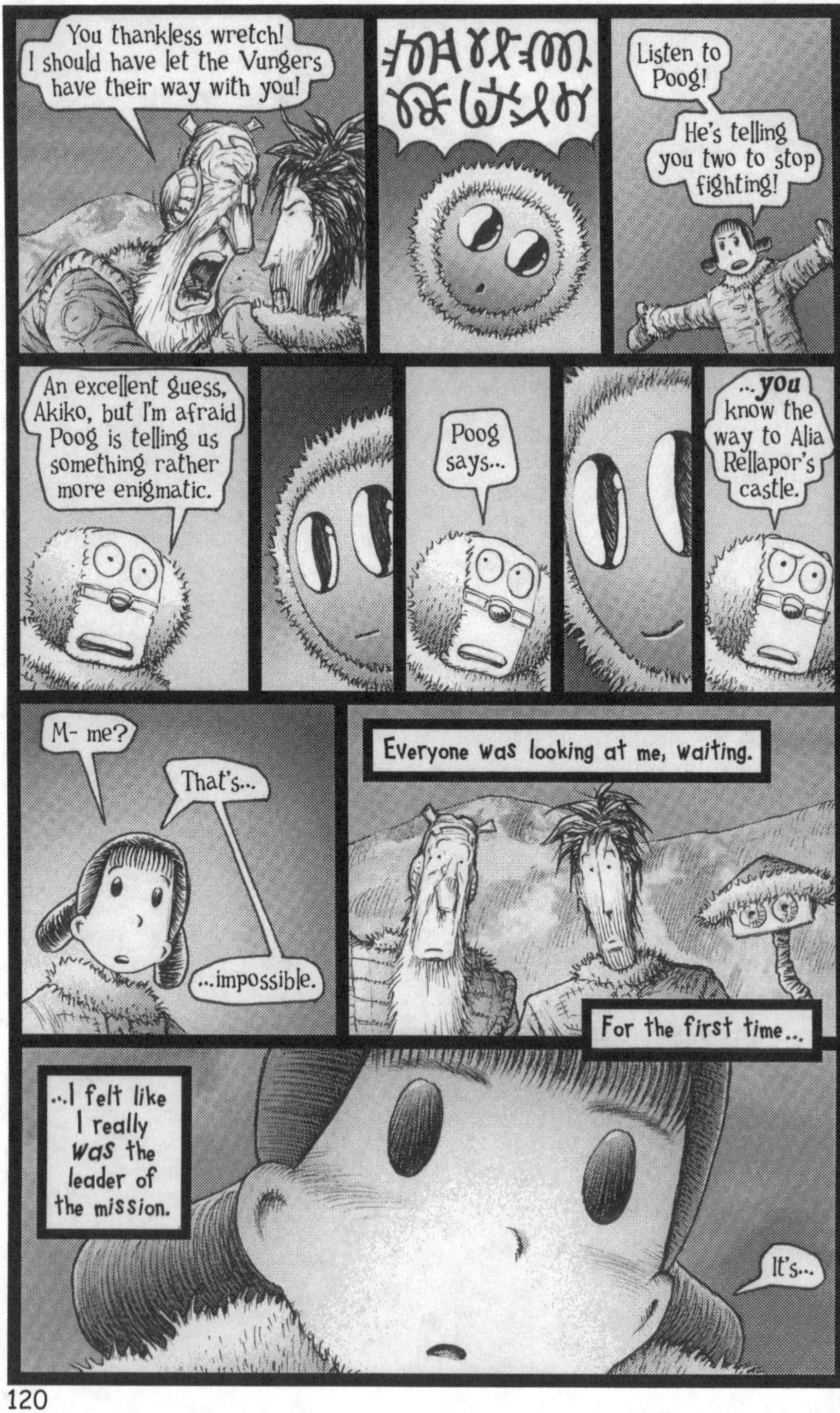
You thankless wretch! I should have let the Vungers have their way with you!
Listen to Poog!
He's telling you two to stop fighting!
An excellent guess, Akiko, but I'm afraid Poog is telling us something rather more enigmatic.
Poog says...
...you know the way to Alia Rellapor's castle.
M- me?
That's...
...impossible.
Everyone was looking at me, waiting.
For the first time...
...I felt like I really was the leader of the mission.
It's...

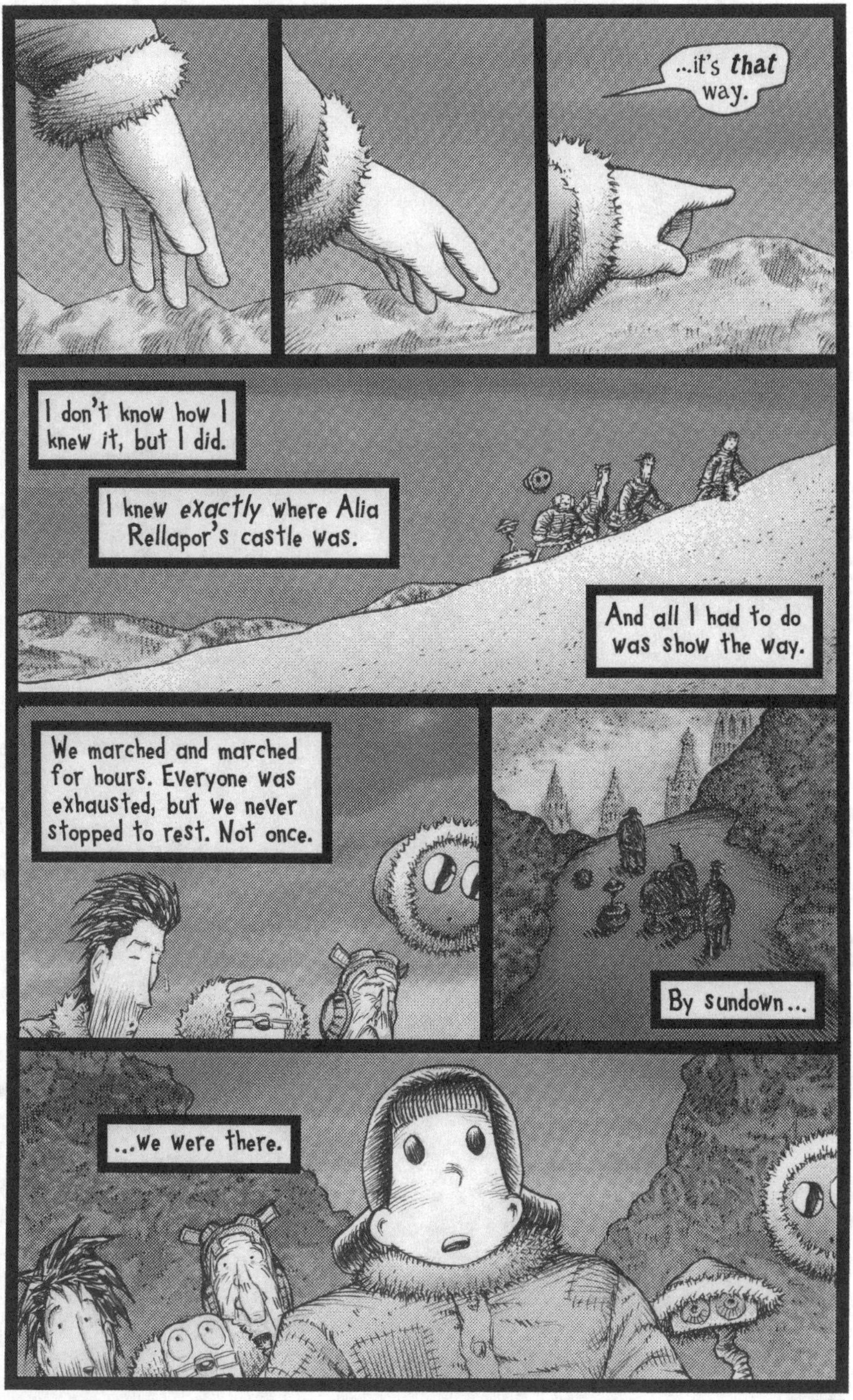

...it's **that** way.
I don't know how I knew it, but I did.
I knew *exactly* where Alia Rellapor's castle was.
And all I had to do was show the way.
We marched and marched for hours. Everyone was exhausted, but we never stopped to rest. Not once.
By sundown...
...we were there.

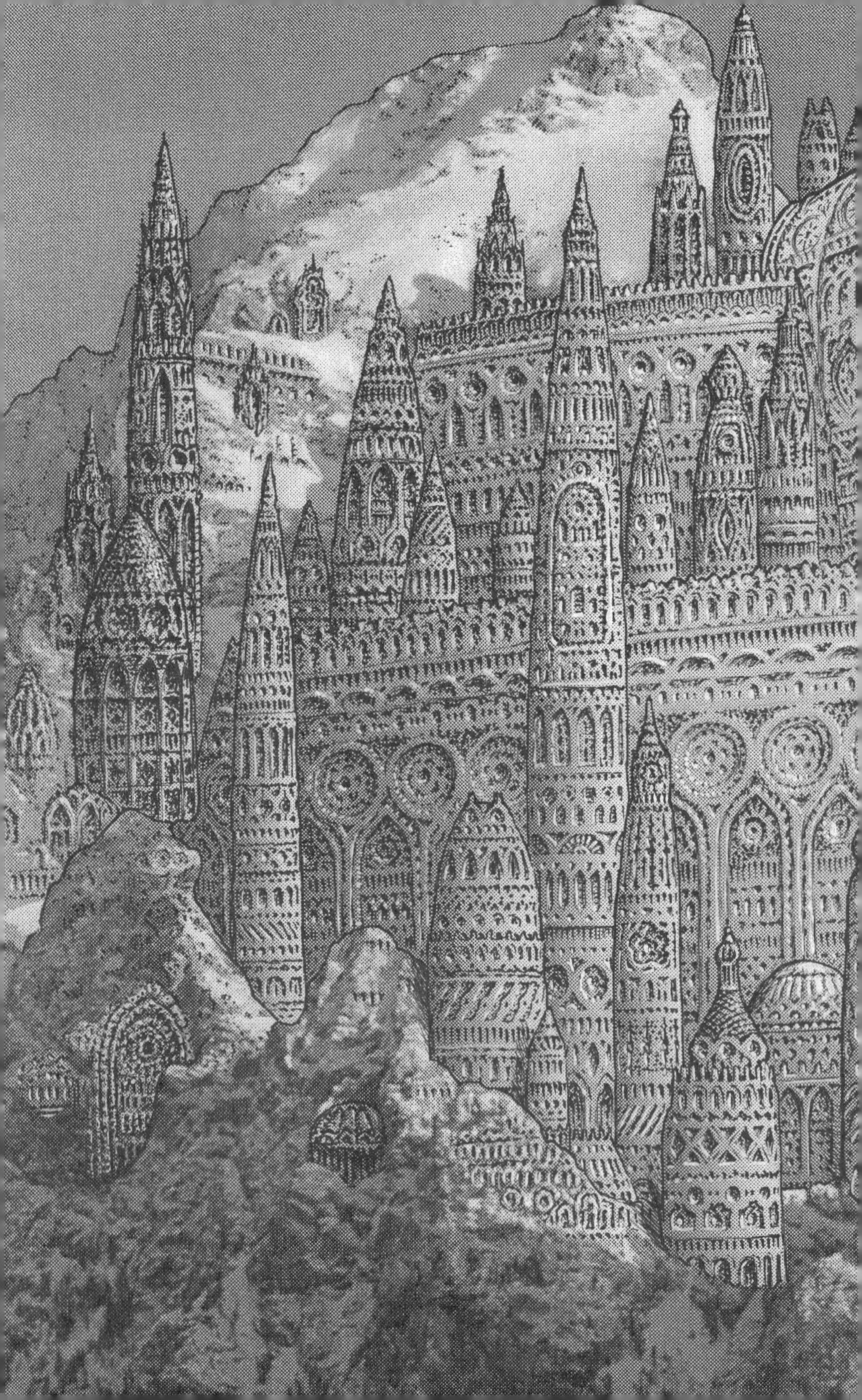

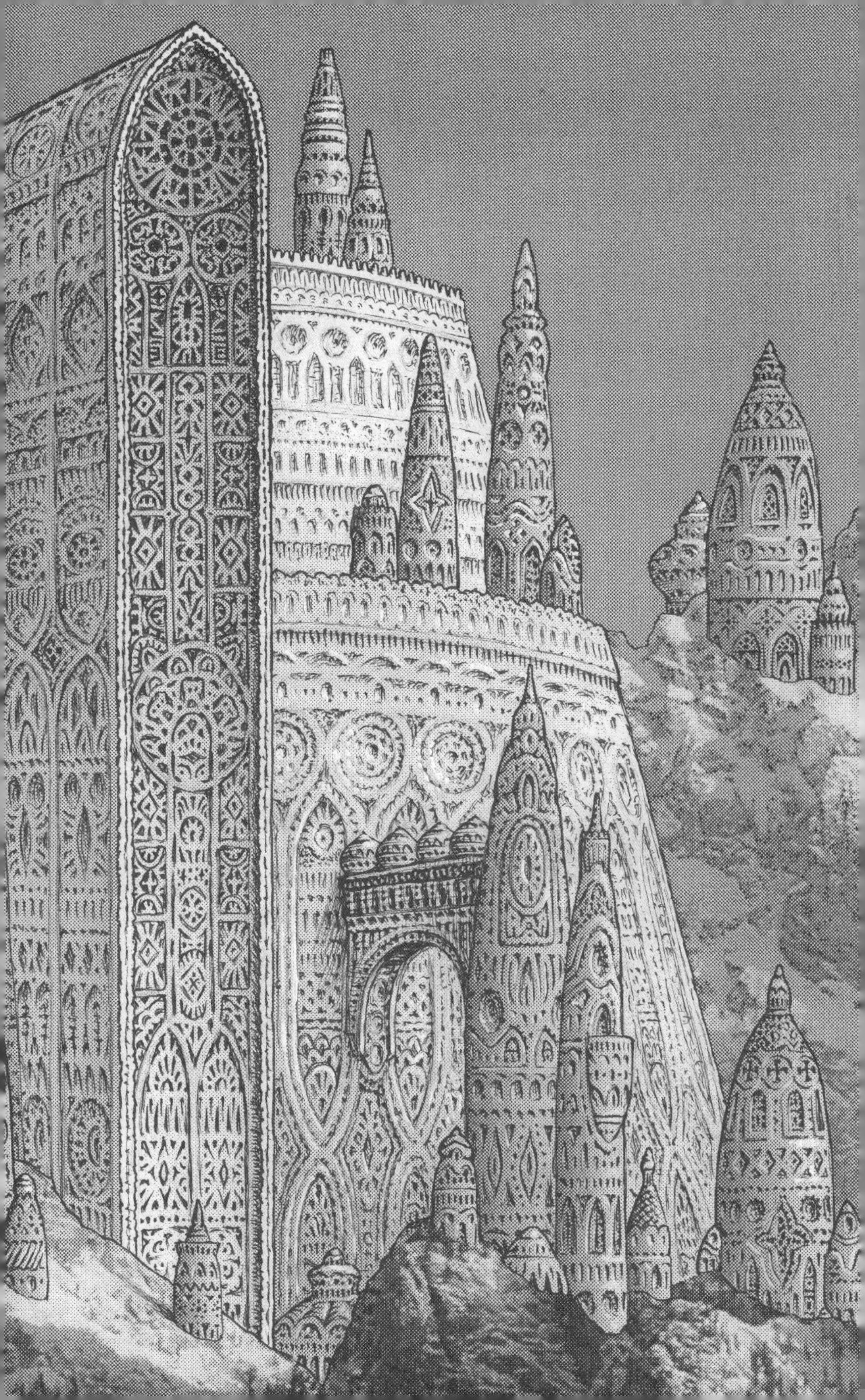

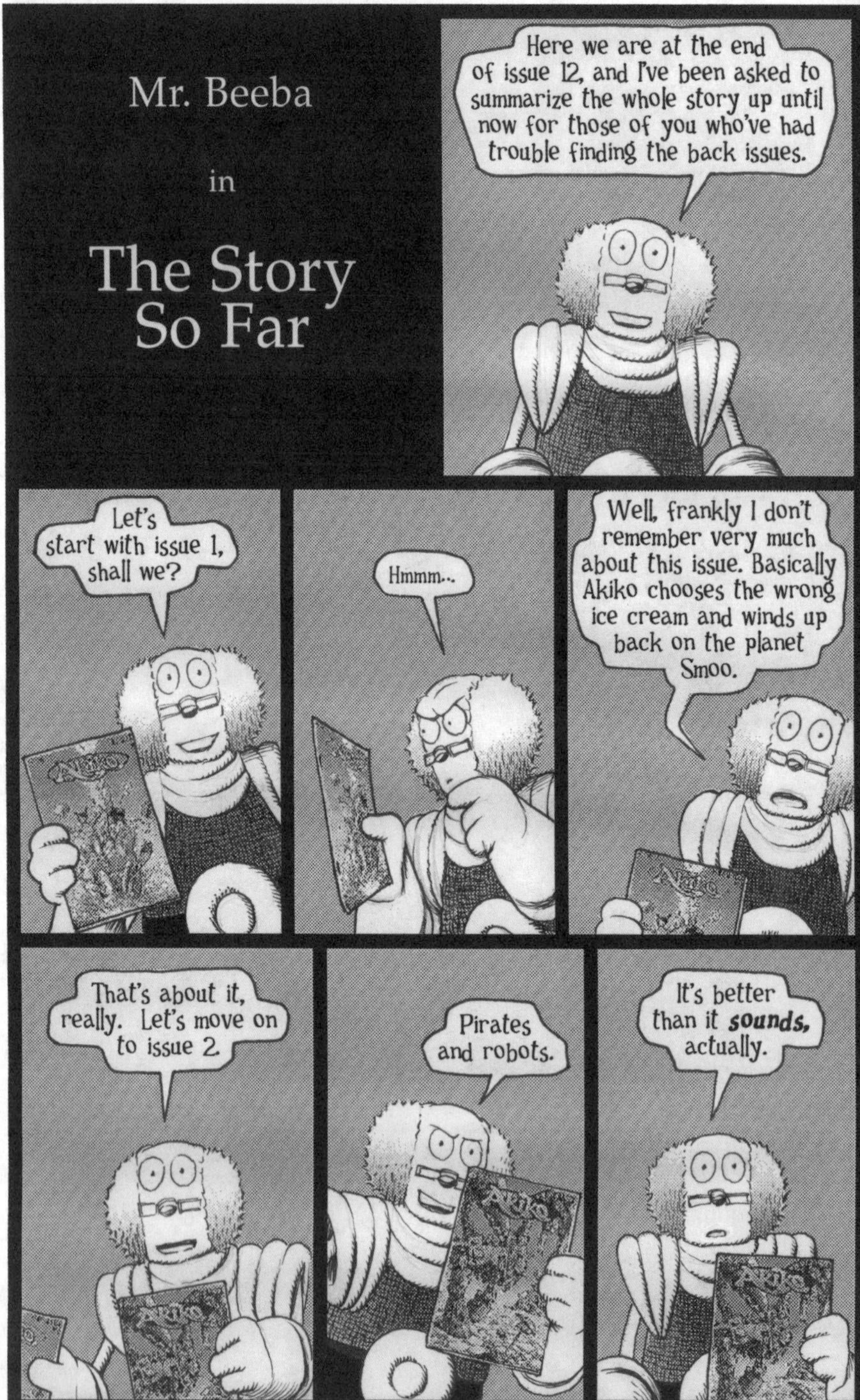
Mr. Beeba
in
The Story So Far
Here we are at the end of issue 12, and I've been asked to summarize the whole story up until now for those of you who've had trouble finding the back issues.
Let's start with issue 1, shall we?
Hmmm...
Well, frankly I don't remember very much about this issue. Basically Akiko chooses the wrong ice cream and winds up back on the planet Smoo.
That's about it, really. Let's move on to issue 2.
Pirates and robots.
It's better than it sounds, actually.

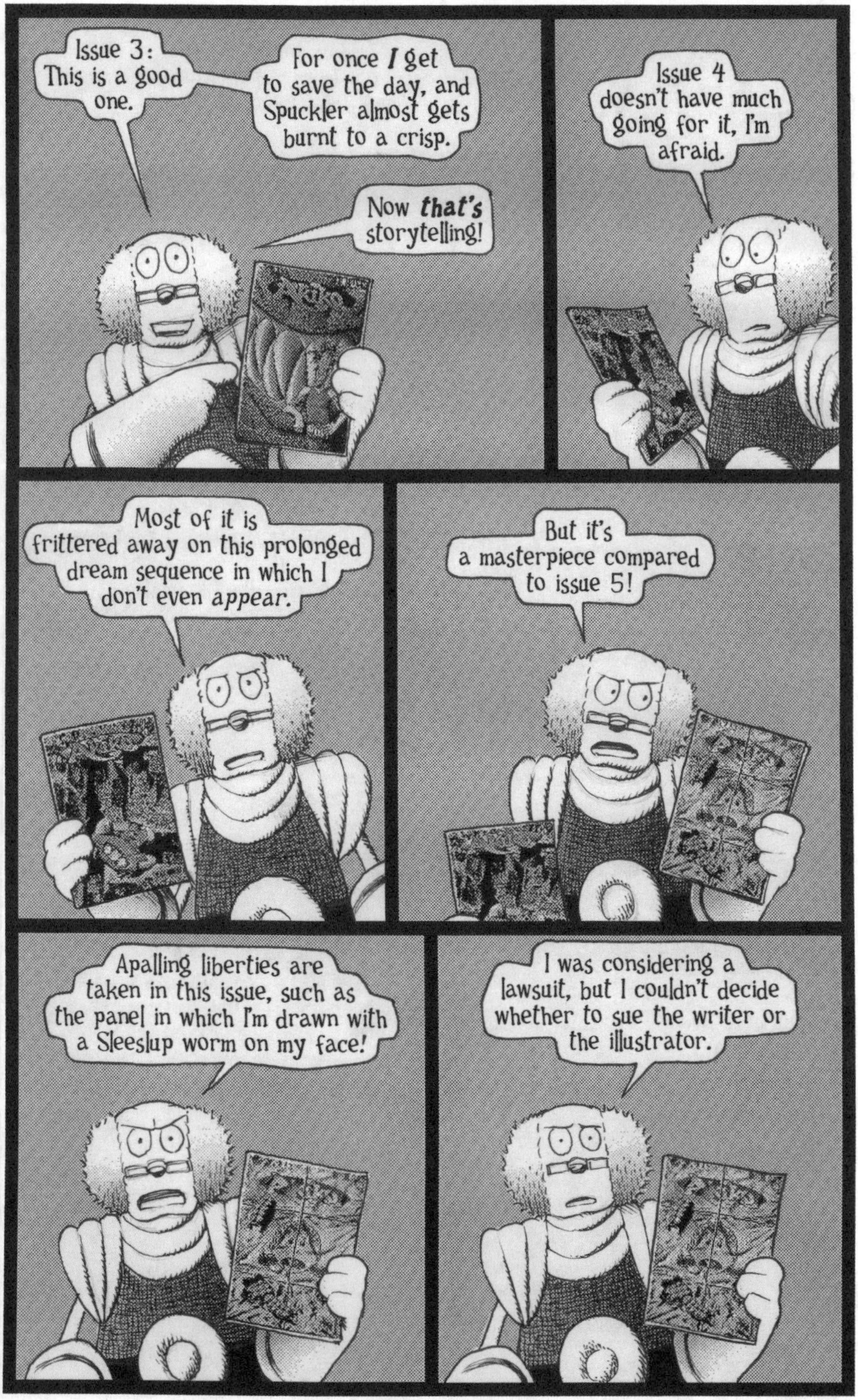
Issue 3: This is a good one.
For once I get to save the day, and Spuckler almost gets burnt to a crisp.
Now that's storytelling!
Issue 4 doesn't have much going for it, I'm afraid.
Most of it is frittered away on this prolonged dream sequence in which I don't even appear.
But it's a masterpiece compared to issue 5!
Apalling liberties are taken in this issue, such as the panel in which I'm drawn with a Sleeslup worm on my face!
I was considering a lawsuit, but I couldn't decide whether to sue the writer or the illustrator.

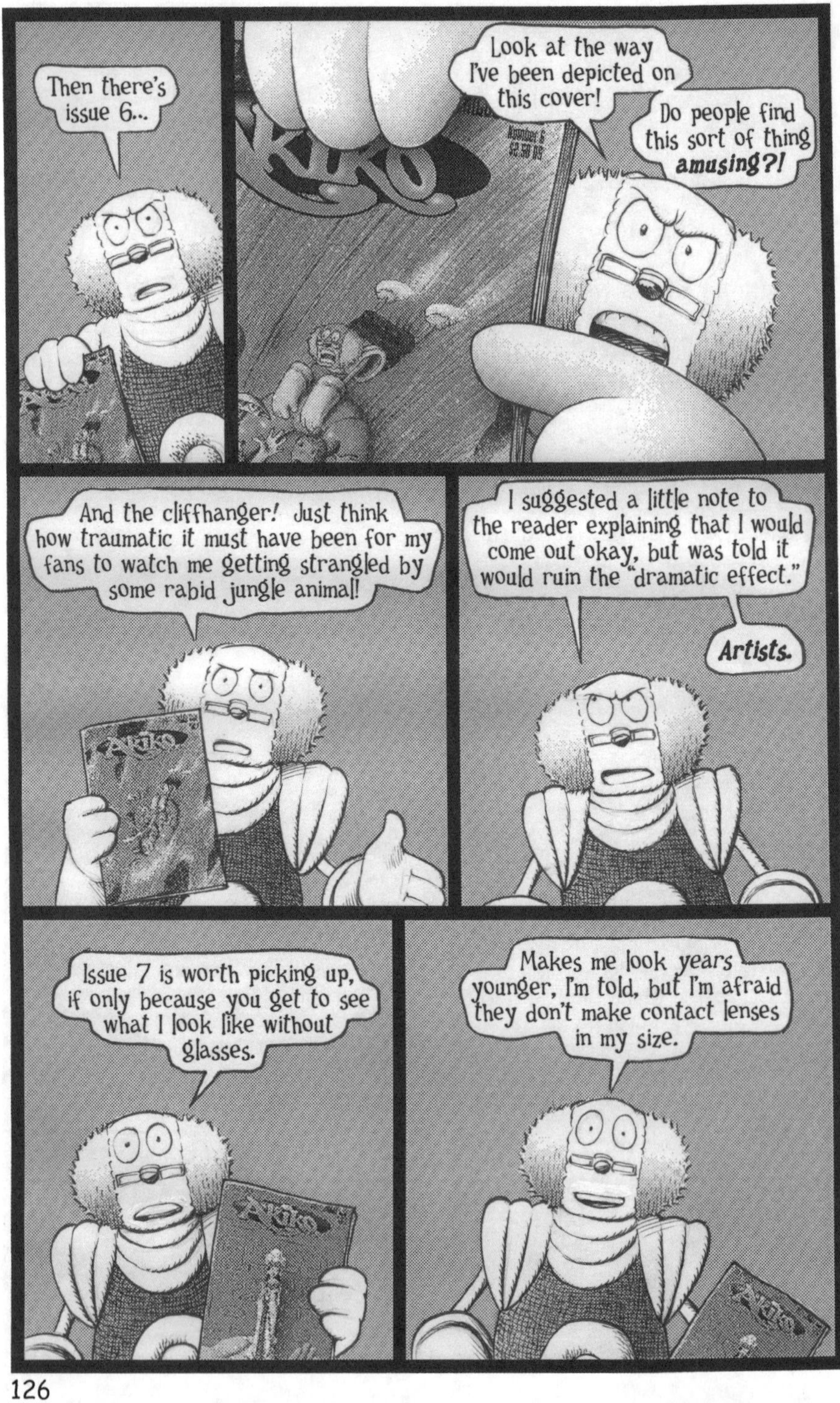
Then there's issue 6...
Look at the way I've been depicted on this cover!
Do people find this sort of thing *amusing?!*
And the cliffhanger! Just think how traumatic it must have been for my fans to watch me getting strangled by some rabid jungle animal!
I suggested a little note to the reader explaining that I would come out okay, but was told it would ruin the "dramatic effect."
Artists.
Issue 7 is worth picking up, if only because you get to see what I look like without glasses.
Makes me look *years* younger, I'm told, but I'm afraid they don't make contact lenses in my size.

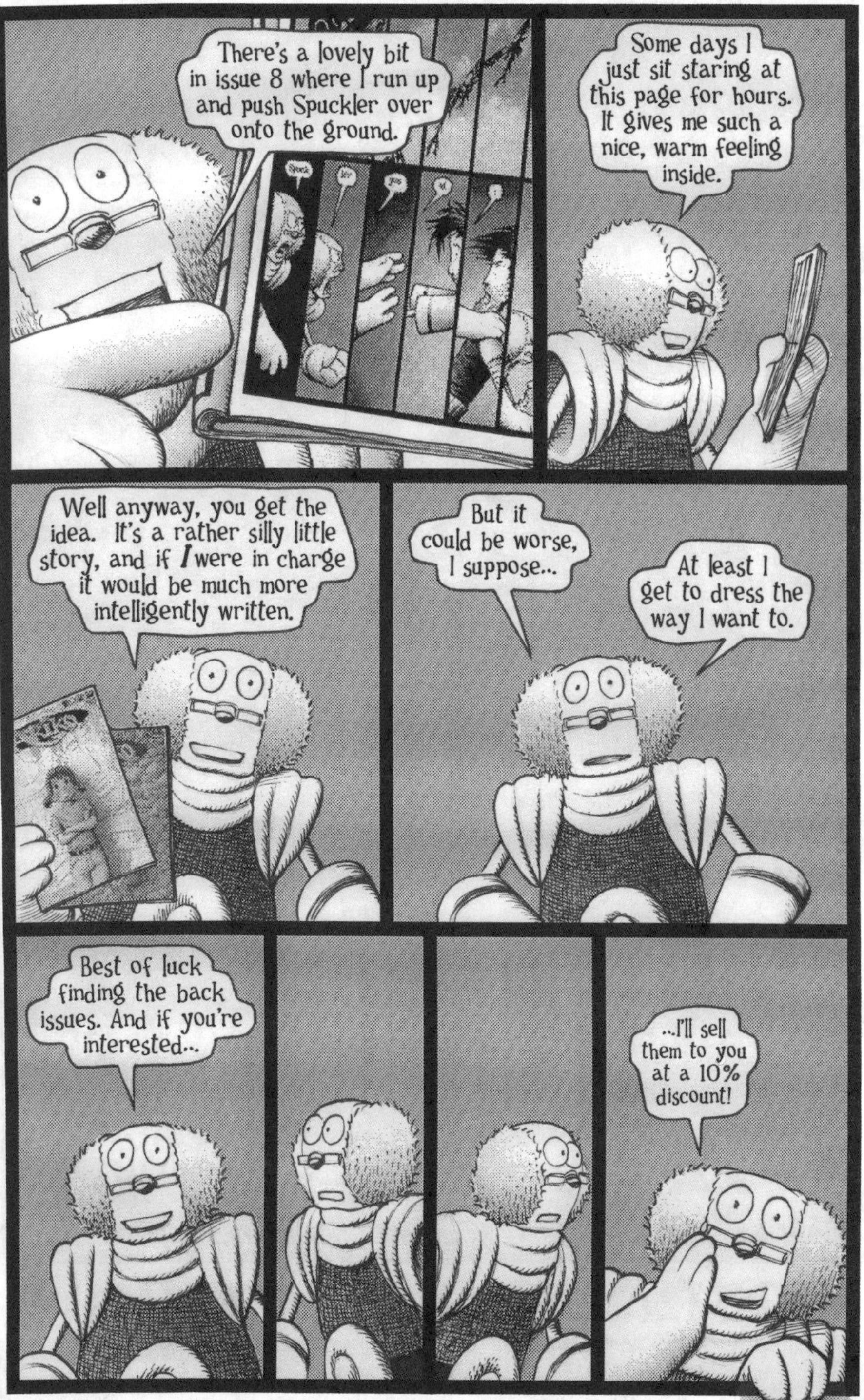
There's a lovely bit in issue 8 where I run up and push Spuckler over onto the ground.
Some days I just sit staring at this page for hours. It gives me such a nice, warm feeling inside.
Well anyway, you get the idea. It's a rather silly little story, and if I were in charge it would be much more intelligently written.
But it could be worse, I suppose...
At least I get to dress the way I want to.
Best of luck finding the back issues. And if you're interested...
...I'll sell them to you at a 10% discount!
The End

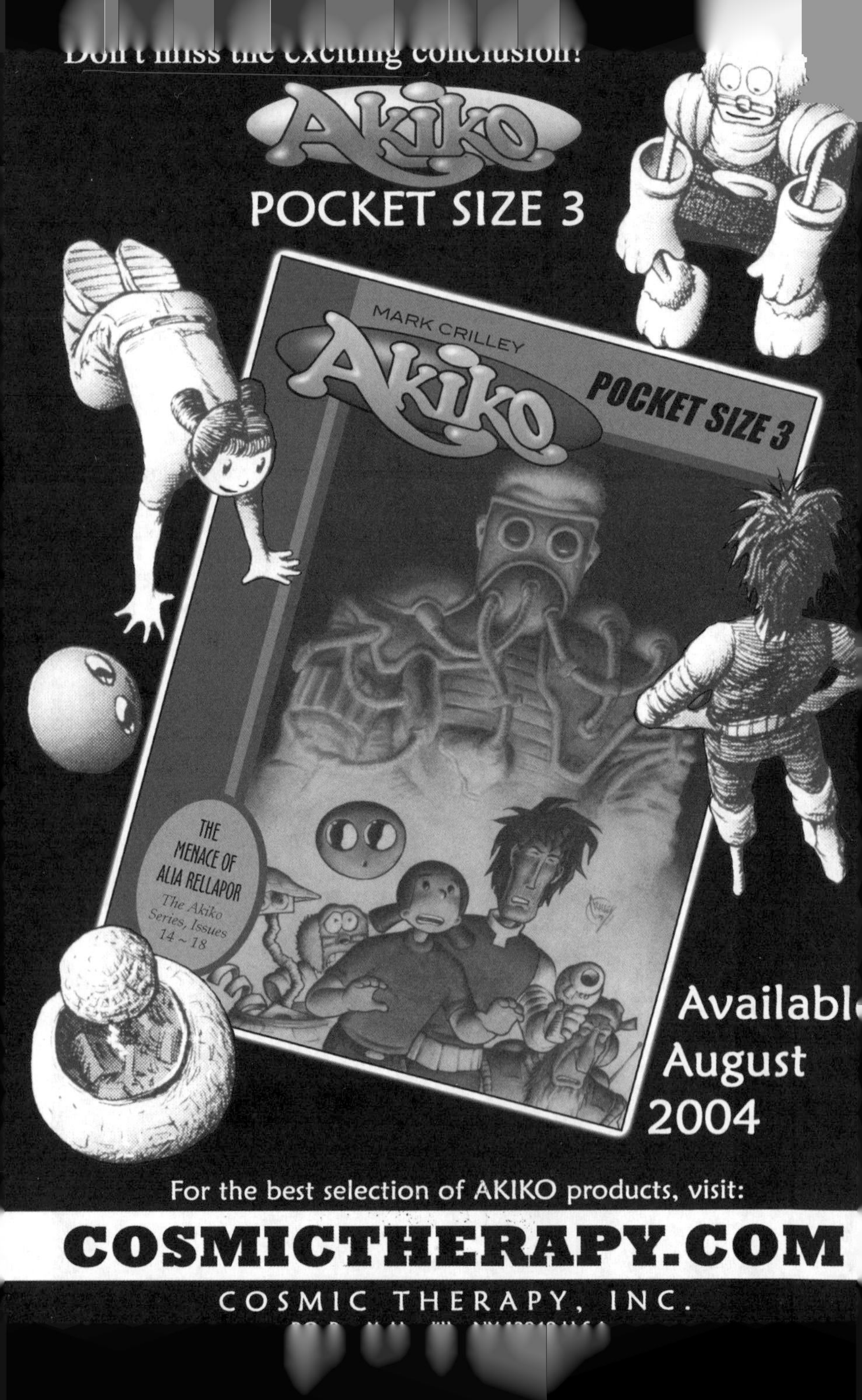

Akiko
POCKET SIZE 3
MARK CRILLEY
Akiko
POCKET SIZE 3
THE MENACE OF ALIA RELLAPOR
The Akiko Series, Issues 14 ~ 18
Availabl
August
2004
For the best selection of AKIKO products, visit:
COSMICTHERAPY.COM
COSMIC THERAPY, INC.